THE EU &
MOLDOVA

On a Fault-line
of Europe

edited by
Ann Lewis

THE FEDERAL TRUST
europe's eastern borders

This book is published by the Federal Trust, whose aim is to enlighten public debate on federal issues of national, continental and global government. It does this in the light of its statutes which state that it shall promote 'studies in the principles of international relations, international justice and supranational government.'

The Trust conducts enquiries, promotes seminars and conferences and publishes reports and teaching materials. The Federal Trust is the UK member of the Trans-European Policy Studies Association (TEPSA), a grouping of fifteen think-tanks from Member States of the European Union.

Up-to-date information about the Federal Trust can be found on the internet at www.fedtrust.co.uk

© Federal Trust for Education and Research 2004

ISBN 1 903403 54 5

NOTE: All contributors to this volume are writing in a personal capacity. Views expressed should not be taken as those of their government or institution.

This book is the fifth title in the Federal Trust series *Europe's Eastern Borders*. The three previous volumes are available from the publisher: *The EU & Kaliningrad: Kaliningrad and the Impact of EU Enlargement* (2001, 0 903573 18 3) edited by James Baxendale, Stephen Dewar and David Gowan; *The EU & Ukraine: Neighbours, Friends, Partners* (2002, 1 903403 18 9) edited by Ann Lewis; *The EU & Russia: The Promise of Partnership* (2002, 1 903403 14 6) by John Pinder and Yuri Shishkov; and *The EU & Belarus: Between Moscow and Brussels* (2002, 1 903403 02 2) edited by Ann Lewis.

The Federal Trust is a Registered Charity No. 272241

7 Graphite Square, Vauxhall Walk,

London SE11 5EE

Company Limited by Guarantee No.1269848

Typeset and printed by J W Arrowsmith Ltd

Contents

Foreword

Chris Patten

The European Union completes its first major expansion eastwards in 2004.

The Member States and the Commission, together with the acceding countries themselves, can already look back with some satisfaction on a successful transition process preparing these new Member States for entry. Notwithstanding the challenge of dealing with the crisis in the Balkans and the introduction of a single currency, European political and diplomatic attention in recent years has inevitably and rightly focused on these countries.

Now that this round of accessions will take place, and once Romania and Bulgaria have, subject to a continuation of their efforts, joined the Union in 2007, Moldova will become a 'New Neighbour' for the European Union. Like Belarus and Ukraine, Moldova may have seemed just over the horizon, just outside our field of vision in recent years while our attention has been focused on other, major, changes. But now it is moving closer to the centre of European attention. This book is therefore timely.

I am delighted that the Federal Trust is following its excellent volumes on EU relations with Ukraine and Belarus with this volume on the EU's relations with Moldova, a future neighbour and a country with which the EU has intense and I hope constructive relations. Moldova became a member of the WTO in 2001, and successfully held the Chairmanship of the Ministerial Committee of the Council of Europe in 2003. Those are important developments to its credit, and show its potential. But it also faces a number of serious problems, widespread poverty being a matter of particular concern. The long-standing and still unresolved problem of Transdniestria also is a potentially dangerous source of instability, which must be addressed and positively resolved. The EU needs to engage more with Moldova and Moldova needs to engage more with the EU in overcoming these problems. The EU is strongly committed to further reinforcing the EU – Moldova relationship. The European Neighbourhood Programme opens up new avenues for doing so.

It is in all our interests that Moldova plays a positive part in Europe. Moldovans, like all Europeans, desire peace and prosperity, and their country can contribute to the security and stability of both the region and the wider continent. But there are issues to resolve and problems to solve along the road. These need honest discussion and open debate. I welcome this book as a useful contribution to the growing public debate on how best to assist the process and steer towards a peaceful and progressive future for relations between the European Union and Moldova.

Chris Patten
EU Commissioner for External Affairs

Introduction

Moldova? Why Moldova? Moldova is very small (population 4.3 million). It is the poorest country in Europe. It is tucked away between Romania and Ukraine on the eastern fringes of non-Russian Europe. Its largely agricultural economy provides little of interest to western trading partners. Tourism is barely a gleam in the eye.

But while Moldova remains where it is, the European Union is gradually getting nearer. In 2007, if Romania is, as expected, part of the second major wave of EU expansion eastwards, Moldova will become our immediate neighbour. Its affairs are therefore no longer a matter of indifference to the Union. This book is intended to provide an overview of where Moldova stands and where it might be going, and consider how the EU might respond to the challenges it presents.

But first: what is 'Moldova'? The name is used for three current entities: the Republic of Moldova, the country which was formerly part of the Soviet Union as the Moldavian Soviet Socialist Republic (itself an artificial creation) and gained its independence in 1991; that part of the Republic of Moldova inhabited by a majority of Romanian(Moldovan)-speakers and governed from Chisinau; and a region of Romania itself. In this book 'Moldova', unless otherwise specified, refers to the Republic of Moldova.

Moldavia (the Russian form of the name) was a relatively prosperous part of the Soviet Union. The products of its rich agricultural land found a ready market, and its factories fed the Soviet military and industrial base. Ethnic differences and any political aspirations were suppressed by russification and the stranglehold of the communist party machine directed from Moscow.

In the late 1980s, once Gorbachev had lifted the lid, the long-suppressed Romanian-speaking majority finally found a voice, one whose radicalism (sometimes extending to calls for union with Romania) alarmed the large Russian-speaking minorities. For the former, independence was an opportunity; for the latter, a threat. Ethnic and political tensions, escalating briefly into violent conflict, led to the establishment of a separatist administration in the area east of the River Dniester known as Transdniestria, a region which was not part of pre-war Romania. Despite a decade of on-off negotiations, this split remains to this day, and threatens the stability of the region.

Alarmed at the consequences of radicalism, the Moldovan population seemed ready to rally round a moderate political consensus in the mid-nineties. But political fragmentation and personal ambition combined to produce a series of weak governments which largely failed to tackle the problems of a rapidly-declining economy. Widespread frustration and disillusion led to growing support for the only cohesive political force and the eventual triumph in the 2001 elections of the Communist Party and President Voronin, the first freely-elected communist administration in any post-Soviet state.

Against this background, Moldova was not high on the EU's list of priorities at a time when the Union was preoccupied with its own internal development, with supporting democratisation and eventual accession in Central Europe, and with the conflict in the Balkans. A standard Trade and Cooperation Agreement was signed in 1994 but only came into force in 1998. Moldova missed out altogether when the EU adopted Common Strategies for most of its prospective neighbours. It was however included in the wider 'Stability Pact' for South-Eastern Europe. It is also very much included in the EU's latest 'Wider Europe' initiative, and has risen up the EU agenda as the Union has recognised that the problems it poses will become more acute once Moldova becomes an immediate neighbour after 2007.

This book presents a wide-ranging and multi-faceted view of Moldova and its relations with the EU, with contributors from Moldova itself (official and unofficial), elsewhere in Europe and beyond. The authors include academics and analysts, politicians and practitioners. Each article is intended to be self-standing, so that it can be read in isolation. This makes for a certain amount of overlap, but that is inevitable since many issues are relevant in a variety of contexts. The aim is to give the reader a well-rounded picture, reflecting various strands of often quite conflicting opinion.

The book is divided into four sections, covering politics and society, the economic situation, Moldova's international relations, and its relations specifically with the EU. Each section starts with a broad overview, followed by a more detailed examination of particular topics.

The book opens with a short history of what is now Moldova. This is a complicated subject, and readers unfamiliar with the country are strongly advised to read this first, since the history is vital to an understanding of modern Moldova.

Part 1 opens with a survey of the roller-coaster of political developments in Moldova since independence, written by Professor William Crowther, a leading American expert in the field. This is followed by an article by Professor Maggs on law and human rights in Moldova; one by Petru Clej and Alexandru Canţîr of the BBC casting a critical eye on the media; one by Angelina Zaporojan-Pirgari on the vital issue of the country's minorities; and a heartfelt piece by Ala Mîndîcanu on the dire situation of women in Moldova. The internal affairs of Transdniestria are covered by the German analyst Gottfried Hanne.

Part 2 deals with the economy, with a broad look at progress and prospects by the Canadian-Moldovan duo of Stuart Hensel and Anatol Gudîm, a shorter look at key issues by the economist Vlad Spanu, and a survey of international economic relations by former prime minister Ion Sturza and Veaceslav Negruta.

Part 3 begins with an overview of Moldova' foreign policy by Deputy Foreign Minister Ion Stăvilă. This is followed by a more detailed look at relations with Russia and the CIS by Claus Neukirch; relations with Ukraine by Rostyslav Khotin of the BBC Ukrainian Service; and relations with Romania by President of the Social-Liberal Party Oleg Serebrian. Liliana Viţu examines Moldova's perception of itself as akin to the Baltic states. Adrian Severin, Romanian MP and former President of the OSCE Parliamentary Assembly, traces the history of the OSCE's involvement with Moldova, especially over Transdniestria.

In Part 4 we turn to Moldova's relations with the EU, with three initial contributions: Marius Vahl presents a cool academic analysis; Andrei Neguţa, Chairman of the Foreign Affairs Committee of the Moldovan parliament, and Alexandru Simionov put a quasi-official Moldovan view; and Jan Marinus Wiersma gives his own perspective as a Member of the European Parliament in Strasbourg. Following that come detailed studies of two key aspects of Moldova/EU relations: border issues, covered by the Moldovan duo Oxana

Guţu and Valeriu Gheorghiu, and EU assistance programmes, by a former practitioner from the UK, Vic Heard.

The book closes with some personal comments by way of conclusions.

A note on the spelling of names. I have, largely for practical reasons, used 'Transdniestria', which is neither Romanian nor Russian but common in international usage, as the name of the region in Moldova east of the River Dniester (Romanian *Nistru*, Russian *Dnestr*). Other names appear in Romanian or in a form transliterated from the Russian or Ukrainian as seems most appropriate in the context.

All contributors to this book are writing in their personal capacity and the views expressed should not be taken as those of their government or institution.

I am grateful to all those who have helped in the production of this book, and in particular to Liliana Viţu for her constant interest and practical assistance, including with translation. Finally, my thanks to all the authors not only for their contributions to the book but also for many interesting discussions along the way.

Ann Lewis
London
November 2003

Republic of
Moldova, 2004

- Transdniestria
- Gagauzia

Moldova: a Brief History

Elizabeth Teague

Since the late Middle Ages, the name Moldova has denoted a shifting succession of political units, each situated within slightly different territorial borders. Today, two adjoining parts of South-Eastern Europe both bear the name. Though they are divided by the River Prut, the two share much common history and were, for substantial periods of their history prior to 1940, politically united. Since then, however, they have been divided by an international frontier that will assume increased significance when Romania joins NATO and, later, the European Union.

One of these two territories, the subject of this book, is today's Republic of Moldova. Until 1991, it formed part of the Soviet Union (USSR); in that year, it became an independent, internationally recognised state. The other is a province of Romania; along with Wallachia to the south and Transylvania to the west, it was one of the mediaeval principalities that historically constituted the territory known as Greater Romania.

Both trace their origins to the mediaeval principality of Moldova. United until 1812, they began to go their separate ways when the territory east of the River Prut was annexed by the Russian Empire and renamed Bessarabia. They were reunited from 1918 to 1940 and again from 1941 to 1944, a period of war and devastation. But in the intervening periods, while the lands to the west of the Prut were uniting in the kingdom of Romania, Bessarabia was undergoing intense russification. Eventually, it was made an integral part of the Soviet Union. Thus it was that Bessarabia, which forms the core of the modern Moldovan state, was excluded from the processes whereby the modern Romanian nation was formed.

When the USSR fell apart in 1991, many people assumed that the two Moldovas would automatically unite within a Greater Romania. After all, their

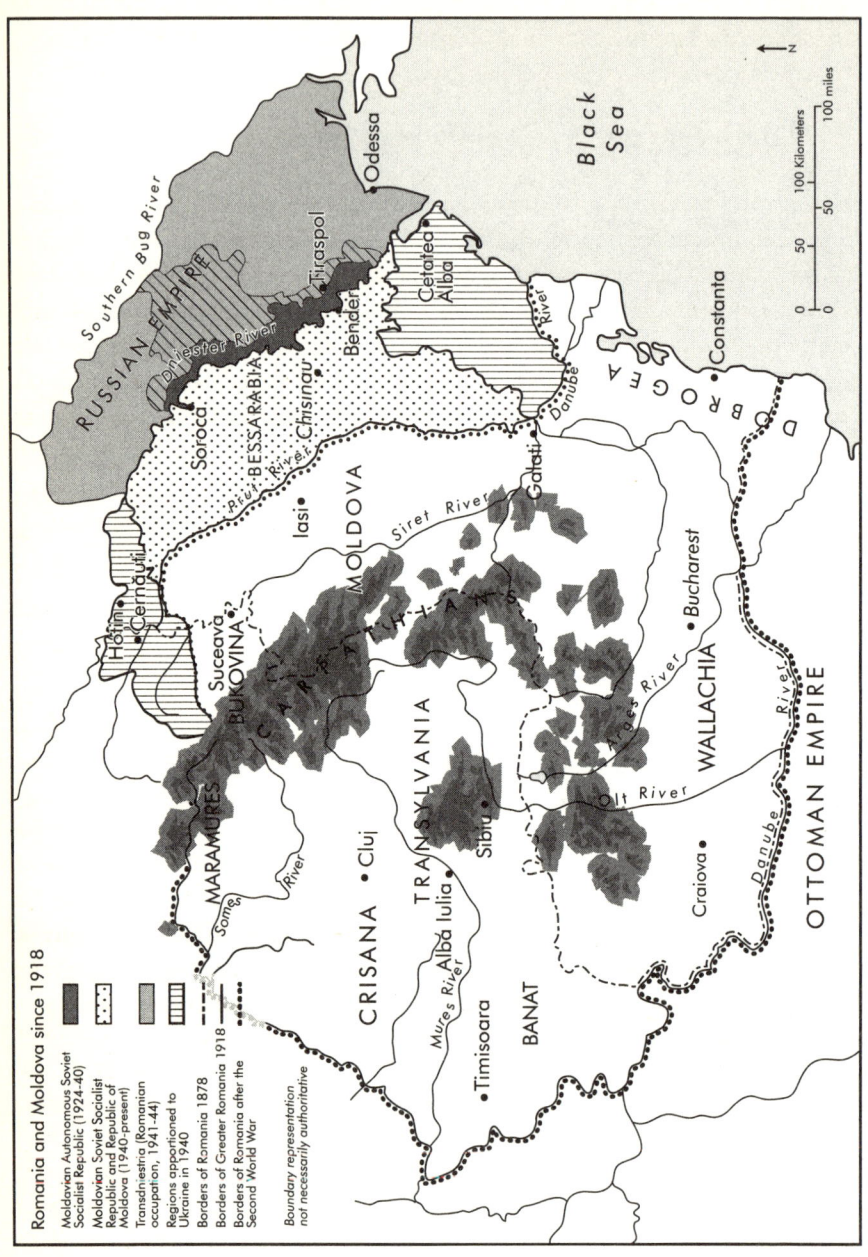

Romania and Moldova since 1918

Moldavian Autonomous Soviet Socialist Republic (1924-40)

Moldavian Soviet Socialist Republic and Republic of Moldova (1940-present)

Transdniestria (Romanian occupation, 1941-44)

Regions apportioned to Ukraine in 1940

Borders of Romania 1878

Borders of Greater Romania 1918

Borders of Romania after the Second World War

Boundary representation not necessarily authoritative

populations speak a common language, Romanian, even though the language spoken in the Republic of Moldova differs sufficiently from that spoken west of the Prut for some people to have argued that Moldovan is a language in its own right, and during the post-war period was written in the Cyrillic rather than the Latin script, by Moscow's decree.

The language issue is highly politicised, but most linguists dismiss this claim. They acknowledge that the language spoken in Moldova has many features that are peculiar to the region, and that its grammar and vocabulary have been influenced by the Russian and Ukrainian languages with which it has for centuries been associated. This is natural, given that the Moldovans have traditionally been Orthodox Christians and that Old Church Slavonic was used in official documents until the early seventeenth century. Russian was declared the official language of Bessarabia in 1854 and later served again as Moldova's *lingua franca* during the Soviet period. Under this influence, Moldovan acquired many Russian loan words, especially for scientific and technical concepts. Most linguists nonetheless agree that the language spoken east of the Prut shares the same fundamental structure as the Romanian language spoken across the border to the west.

It turned out however, after the Soviet collapse of 1991, that history had taken the two Moldovan societies in such different directions that most of their inhabitants were aware more of their differences than of their similarities. While those living to the west of the Prut felt Romanian and identified with Romania, no more than ten percent of those to the east felt such a loyalty. This was particularly true of the predominantly Russian-speaking populations living both in the south of the country and in Transdniestria – the sliver of land on the east bank of the River Dniester, which runs through the eastern part of Moldova. Yet many Moldovans from the region between the Prut and the Dniester, while recognising that they shared many elements of their cultural heritage with their Romanian neighbours, felt distinctively Moldovan and wanted their country to assert its sovereignty and independence.

Some of their antipathy to union with Romania was inspired by the fact that much of the history Moldova shared with Romania had been painful. Their recent history had been very different, a fact that was unlikely to receive much recognition from a post-communist Romanian government with strong centrist tendencies, due in part to sensitivities in relations with Hungary, its neighbour in the west, over Transylvania, with its ethnically mixed population. The perceptions of those living to the east of the Prut were also influenced by the fact that substantial portions of Moldova's inhabitants – the Christian Turkic Găgăuz in southern Moldova and the predominantly Russian-speaking inhabitants of Transdniestria – opposed the idea of union with Romania so strongly that, rather than run such a risk, they were prepared to threaten to secede (in the case of the Găgăuz) or indeed (in the case of the Transdniestrians) to declare themselves a separate state. As this book shows, the tensions arising from these conflicting emotions, and from Moldova's emergence as an independent state of South-Eastern Europe, have yet to be resolved.

Early history

Today's Moldovans and Romanians trace their ancestry to the Dacians: early inhabitants of the region to the north of the Danube stretching through modern Romania to the Black Sea. The Emperor Trajan fought two military campaigns before conquering the region in 106 AD and incorporating it into the Roman Empire. His victory was celebrated in Rome by the erection of Trajan's column and marked the beginning of nearly two centuries of Roman occupation. The Romans intermarried with the indigenous population and exploited the gold and salt of the Carpathian Mountains. Their legacy lives on in the Latin roots of the modern Romanian language spoken in both Moldova and Romania.

The Romans were driven out of the Danube region toward the end of the third century by successive waves of nomadic Gothic invaders. What happened to the indigenous Latin-speaking populations after the Romans left in 271 is a subject of historical controversy. While some may have moved south of the Danube, others sought refuge in the forests and mountains of Transylvania where they established themselves as shepherds and hill-farmers. From these tribes emerged in the twelfth century the proto-Romanian people known as Wallachs or Vlachs, a name that derives from a mediaeval Germanic word for foreigners (it is also found in 'Welsh' and 'Walloon'). The Vlachs spread into the plains to the south and east of the Carpathians. There, in the mid-fourteenth century, they established the principalities of Moldova (in the land lying to the east of the Carpathians) and Wallachia (lying to the south, between the Carpathians and the Danube). These independent chieftainships flourished thanks to their advantageous location on trading routes connecting the Hanseatic states in the north with the Byzantine Empire to the south.

This first Moldova was founded on territory that today constitutes the Romanian province of Bucovina. By the beginning of the fifteenth century, however, it had extended as far as the River Dniester (Nistru in Romanian, Dnestr in Russian). That is, it included most of both of today's Moldovas.

As the power of Byzantium waned, a new threat appeared, that of the Ottoman Empire. The Moldovan and Wallachian princes, who professed Orthodox Christianity, joined forces with their Christian neighbours in an attempt to defend their territories and exclude the Ottoman Turks from Central Europe. The method favoured by Wallachia's prince Vlad for killing captured Turks earned him the nickname 'Impaler'. Moldova flourished at this time under the leadership of the king revered to this day as the country's greatest hero, Stephen the Great (1457–1504). His statue stands today in the centre of Chișinău, capital of the Moldovan Republic, where the main street bears his name, and his portrait appears on all of Moldova's banknotes.

The Ottomans reached the south bank of the Danube in 1396 and, following the fall of Constantinople to the Turks in 1453, the Romanian principalities were forced to accept Turkish suzerainty. But while they remained subjects of the Ottoman Empire for the next three hundred years, they did not become Turkish provinces. Instead they were allowed, in return for an annual tribute, to elect their princes and to maintain their own military and administrative systems. For much of the time they were ruled by (Greek) Phanariot princes. Their leaders made occasional, unsuccessful attempts to assert their independence. In his illuminating study of the Moldovans, however, Charles King cautions against the idea that a Moldovan or Romanian nation existed in these early years. It was not, King points out, until the eighteenth and nineteenth centuries, with the rise of modern notions of the nation-state, that such concepts began to assume political significance.

Meanwhile, the Russian Empire was beginning to make itself felt in South-Eastern Europe. The rapid expansion of Russia's frontiers under Peter the Great (reigned 1682–1725) and Catherine the Great (reigned 1762–96) brought Russia into conflict with the Ottoman Empire. By the end of the eighteenth century, the whole of the northern coast of the Black Sea was in Russian hands. At this point, Russia began to demand commercial rights in the Ottoman Empire and the right to protect the Ottomans' Christian subjects, including those in the principalities of Moldova and Wallachia. Russia's main aim was to gain control of the Bosporus and the Dardanelles. Known to the ancient world as the Clashing Rocks and the Hellespont, these are the Straits that lead from the Black Sea to the Mediterranean; control over them would secure Russia the year-round access to warm waters that Nature had denied her. A series of Russo-Turkish wars ensued. Defeated in the war of 1806–12, Turkey was forced in 1812 to cede the eastern half of Moldova – the area between the Prut and the Dniester, which forms the core of today's Republic of Moldova – to Russia, which renamed it Bessarabia. Romania's claim to the territory as Romanian *irridenta* dates to this time.

At first, Russia appeared in the region as a liberator. Before long, however, it began to subject Bessarabia to intense russification. Russian settlers and administrators poured into the region, and Cossacks patrolled the borders.

Under the Treaty of Adrianople of 1829, Russia secured some access to the Straits, and for a brief period occupied western Moldova and Wallachia as well as Bessarabia. Russia was unable, however, to hold onto the two Romanian principalities permanently, and in 1841 they reverted to the Ottoman Empire under the terms of an international agreement to demilitarise the Black Sea. Bessarabia remained under Russian control until 1853, when Russia, still intent on extending its influence into the Black Sea, moved its troops back into Moldova and Wallachia and thereby triggered the Crimean War (1854–56).

Following its humiliating defeat in that war, Russia was forced to cede part of Bessarabia to the Ottomans. Britain and France encouraged nationalist sentiment in the Romanian principalities, imagining an independent Romania as a handy buffer between Russia and the Straits. In 1859, Moldova and Wallachia united under a single ruler; they finally won their independence in 1878, following Turkey's defeat in the Russo-Turkish War of 1877. Under the Treaty of Berlin that ended that war, Bessarabia returned to Russia. The Kingdom of Romania was created in 1881; in 1919, following the First World War, it was joined by Transylvania.

It is a consequence of Moldova's borderland status that its population has always been ethnically mixed. For centuries there was a strong Jewish community in the region. The first Jews arrived with the Romans; more came after they were expelled from Poland and Hungary in the fourteenth and seventeenth centuries; most settled in Bucovina and Bessarabia. The southern parts of Moldova, where the soil is less fertile than in the north, has been inhabited since the late eighteenth century by the Găgăuz, a Turkic people who sought refuge in what was then an outpost of the Russian Empire when their Ottoman overlords tried to force them to abandon Christianity for Islam. Bulgarians, who also fled Ottoman rule, live alongside the Găgăuz, and there are substantial Ukrainian and Roma communities in the north of the country.

The impact of World War I

The First World War had a profound impact on all the borders in South-Eastern Europe. As the Russian, Ottoman and Austrian Empires collapsed, Romania, Ukraine and Bolshevik Russia all staked claims to all or part of Bessarabia. In October 1917, Bessarabia declared itself independent of Russia; the following March, it joined Romania under an act of union. In the years between the First and Second World Wars, Bessarabia accordingly formed part of Romania. It was and remained the most backward part of a country that was, in the depressed economic conditions of the 1930s, moving toward fascism.

The Soviet leaders refused to recognise Bessarabia's union with Romania. As a way of underscoring this refusal and staking their own claim to Bessarabian territory, the Soviet authorities in 1924 created the Moldovan Autonomous Soviet Socialist Republic (MASSR) out of a small piece of territory on the east bank of the Dniester. The population of the MASSR became the subject of a remarkable exercise in Soviet nation-building when the Soviet authorities began to assert the existence of a separate Moldovan nation linked historically not to Romania but to Russia.

Until that time, the language spoken by Moldovans had generally been seen as a dialect of standard Romanian. Now, the Soviet authorities began to insist that Moldovan, with its large number of words derived from Slavic languages, was a language in its own right. They backed this assertion by publishing a stream of Moldovan histories, textbooks, grammars and newspapers; there was even a Moldovan-Romanian dictionary.

World War II

In August 1939, Germany and the USSR shocked the world by signing the non-aggression treaty commonly known as the Molotov-Ribbentrop Pact, which opened Hitlers's path to war. Secret protocols to that treaty divided the lands between the two countries, along with others, into Soviet and German spheres of influence. Bessarabia fell into the Soviet sphere and Soviet troops moved into the region in June 1940.

In June 1941, Germany tore up the non-aggression treaty and invaded the Soviet Union. Romania, desperate to regain its lost territory, joined Germany in the attack. Romanian troops not only moved into Bessarabia but also crossed the Dniester into the MASSR. The establishment of Romanian rule in this region, which had never historically been part of the Romanian lands, was an especially bloody business. This helps to account for the strong hostility in Transdniestria to this day to any idea of a merger of Moldova and Romania.

The tide of the war turned in 1943 with Germany's defeat by Soviet troops at the battle of Stalingrad, spelling disaster also for Romania. That year, the Romanian government was overthrown in a coup and the Soviet Army occupied Bessarabia. At the end of the war, a communist government was installed in Bucharest and, under a peace treaty signed in 1947, Romania was forced formally to cede Bessarabia to the USSR. At the same time it also lost Northern Bukovina to what is today Ukraine.

Moldova under Soviet rule

Having seized Bessarabia from Romania, Stalin combined it with existing Soviet territory – the sliver of land on the left bank of the Dniester which had earlier, as mentioned above, been given the status of an autonomous region. The two units were declared the Moldavian Soviet Socialist Republic (SSR), one of the fifteen constituent republics of the USSR. This is the territory of today's Republic of Moldova. But first, lest the population should nurse ideas of independence, Stalin took the precaution of incorporating two districts of southern Bessarabia, between the Dniester and Danube deltas, into Ukraine, where they remain to this day. This ensured that the Moldavian SSR was landlocked and in Stalin's eyes reduced the danger that its inhabitants might one day seek self-determination or unification with Romania. As a further precaution, Moldova was subjected to intense sovietisation. After 1945, thousands of ethnic Romanians were deported to Siberia. Their places were taken by an influx of mainly ethnic Russian workers and professionals who were brought to Moldova and settled chiefly in the cities, Chişinău, Bălţi, and Tiraspol. Use of the Russian language was made obligatory in the schools, in the administration and, of course, in dealings with Moscow. Any sign of nationalist sentiment or opposition to Communist Party rule was ruthlessly suppressed. Linguistic assimilation was high, as was the level of interethnic marriage.

During the Soviet period Moldova was, like the other republics of the USSR, governed by the Communist Party leadership in Moscow, acting through subordinate local party and government bodies. The economy was also run from Moscow, where central planners saw Moldova as a source of cheap agricultural labour. Moldova is characterised by fertile soil and rolling steppe-land (grassy plains), relatively mild winters and long, warm summers. It produces excellent wine, fruit, grain, sugar beet, sunflower seed, beef, dairy goods and tobacco. But it has no major mineral deposits and is dependent on imports for all its energy supplies, most of which come from Russia. During the Soviet period, the republic received little investment and its level of industrial development was low. Such investment as did take place was concentrated in Transdniestria, on the left bank of the Dniester.

Change came in the late 1980s when Soviet Communist Party leader Mikhail Gorbachev began to ease the political climate in the USSR as a whole. His attempts to reform and liberalise single-party rule led, in 1991, to the collapse of the entire Soviet political system and the demise of the USSR. A significant role was played in this process by the upsurge of nationalist sentiment that Gorbachev's reforms provoked in the USSR's non-Russian republics. National sentiment was strongest in those republics, such as the Baltic states, that had prior experience of independent statehood or where, as in Georgia, Armenia and western Ukraine, substantial numbers of the titular nationality were urbanised and relatively untouched by russification. It occurred less readily in republics such as Moldova with no prior experience of independence and where the titular nationality was predominantly rural. The Central Asian republics fell into the same category.

By 1988–89, a Moldovan Popular Front movement had nonetheless begun to coalesce around Moldova's small cultural elite and younger generation of Romanian-speaking anti-communist intellectuals. Once the process began, it made rapid strides. In January 1989, Romanian was declared the state language of the republic. That is, the authorities officially recognised the Moldovan and Romanian languages as one and the same. At the same time, the Latin alphabet was reinstated, in place of Cyrillic, as the script in which the state language was officially written. This was significant since the use of Cyrillic was one of the key features used to distinguish the Moldovan language from standard Romanian. (Today, Cyrillic is used to write Romanian only in Transdniestria, where the language is called Moldovan.) In June 1990, the Moldovan parliament declared state sovereignty, that is, that Moldovan laws should take precedence within the republic over all-Union (Soviet) laws; it also asserted the republic's exclusive right to control its own natural resources. In October 1990, Mircea Snegur, a former Communist Party official who had embraced the idea of Moldovan independence, was elected head of state by parliament. In spring 1991 the Moldovan government announced, as did the governments of the Baltic states, Georgia and Armenia, that their country would not sign the Union Treaty, the agreement which President Gorbachev hoped would preserve the Soviet Union by placing it on a new footing.

At that time, many members of the Popular Front favoured not just close cultural links with Romania, where the Communist leadership had been overthrown in December 1989, but political union within a single Romanian state. Such a policy was bound to be controversial, given Moldova's multiethnic composition and the country's complex and often turbulent history. It caused particular alarm in mainly Russian-speaking Găgăuzia and Transdniestria.

Moldova declares independence

Moldova declared itself an independent country on 27 August 1991, following the abortive coup in Moscow that precipitated the collapse of the Soviet Union. The following day, Snegur as head of state promulgated a decree promising equal treatment for the entire republic's minorities, including the protection of minority languages (which of course included Russian and Găgăuz). In December 1991, Moldova joined Russia and most of the other former Soviet republics in the loose (and largely ineffectual) association known as the Commonwealth of Independent States. Its purpose was to ensure the peaceful regulation of any other disputes arising from the collapse of the Soviet Union. Meanwhile, Snegur's opposition to immediate unification with Romania provoked a split with the Popular Front and led him to stand as an independent in the December 1991 presidential election. Snegur's stance was supported by the majority of the electorate. Running unopposed, he was elected president after the Popular Front failed to organise a voter boycott.

Transdniestria, which in September 1991 proclaimed itself the 'Dniester Moldovan Republic', held a referendum in December 1991 demanding to remain part of the Soviet Union. When the USSR finally collapsed at the end of that year, Transdniestria's leaders began to call instead for complete independence. Having seized control of most of the territory on the left bank of the Dniester, the separatists moved to the right back, where they overpowered Moldova's poorly equipped police force and captured the town of Bendery. The Moldovan authorities dispatched troops and volunteers, and fierce street-to-street fighting followed. The separatists were able to stand their ground because they had the backing of Russia's 14th Army, stationed in Transdniestria under its charismatic commander, General Lebed. Hundreds of people were killed or injured before a ceasefire was agreed in July 1992. This established a tripartite peacekeeping force made up of Russian, Moldovan and Transdniestrian units. Negotiations over a resolution of the conflict have continued on a sporadic basis ever since but had not, at the time of writing, reached a solution.

Moldova's conflict with its Găgăuz minority, who in 1990 declared a separate Găgăuz Republic and threatened to secede from Moldova should Moldova leave the USSR, was peacefully resolved in December 1994, when the Moldovan parliament adopted a law granting special autonomous status to the Găgăuz-dominated region.

Today's Moldova has a population of some 4.3 million. In 1989, when the most recent census was taken, 64 per cent of the population described themselves as Moldovan, 14 per cent as Ukrainian, 13 per cent as Russian, 3.5

per cent as Găgăuz, 2 per cent as Bulgarian, and 1.5 per cent as Jewish. Many members of Moldova's once substantial Jewish community have since left the country, as have some Russians and Ukrainians; as a result, the Moldovan share of the population is currently estimated at around 67 per cent. The number of Roma inhabitants is officially put at no more than 12,000, but the true number could be closer to 100,000. A precise figure is hard to reach since the Roma are widely dispersed throughout Moldova; moreover, they are linguistically highly assimilated, speaking mainly Romanian or Russian, like many of Moldova's other ethnic minorities.

Moldova's leaders were forced to abandon the idea of uniting Moldova with Romania not only because of the hostile reaction of Moldova's ethnic, linguistic or territorially-based minorities, but also because opinion polls revealed that a majority of the Moldovan population opposed union with Romania. Many Romanian-speaking Moldovans, it turned out, preferred to maintain their independence from their bigger neighbour.

The territory occupied by today's Moldovan Republic has been fought over for centuries, tossed back and forth between the imperial powers without thought for the interests or wishes of its multiethnic population. Its borderland status is exemplified by the fact that, when the poet Ovid was banished from Rome in 8 AD by the Emperor Augustus, he was sent in disgrace to the nearby Black Sea port of Constanta, then on the south-eastern fringe of the Roman Empire. Eight centuries later, in 1820, the poet Pushkin was exiled from St Petersburg and packed off to Chişinău, then on the south-western fringe of the Russian Empire. Until 1991, Moldova's population had never known independence. They had had no experience of democratic government, nor any opportunity of developing a sense of themselves as citizens with a stake in their own nation-state. Yet a majority of them felt not Romanian, but Moldovan, and wanted to run their own affairs within their own newly-independent country. Their subsequent history is detailed in the chapters that make up this book.

Further Reading

Davies, Norman, *Europe: A History*, London: Pimlico, 1997.

Day, Alan J. (ed.), *Border and Territorial Disputes*, second edition, Harlow: Longman, 1982; section on Bessarabia, pp. 85–90.

Fernandez-Armesto, Felipe (ed.), *The Times Guide to the Peoples of Europe*, London: Times Books, revised edition, 1997.

Juler, Caroline, *Blue Guide to Romania*, London: A. & C. Black, 2000.

King, Charles, *The Moldovans: Romania, Russia, and the Politics of Culture*, Stanford, CA: Hoover Institution Press, 2000.

Socor, Vladimir, Chapters 17 and 26 in Vera Tolz and Iain Elliot, *The Demise of the USSR*, London: Macmillan, 1995.

Thomson, David, *Europe Since Napoleon*, Harmondsworth: Penguin, 1966.

Part 1:
Politics and Society

Moldova's Post-Communist Transition: Ambiguous Democracy, Reluctant Reform

William Crowther

The politics of transition: from Soviet Moldavia to the Republic of Moldova

On the eve of the transition from communism, Moldova suffered poor economic development, serious ethnic divisions, and a wide gap separating the population from the entrenched Soviet-era elite. Furthermore, unlike other Central European states emerging from Soviet dominion, Moldova had no history of independent national government to fall back on. Its inter-war experience of rule from Bucharest provided little useful guidance in developing sovereign institutions.

As in other former Soviet republics, Moldovan nationalists began to seek independence in the context of the widespread Soviet reforms of the late 1980s. Serious opposition began to crystallise in the context of elections to the USSR Congress of People's Deputies in the spring of 1989. Members of the nascent opposition employed the relative security conferred by the electoral process to publicise their reform message. The electoral victory of a handful of reformers proved critical in legitimising opposition activity. Building on their success, in early June 1989 opposition leaders sought and obtained official registration for the Popular Front of Moldova. The Popular Front championed the Romanian-speaking majority (64.5 per cent of the population) and benefited from heightened ethnic activism. In their efforts to attract mass support, opposition leaders focused on the highly-charged language issue, demanding the status of 'state language' for Romanian. While expedient in the short run, playing the language card imposed a high price in terms of undermining ethnic unity. The heavily nationalist appeal of the anti-Soviet opposition almost instantaneously generated a sharp increase in inter-ethnic conflict. The Republic's main minority groups, Ukrainian (13.8 per cent), Russian (13 per cent), Găgăuz (5.2 per cent) and Bulgarian (2 per cent), were largely russophone or bilingual in Russian and their native language. Faced with the prospect of domination by the Romanian-speaking majority, many Russian-speakers gravitated toward the pro-Soviet mass movement *Edinstvo*, which became the main political vehicle of the russophone population. A second anti-Romanian movement, *Găgăuz-Halki*, was formed to represent Moldova's Turkic Găgăuz minority in the south. Ethnic polarisation intensified in the context of the 1990 campaign for the republican legislature. While this focused in part on reform, it quickly took on a strongly ethnic character.

The 1990 elections fundamentally altered the Moldovan political landscape. The law governing the election provided for quite substantial competition. As the prospect of dramatic change became increasingly evident, an alliance began to take shape between key figures in the Soviet regime and the Popular Front. Among these was Mircea Snegur, a Central Committee Secretary since 1985, who was appointed President of the Moldovan Supreme Soviet in July 1989. By early 1990 he had clearly associated himself with the Popular Front and its political programme. Approximately one third of deputies elected to the republican Supreme Soviet were Popular Front members. With the support of allies among the deputies of the Communist Party, the Popular Front was able to command a majority of the votes in the new legislature. Snegur, still a Communist, was named President of the Supreme Soviet. Mircea Druc, a Popular Front leader and vocal proponent of unification with Romania, was appointed Prime Minister. Under the influence of Druc and other nationalist deputies, the legislature introduced a series of extremely divisive measures, which heightened the growing anxiety of the Russian-speaking minorities.

Anti-Soviet efforts by the majority population thus reinforced ethnic divisions in Moldova. Extremists among the Popular Front leaders became increasingly open and aggressive in their pursuit of power, hastening the descent into violence. When Popular Front leaders organised demonstrations in central Chişinău to intimidate their opponents, russophone deputies withdrew from the Supreme Soviet. In localities with a Russian-speaking majority, the authorities began to set up independent political institutions. The cities of Tiraspol, Bender and Ribniţa all passed laws suspending the application of central government edicts within their boundaries. In August 1990 the Găgăuz minority went even further, declaring the formation of an independent republic in the southern region. The local Communist Party leadership on the east bank of the Dniester (Transdniestria) followed suit, forming the Dniester Moldovan Republic. Ethnic polarisation was brought to a head by the August 1991 anti-Gorbachev coup. In Chişinău, the Popular Front controlled government denounced the coup and declared independence on 27 August 1991. The separatist leaders pursued the opposite course with equal vigour, declaring for the coup plotters and asserting their independence from the new Republic of Moldova.

Post-Soviet Moldova: ethnic division and elite conflict

The transition from Soviet rule to independence in Moldova produced a complex network of competing interests and no clear victor. At the popular level, ethnic divisions were evident. But conflict also arose between those favouring political and economic reform on the one hand, and those committed to resisting it on the other. The Romanian and Russian-speaking communities were deeply divided on fundamental questions of sovereignty and statehood. Divisions on reform issues were less substantial overall, and tended not to coincide with ethnic divisions. In general, the population was highly cautious with regard to reform. While a majority favoured reforms in principle, in 1992 less than 10 per cent of the population favoured total privatisation of industrial property, while about half favoured retaining state ownership intact. Despite their characterisation as supporters of the successor communists, in fact ethnic Russians expressed a slightly more reformist disposition than Romanian-speakers.

Controversy over ethnic identity was not confined to the russophone versus Romanian-speaking division, but divided the Romanian-speaking majority as well. Despite the pan-Romanian convictions of the Popular Front leadership, the self-identification of Romanian-speakers in Moldova was overwhelmingly 'Moldovan' rather than Romanian. The strongly pan-Romanian agenda of the Popular Front therefore failed to inspire broad popular support, even at a time when inter-ethnic conflict was relatively intense.

These competing divisions established the parameters within which elite factions contested for power. For as long as political discourse focussed on inter-ethnic issues, moderate elites were at a tactical disadvantage to extremists. But opinion on key reform issues cut across rather than reinforced ethnic division, which clearly provided the basis for a non-ethnic appeal. Similarly, divisions within the majority community on national identity worked against the interests of ethnic extremists.

As in many post-Soviet republics, Moldova's newly-emerging political elite was deeply fragmented, and the country lacked any coherent opposition organisations. Nothing like the institutionalised civil society produced in Poland under the sway of the Solidarity movement was in evidence. When the effectiveness of Soviet-era institutions inevitably eroded, Moldovan politics became increasingly disordered. Competition for power took place in an environment of escalating social crisis. As elsewhere during the first phase of transition, the economy suffered massive dislocation. In part this was a result of the generalised failure of the Soviet economy. Simultaneously, the loss of the territory on the left bank of the Dniester to the secessionist Transdniestrian regime dislocated industrial production throughout the entire republic. As the economic crisis deepened (GDP declined by approximately 14 per cent in 1991), the government vacillated, unable to produce a comprehensive reform policy. Faced with this looming crisis, pro-reform and anti-reform factions proposed radically different policy directions, and failed to reach any consensus.

Ethnic conflict also played a role in the competition for political power among members of the elite. Clearly, escalation benefited radicals within the Popular Front, many of whom favoured reunification of Moldova with Romania and the construction of a single 'Greater Romanian' state. The greater the level of conflict, the stronger their hold on the Romanian-speaking majority. Just as clearly, moderates (mostly drawn from among former communists) recognised their vulnerability, and therefore promoted consensus between the majority and minority communities. Mircea Snegur, a key figure in the reformist camp, achieved a first step in reorienting the government. His confidence-building measures included a broadly inclusive citizenship law passed in June 1991. In an effort to establish a power base independent of the Popular Front, Snegur successfully argued for direct presidential elections, and was elected to the office unopposed in December 1991. Unable to counter the moderates' initiative, the Popular Front lost the ability to dominate policy unilaterally, though its members remained a powerful force within the legislature.

In Tiraspol there were few signs of such moderating tendencies. On the contrary, under the leadership of Igor Smirnov, the separatist regime became increasingly aggressive. Smirnov was elected president in elections engineered by the region's former communist party nomenklatura and not recognised internationally. While maintaining the pretence of democratic governance, he and his closest lieutenants established an extremely repressive regime based on their direct personal control of the military and security services. The Transdniestrians were quick to build bridges to nationalists in Moscow, recruiting volunteers and seeking to influence Russian political and military leaders. Moscow provided access to an alternative financial infrastructure that mitigated the impact of the secession. Assured of external support, Transdniestria aggressively pursued the goal of complete independence. The Smirnov leadership's increasing intransigence, and conflict over control of the contested city of Bender (Tighina), led to a major escalation in the Transdniestria conflict in 1992. With nationalists in parliament demanding action, President Snegur undertook to disarm units of the separatist militia by force. This attempt met with armed resistance, and by May 1992 the conflict had escalated into full-scale civil war. Resolving the separatist issue was profoundly complicated by the involvement of Russia, whose forces intervened on the side of the Transdniestrians. The July 1992 cease-fire agreement which ended the worst of the fighting was reached with the support of President Yeltsin, but no final resolution of the conflict was achieved. Russian negotiators publicly supported a settlement based on substantial Transdniestrian autonomy within Moldova, but were not willing to impose this on the separatists.

Widespread popular discontent with the conflict provided a crucial opportunity for ethnic moderates to consolidate their influence. A new government formed under Andrei Sangheli in June 1992 immediately distanced itself from the Popular Front. Sangheli increased russophone representation and pursued a strategy based on reducing inter-ethnic tensions. His government also promised more thoroughgoing economic reform. Seeing their support diminish, Popular Front deputies pursued a course of legislative obstructionism that brought work in the parliament to a near standstill. President Snegur joined in the migration to the political centre. He made overtures to the former communists, and warned against the extremes of either unification with Romania or closer integration into the CIS. When the pro-Popular Front president of parliament offered his resignation in protest against the emerging policy direction, former Communist Party First Secretary Petru Lucinschi returned from his post as Ambassador to Russia to assume leadership of the legislature.

The newly-formed executive triumvirate of Snegur, Sangheli, and Lucinschi quickly determined that the transition legislature was no longer viable. At their urging, new elections were called for 27 February 1994. Entering the legislative campaign, supporters of the government, drawn primarily from Romanian-speaking members of the former regime's rural apparatus, organised the Agrarian Democratic Party. United by common interests and drawing on infrastructure inherited from the Soviet regime, the Agrarians were able to maintain cohesion. The Popular Front, by contrast, fell into disarray. Moderates among its deputies, distressed with its increasingly provocative agenda, defected to form the Congress of Intellectuals. Several liberal MPs, discouraged by the Front's failure to pursue economic reform, established independent centre-right parties promoting their agenda. The Popular Front's parliamentary representation was thus reduced to only 25 deputies.

The rules governing the 1994 legislative elections called for a dramatically smaller legislature than before (104 against 380 deputies), elected by closed-list proportional representation. In order to avoid an impasse over representation from Transdniestria and the Găgăuz region, the legislature established a single national electoral district. The campaign focussed on alterative approaches to the separatist crisis and on economic reform. The left-wing Socialist and Agrarian Democrats called for cautious reform, social protection, and a slow transition to market capitalism. These parties also favoured close relations with Russia, full participation in the CIS, and a conciliatory approach to majority/minority relations and the separatist crisis. At the opposite ideological extreme, the Popular Front and the National Christian Party argued for unification with Romania. In addition, several small liberal parties, mostly supported by urban professionals, campaigned for rapid marketisation and privatisation.

The outcome of Moldova's first truly democratic legislative election marked a dramatic shift away from the politics of the early transition. The campaign appears to have been fairly contested for the most part. The single most significant outcome was popular rejection of the parties identified with 'pan-Romanianism' in favour of those supporting an independent Moldovan identity and ethnic accommodation. The Agrarian Democrats won approximately 43 per cent of the vote and 56 seats in the new parliament. A second left-wing party, the Socialist Bloc (the Socialist Party and *Edinstvo*) captured 22 per cent of the vote and 28 seats. The Socialist Bloc dominated the urban vote, taking first place in five of Moldova's seven cities (in essence, areas where industrial workers and Russian-speakers were concentrated). The Agrarian Democrats won in all the rural districts, and in the two cities not won by the Socialists. Pro-Romanian nationalists suffered a massive defeat. The Bloc of Peasants and Intellectuals (vehicle of the moderately pro-Romanian Congress of Intellectuals) did best, garnering a little over 9 per cent of the vote and eleven seats. The Popular Front was reduced to less than 8 per cent of the vote and nine seats in parliament. No other party or bloc surmounted the 4 per cent threshold.

The 1994 parliamentary election ended the first phase of post-communist political realignment. While committed minorities continued to support extremist positions, the overall distribution of popular opinion worked substantially to the advantage of the more moderate Agrarian Democratic Party. The Agrarians (and their sponsors within the republic's leadership) were able to turn this advantage into a massive electoral success in 1994. Thus the outcome of electoral competition in Moldova produced a strategy of ethnic inclusion, while ethnic extremists within the majority community were effectively marginalised.

Institutional deadlock, elite competition and the failure of politics

The 1994 legislative election brought to an end (at least briefly) competition between the executive and legislative branches, and provided a working majority in parliament. Previously deadlocked legislation was revived and enacted, including an agreement giving local autonomy to the Găgăuz region. This accord was seen by many at the time as the model for a future Transdniestrian settlement. It recognised an autonomous Găgăuz region with the right to elect its own representatives, local linguistic rights, and the right to seceed should Moldova unify with Romania.

On 29 July 1994 parliament ratified a new post-Soviet constitution which had previously been blocked. In broad outline, it called for the formation of a democratic republic guaranteeing human rights and representative political pluralism. Institutionally, power at the national level was to be divided between the president of the republic, a unicameral legislature, and a constitutional court.

Moldova's legislature is the Parliament of Moldova (*Parlamentul Moldovei*), described in the constitution as the supreme representative body of the republic. Deputies are elected to four-year terms by direct universal vote. It elects a president of parliament by secret majority vote of the deputies, and may remove him by a two-thirds vote. Parliament passes laws, may call for a referendum, and exercises control over the executive as laid down in the constitution. Ten permanent commissions scrutinise legislation in various specialist areas.

The president is described in the constitution as the chief of state. Under the terms of the 1994 constitution (since amended) the president is elected by direct universal vote for a four-year term. He is charged with guaranteeing the independence and unity of the republic, and overseeing the efficient functioning of public authorities. The president may be impeached by vote of two-thirds of the deputies in parliament. The president can take part in meetings of the government, and presides when he does so. He nominates the prime minister following consultation with the parliamentary majority and names the government subject to a vote of confidence by parliament. The president can dissolve parliament if it cannot agree a government within 60 days. This can be done only once in a year, not during the last six months of the life of a parliament, and not during a state of emergency or war.

The government consists of the prime minister, and other ministers as determined by law. Once chosen by the president the prime minister selects a government and draws up a programme which is then submitted to parliament for a vote of confidence. The government and its members are responsible to parliament. They must submit to parliamentary questioning on request, and must participate in the work of parliament. Parliament has the power to dismiss the government through a majority vote of no confidence.

The constitution sought the middle ground in inter-ethnic relations. Forsaking the references to the 'Romanian' language prominent in earlier drafts, the final document substituted 'Moldovan'. This both calmed the minorities' fears of incorporation into a unified Romanian state and promoted the concept of a Moldovan civic identity independent of Romanian national identity. For similar reasons, references to a 'national' state were eliminated in favour of more inclusive terminology. In a further gesture to the minorities, Article 13 committed the state to 'recognise and promote' the development and functioning of Russian and other languages spoken in the country.

In addition to breaking the legislative deadlock, the Agrarian-dominated government initially appeared more committed to economic reform than its predecessor. A new ministry of privatisation was established in April 1994, and a more vigorous programme of economic transformation was initiated. In the rural sector the first steps were taken in agricultural privatisation through the conversion of state enterprises into joint stock companies. By the close of 1995 the impact of the change in policy direction was evident. Moldova was widely considered by Western governments and international agencies to be among the more progressive of the post-Soviet states, and began to receive substantial Western support.

Yet even while Moldova appeared to be on a positive trajectory, a number of factors in the immediate aftermath of the 1994 elections undermined progress. Most important among these was an unrelenting power struggle among the top elite. As in a number of post-communist countries, Moldova's political class was drawn largely from members of the former regime. In an environment only loosely constrained by the rule of law, influential politicians were quick to form personalised factions linking members of the state administration, powerful individuals in the private sector, and elected officials.

Increasingly it was the interests of these 'elite cartels' that determined policy. Discord at the pinnacle of power was further exacerbated by the country's semi-presidential system, which left lines of authority between the president and the legislature unclear. These conditions, in conjunction with Moldova's lack of a constitutional tradition, created a situation in which no actor was able to impose definitive decisions. Lines of authority blurred, and policy stalemate rapidly ensued. While civil liberties remained largely intact, public accountability became increasingly difficult to enforce.

Finally, the unresolved Transdniestria issue both undermined efforts to revive the economy and added to the popular perception of government deadlock. The crisis was profoundly complicated by Russian involvement. Moscow's record in Transdniestria was ambiguous at best, despite official support for conciliation. In the negotiations following the July 1992 cease-fire agreement, Russia publicly supported a political settlement of the crisis based on Transdniestrian autonomy within a sovereign Moldova. But Moscow continued to provide substantial behind-the-scenes support to Transdniestria. Meanwhile the continued presence of Russia's 14th Army made the military suppression of the Tiraspol government impossible and encouraged the Transdniestrians not to compromise. In a major concession, Moldova accepted that Russian troop withdrawal should be synchronised with a political solution to the separatist conflict. But this agreement, which was immediately denounced by leaders in Tiraspol, was followed by more months of controversy, and little or no actual progress.

Given this uncertain environment, it is hardly surprising that an open struggle for power broke out during the run-up to the 1996 presidential election. President Snegur began his fight for a new term of office by shifting toward the pro-Romanian political niche formerly occupied by the increasingly marginalised Popular Front. Taking nearly all political observers by surprise, Snegur reversed his previously-held position on the highly sensitive national language issue. Abandoning 'Moldovanism', he introduced legislation that declared Romanian the official language of the republic. This act, intended to attract the support of the more nationalist Romanian-speaking voters, was rebuffed by parliament in early February. Putting his confrontation with the rest of the leadership at the centre of his campaign, Snegur argued that his rivals were using the legislature to block reform. He proposed that the constitution should be amended to turn Moldova into a 'presidential republic'. Snegur also came out in favour of more thoroughgoing economic reform, and more rapid integration into West European political and economic structures.

The 1996 presidential election highlighted both the evolution of public opinion and the weakness of Snegur's position in relation to his rivals. The strength of the left-wing parties was attributable both to the continued influence of Soviet-era ideology on the electorate, much of which remained attached to socialist-egalitarian values, and to widespread concern that thoroughgoing economic reform would mean further hardship. In the first round on 16 November, President Snegur came in first of nine candidates with 38.8 per cent of the vote, followed by Lucinschi with 27.7 per cent and Vladimir Voronin, leader of the Communist Party (which returned to activity in April 1994 after being banned in 1991), with about 10 per cent. Sangheli, supported by the Agrarians, was able to attract only 9.5 per cent of the vote. In the second round President Snegur, limited to the Romanian-speaking ethnic base, was only able to increase his share of the vote by about 6 per cent, bringing his total to 46 per cent. By contrast, Lucinschi attracted support from across the entire centre-left, including moderates within the russophone population, as well as those Romanian-speakers who were less supportive of rapid reform. As a former Communist Party First Secretary, he also benefited from a general perception that his high-level CPSU connections would enable him to resolve the Transdniestria dispute. Lucinschi thus captured 54 per cent of the second round vote and assumed the presidency.

Despite the hopes invested in him by the electorate, Lucinschi did not manage either to bring an end to the infighting and institutional deadlock that had plagued Moldova for the previous four years or to resolve the Transdniestria conflict. The new government established under Prime Minister Ion Ciubuc (formally an independent) and backed by President Lucinschi was composed largely of hangovers from the previous cabinet, but with the addition of two ministers from the Communist Party of the Republic of Moldova (CPRM). To the consternation of most observers, while the configuration of leadership changed following the election, the prevailing pattern of elite politics immediately reasserted itself. Factionalism and institutional disorder continued to undermine policy-making. While officially pro-reform, Ciubuc's government proved largely indecisive, especially with regard to privatisation and budgetary issues. Reform also continued to be hindered by parliament, due both to the continued strength of anti-reform deputies and the growing political fragmentation of its membership.

In the absence of decisive government action, the economy continued in free-fall. First, Moldova is virtually entirely energy-dependent, having no hydrocarbons and almost no other sources of power. Second, within the former Soviet Union Moldova had been a large-scale producer of agricultural commodities. The collapse of the USSR and the decline of Russia's economy devastated Moldovan agricultural exports. Its balance of trade became highly negative, and it began to accrue enormous debts, particularly in the energy sector. As elsewhere in the region, official corruption quickly grew to epidemic proportions. Members of the former nomenklatura took advantage of their positions to sell access to the state, and to profit from trade between the economically failing but publicly-subsidised state-owned enterprises and the private sector. Finally, in addition to causing the loss of sizeable industrial capacity and disrupting production in the republic as a whole, Transdniestria presented an increasingly grave criminal justice problem. As the crisis dragged on, the break-away region became a magnet for illegal economic activity linking individuals from the Transdniestrian separatist region, the rest of Moldova, and Russia. Smuggling, customs fraud, arms trafficking and other activities were carried on outside the administrative reach of Chişinău, but had a significant impact on the economy of the whole country.

According to World Bank figures, Moldova's real GDP (excluding Transdniestria, for which no reliable figures are available) fell on average by 10 per cent per year through the 1990s (more than 30 per cent in 1994 alone). By 1997, Moldova was poorer than any other country in Central Europe, and poorer than any former Soviet republic except Tajikistan and Uzbekistan, with a per capita GDP of $527. The 1988 Russian economic crisis delivered a further blow. While unemployment was kept relatively under control, the impact on the standard of living was disastrous. Outside Chişinău access to electricity and gas for heating became problematic for long periods each winter. Conditions were particularly harsh in the villages, where land reform had fragmented agricultural property and new market-based production was slow to take hold. With little or no alternative to agricultural employment, many rural dwellers shifted to subsistence farming, while much of the younger generation abandoned the countryside either for the capital or for work abroad. By the late 1990s rural malnutrition was widespread, and chronic diseases had become pervasive as a result of a breakdown in health care.

Collectively these conditions produced a growing sense of social crisis. The number of Moldovans believing that the country was 'on course' politically or expressing confidence in any of the political leaders declined dramatically. The impact of popular discontent was unmistakable in the 1998 parliamentary contest. Of the 15 parties and electoral blocs, only one could claim the support of more than 15 per cent of the population in the months leading up to the election. This was the CPRM. Under Voronin's leadership, this party became the primary outlet for the many Moldovans who had suffered as a consequence of the transition. As in other post-Soviet states, the Communists' core constituency included pensioners and others dependent on the state and nostalgic for the previous regime. The CPRM was supported disproportionately by Russian-speakers in general, and in particular Russian-speaking industrial workers. In the pre-election period, the Communists campaigned for better social protection, closer integration into the CIS, and joining the Russia-Belarus Union.

The Communist resurgence presented a significant threat to President Lucinschi, who had thus far benefited from the lack of credible alternatives for left-wing voters. Now forced to compete, he established the Movement for a Democratic and Prosperous Moldova (MDPM), which described itself as a social democratic party. Entering the 1998 election, the MDPM campaigned in support of the presidency, for social justice, and for retaining a strong system of social protection. Lucinschi's MDPM was more neutral than the Communists with respect to foreign policy alignment. This had the advantage of appealing to leftist elements in the more Western-oriented Romanian-speaking majority. The MDPM argued that strengthening the institutional role of the president would resolve the republic's policy deadlock and provide more efficient government.

The centre-right remained deeply divided entering the 1998 elections. Like Lucinschi, former President Snegur had also established his own political party, the Party for Revival and Conciliation in Moldova (PRCM), following his break with the Agrarian Democrats in 1995. In addition to its personalised appeal to Snegur's admirers, the PRCM espoused a pro-reform and pro-Romanian platform. The PRCM campaigned within an electoral bloc, the Democratic Convention of Moldova (CDM), that reunited Snegur in an uneasy partnership with former Popular Front allies, now rechristened the Christian Democratic People's Party (PPCD). Yet a third right-wing party, the Party of Democratic Forces (PDF), headed by Valeriu Matai, decided to run separate candidates. Matei took an extremely critical public stance on the political establishment, focussing primarily on corruption. His party argued for near-term independence but eventual reunification with Romania. Positioning himself in this way Matei hoped to become the choice of the moderately nationalist segment of the Romanian-speaking majority.

The election result was mixed. Four parties got the 4 per cent necessary to enter parliament; the Communists with 30 per cent (40 seats), the Democratic Convention with 19.4 per cent (20 seats), Lucinschi's MDPM with 18.2 per cent (24 seats), and finally the PDF with 8.8 per cent (11 seats). This outcome reflected the abiding divisions in Moldovan society, in essence giving the main left-wing parties 48.9 per cent of the vote and a potential 64 seats, and the main right-wing parties 28.3 per cent and a potential 37 seats. In the normal course of events one would assume continued government by the centre-left. Intra-elite politics, however, dictated otherwise. Despite their internal differences, the non-communists united in opposition to the CPRM's assumption of a central political role. In order to hold Voronin in check they joined to form a new vehicle, the Alliance for Democracy and Reform (ADR). The ADR comprised 61 deputies representing the CDM, the PDF and MDPM. A coalition agreement signed on the day of the new parliament's inaugural sitting, 21 April 1998, called for development of a joint programme and the allocation of offices proportionally to all three factions. Dumitru Diacov, the legislative leader of the MDPM, was voted in as parliamentary chairman, with Valeriu Matai and Iurie Roşca (head of the PPCD) as his deputies.

Combining pro-reform and anti-reform, and pro-nationalist and anti-nationalist factions, the ADR was in fact an alliance in name only. While Diacov and the MDPM at least formally supported the president's policy agenda, the leaders of each of the other coalition parties were longstanding opponents of Lucinschi with their own aspirations to rule. They had no interest in promoting the president's legislative programme or in seeing his governmental initiatives succeed. Even Lucinschi's own lieutenant, Diacov, quickly came to see his position as legislative leader as a platform from which he might pursue independent power. After several months of wrangling, Diacov publicly broke with Lucinschi to form his own party, the Democratic Party of Moldova (PDM). Diacov's defection further aggravated both the factional dispute within the legislature and the dispute between the president and parliament. Thus, rather than clarifying lines of authority and providing a stable basis for governance, the 1998 legislative outcome condemned Moldova to further elite infighting and aggravated the prevailing institutional deadlock. Blocking an effort by the Democratic Convention to name one of its supporters as prime minister, President Lucinschi engineered the reappointment Ion Ciubuc. Ciubuc's new government, unmanageable from the outset, included ministers from all three of the coalition parties. While Ciubuc struggled to address the concerns of the IFIs and Western governments regarding reform and fiscal discipline, the country's economy continued to decline. His cabinet's ability to either cut services or reduce subsidies to failing enterprises was limited by its dependence on left-wing deputies (for the most part associated with Lucinschi) who would, if pushed too far, abandon the coalition. No workable formula was found to deal with the country's ever-mounting international debt. In particular, Moldovan imports of natural gas from Russia made the country both economically and politically vulnerable. When payment arrears surpassed $500 million, Gazprom threatened to interrupt Moldova's energy supplies. The energy debt could be rescheduled, ensuring an uninterrupted flow of the natural gas that was indispensable both for heating and to fuel Moldova's remaining industrial enterprises, only with backing from the Russian government. This in turn dictated that Moldova should exercise flexibility in other areas of its bilateral relationship in order to retain Moscow's support. Finally, the politicisation of public corruption bitterly divided the elite. Lucinschi and those close to him were charged by members of the coalition with involvement in financial fraud. This was met with counter-charges against the initiators, and a series of what the government's opponents considered to be political prosecutions. Under these conditions the ADR's ability to govern was limited at best.

Prime Minister Ciubuc very quickly found his position at the focal point of this turmoil untenable. Under constant attack from both right and left, he resigned in November 1998 having achieved virtually nothing. Prospects for the successor government under Ion Sturza were hardly any better. Sturza, a successful businessman considered a moderate reformer, retained all but four members of the Ciubuc cabinet. His government was voted into office only after two failed attempts, and with great difficulty. He was opposed by the Communist deputies, and also by the PPCD on the grounds that the proposed government included corrupt members of the preceding cabinets. Sturza undertook a series of actions to stabilise the fiscal situation and speed up privatisation. However, his appointment ultimately did little to resolve the underlying deadlock that had plagued his predecessors. Indeed, even as Prime Minister Sturza began to gain ground in the reform effort, President Lucinschi distanced himself from the government. Lucinschi ever more openly questioned the functionality of the existing constitutional order, arguing that it was no longer possible to govern the country effectively because of the incessant institutional power-struggle.

In a bid to break this stalemate in his own favour, in early 1999 Petru Lucinschi (like Snegur before him) called for a referendum to establish a 'presidential republic'. While the referendum was won by a narrow margin, the verdict was not properly valid because Moldova's constitution required a three-fifths turnout, and in this case only 58 per cent of the population voted. President Lucinschi, however, was not deterred. Rather, he established a special commission to draft a law to strengthen the role of the president. Lucinschi's initiative polarised the elite. Predictably, Lucinschi's rivals were vehemently against increasing presidential powers. The CPRM contended that it would be contrary to democratic principles and lead to a totalitarian regime. Similarly, the Democratic Convention and the PDF both argued that the proposed changes amounted to an effort to introduce in Moldova the type of authoritarian 'super-presidencies' that had emerged in the post-communist

Central Asian republics. Even many nominally pro-Lucinschi MDPM legislators questioned the initiative, causing a schism within that organisation.

In a show of considerable determination in the circumstances, Prime Minister Sturza and his cabinet struggled to stabilise the economy and revive stalled reforms. Once again, however, reform opponents in parliament worked both openly and behind the scenes to undermine what headway the government did make. When parliament failed to pass privatisation legislation affecting major tobacco and wine holdings, the IFIs reacted sharply. Signalling the seriousness of their dissatisfaction, the World Bank postponed structural-adjustment credit, and the IMF suspended its Moldova operations. Under criticism from all sides, Sturza's government was brought down in November 2000 through a vote of no confidence engineered by the Communists and the Christian Democrats. President Lucinschi responded to Sturza's fall by attempting to shift still further to the left. He proposed Vladimir Voronin as Prime Minister, hoping that the Communists' forty-member parliamentary faction would provide the basis for a stable parliamentary majority. But Voronin's candidacy was predictably blocked by the centre-right. When a second candidate failed to accumulate the necessary number of votes, Lucinschi threatened to dissolve parliament and call early elections, which would in all likelihood have resulted in large electoral gains for the Communists. In order to avoid this outcome, in late December a majority in parliament accepted the nomination of Dumitru Braghiş, a compromise candidate, as prime minister.

Braghiş, once head of the Soviet-era Communist Youth League, formed a 'technocratic' cabinet committed to a programme of efficient reform and anti-corruption efforts. Braghiş was supported in parliament by a politically unstable alliance between the Communists and PPCD deputies. On taking office Prime Minister Braghiş faced a daunting task. Public confidence in the political class was at an all-time low, and Moldova's economy was in a state of near-total collapse. The government had accumulated massive arrears in pension and wage payments, and international lenders were increasingly sceptical regarding Moldovan creditworthiness. Furthermore, while the Braghiş cabinet was publicly committed to reform (if nothing else in order to secure the backing of international lenders), its dependence on the support of Communist deputies for survival again severely limited its actions. It is hardly surprising then that despite its liberal rhetoric the Braghiş government failed to push the reform process forward or revive the failing economy. Throughout his term in office Prime Minister Braghiş was plagued by Moldova's seemingly interminable elite infighting, which both hindered his ability to develop a coherent agenda and undermined implementation once a particular course of action was agreed upon.

Ultimately, however, it was the ongoing power struggle between the president and his parliamentary rivals rather than any policy failure by the government that led to the dissolution of parliament. Allegedly under threat from Lucinschi's scheme to establish a presidential republic, his rivals struck back with an alternative initiative. PPCD legislators introduced a counter-proposal to form a 'parliamentary republic'. This idea was immediately seconded by the Communist faction and gained the support of a large parliamentary majority. The basic thrust was simple: break the prevailing institutional deadlock in favour of the legislative branch by reducing the role of the chief of state in domestic affairs, and have the president indirectly elected by parliament. On 22 September 2000 legislation was passed under which parliament elects the president by a three-fifths majority. If no candidate gets the required number of votes, a second round must be organised within three days. This pits the two candidates with the highest number of votes in the first round against each other. If no candidate obtains the required majority in the second round, a repeat election must be conducted within 15 days. If this again fails, then the president must dissolve parliament and new legislative elections are called.

The legislators' intention was clearly to block Petru Lucinschi from winning a second term, but the immediate consequence of their action was the dissolution of parliament. In preparation for the first contest to be held under the new rules in December 2000, Communist deputies nominated CPRM leader Vladimir Voronin. The Democratic Convention and the PDF jointly supported Pavel Barbălat. Neither candidate gained the necessary three-fifths majority in the first or second rounds. In essence, all the non-communists joined together to block Voronin, but the CPRM faction was just large enough to block the election of any other candidate. On the day of the third ballot, the centre-right parties boycotted the legislative session in order to avoid the election of a Communist. After obtaining a ruling from the constitutional court that the third ballot could be considered to have failed, President Lucinschi announced the dissolution of parliament and set early elections for 25 February 2001.

After post-communism

The overwhelming victor in the election contest was the CPRM, which took 50.7 per cent of the vote and 71 of the 101 seats in parliament. The Braghiş Alliance, whose leadership was composed of members of the government and which had the support of President Lucinschi, came in a distant second, with 13.4 per cent and 19 seats. Only one other party, the CDPP, surpassed the 6 per cent threshold. It won 8.2 per cent of the vote and 11 seats. Two parties, the Party of Rebirth and Reconciliation with 5.8 per cent and the DPM with 5 per cent, would have been included in the legislature under the previous threshold rule, but were now excluded.

The factors that led to the CPRM's decisive victory were quite clear. As a consequence of the economic collapse and continual infighting, support for political parties and leaders associated with the government plummeted in the months leading up to the election. The CPRM enjoyed more support than any other party in virtually every demographic category. Eurobarometer public opinion data collected just prior to the election show the Communists enjoyed disproportionate support among the less educated, the older population, and among non-Moldovans. Those dissatisfied with the political parties in general, and those who felt most at risk economically, were also significantly more likely to support the Communists. Finally, the centre-right parties also suffered as a consequence of demographic changes in the country. By 2001, well over 500,000 Moldovans had left the country in search of employment. Disproportionately young, educated, and disaffected with economic conditions, the migrants could have been expected to vote in favour of reformist parties had they remained in Moldova.

The 2001 election redefined Moldova's political landscape. Marginalised during most of the transition, the Communists were now the dominant political force. With 71 seats, the CPRM could not only choose the country's next president but also amend the constitution at will. Vladimir Voronin was immediately elected President of Moldova with the support of all 71 Communist deputies. Dumitru Braghiş, who came second, was able to attract only 15 votes. PPCD deputies, not wanting to add legitimacy to the election of a Communist president, boycotted the proceedings. The new government formed under Prime Minister Vasile Tarlev, a successful business manager, retained eleven members of the previous cabinet. This continuity and Tarlev's selection were seen as concessions to moderates and as a signal of the Communists' willingness to take a flexible approach. At the same time, however, having gained a level of political control unprecedented in Moldova since the beginning of the post-Soviet transition, the CPRM laid out an agenda designed to reverse many of their predecessors' reforms. The new leadership declared its intention to halt decollectivisation, reestablish the state's taxing authority and re-nationalise failing privatised enterprises. The party also proposed to strengthen Moldova's economic ties to Russia and integrate more comprehensively into the CIS. To the dismay of liberals, the symbolism and rhetoric of the Soviet regime also began to reappear in public life. Less controversially, Voronin committed himself to attacking the problem of corruption, and to paying the arrears in state employees' wages and pensions.

Much of this enjoyed widespread popular support. Other proposals greatly favoured by the more dogmatic wing of the CPRM proved highly destabilising. Among the most controversial of these were plans to revise the state language law and join the Russia-Belarus Union. In early June it was decided to return to the previous Soviet pattern of local administration. This move reversed a major administrative reform carried out with the support of the EU and World Bank. The reform, designed to streamline and reduce the cost of local administration, reduced the number of local administrative units from 40 *raions* to 12 larger *judets*. Much of the rural population objected to the reform because it would reduce access to social and administrative services. The Communists' objections were driven by more political concerns as well, in that the *judet* was the traditional Romanian unit of sub-national administration, raising fears of eventual reunification, and the reform would involve the retirement of large numbers of local civil servants associated with the party.

Further raising the Romanian-speaking population's fears of russification, President Voronin made a clear public display of his close attachment to Moscow, and rapidly concluded a bilateral treaty with the Russian Federation which named Russia as the guarantor of the Transdniestria peace settlement and recognised the special status of the Russian language. The ministry of education engaged in a series of equally controversial heavy-handed initiatives. Most alarmingly, the ministry announced its intention to make Russian-language instruction mandatory in lower grades. Soon afterwards a textbook on the history of Romania scheduled for introduction into the national curriculum was withdrawn; a new history of Moldova would be written instead by scholars widely associated with the Soviet regime.

Even moderates in the non-russophone population took these initiatives as a direct assault on reforms seen as central to the national independence movement. Criticism of the initiatives, however, was met by administrative pressure, and by charges that opponents were motivated by nationalist extremism. After vainly opposing President Voronin for months, the Christian Democrats were able to turn these issues into the focal point of a growing popular protest movement. Unable to press their case effectively in the legislature, PPCD leaders began to organise daily demonstrations in Chişinău at which they denounced the return to Soviet communism and called for mass action to save democracy. As the protests escalated through February and

March 2002, isolated incidents of violence occurred and rumours circulated that the regime was preparing to deploy its armed forces against the protestors.

For their part, the leaders of the ruling party showed little tolerance for public dissent, and employed increasingly heavy-handed tactics against their critics. The state-owned media was subjected to increased political control; and both official and unofficial pressure was brought to bear on the regime's adversaries. In late January, the PPCD was banned from political activity for a period of 30 days and its leaders threatened with further sanctions should they continue their protests. The justice minister also suggested that the opposition leaders could be prosecuted for inciting violence. Teachers and educational administrators whose students participated in the demonstrations were threatened with dismissal, as on occasion were the parents of student leaders.

Even at their height these protests were clearly only supported by a politically-aware minority within the Romanian-speaking community. Overall, popular backing for the Communists remained strong. Yet while the party was easily able to contain its opponents, the political cost of its confrontational approach was substantial. The tensions produced by the CPRM programme generated a highly negative response internationally. Even before the protests, plans to reverse the territorial-administrative reform had been badly received, particularly by the EU. Moldova's relations with the IFIs also deteriorated sharply in reaction to the Tarlev government's retreat from economic reform. In the context of an already distrustful relationship with the West, the regime's harsh tactics in dealing with its opponents generated a sharply critical response from the diplomatic community. The Council of Europe registered a series of complaints against Moldova. The Romanian government, reacting to accusations by members of the Tarlev government that Bucharest was encouraging extremists and interfering in Moldova's domestic affairs, issued a communiqué accusing Chişinău of anti-Romanian rhetoric. The international community's forceful reaction to events in Moldova raised the very real possibility of diplomatic isolation. Given the country's economic vulnerability, this was an extremely unpalatable prospect.

Confronted with a nearly universal negative reaction from the West, and finding little indication of support from Russia, the CPRM sharply altered its political course in early 2002. The government's confrontational public approach to dealing with sensitive ethnic issues abruptly disappeared. Plans to make Russian language study mandatory were dropped, along with the offending Moldovan history text. The minister of education publicly apologised for his mistakes and was dismissed by President Voronin. By thus removing the most incendiary issues from public discourse the government dramatically reduced support for anti-communist demonstrations, and was able once again to marginalise its Christian Democrat opponents.

President Voronin took steps to repair relations with the international community as well. Following a series of discussions, the Tarlev government agreed to maintain its budget within limits established by the IMF and to follow IMF recommendations on the management of its international trade inspection regime. Finally, the Communist Party leadership agreed to participate in a mediation effort sponsored by the Council of Europe. This initiative brought the CPRM and the opposition together in Strasbourg in mid-April in an effort to promote civility in political discourse and cooperation between the government and opposition.

----President Voronin and the Moldovan Communists clearly recognised and responded to the constraints imposed by the international environment and their own economic vulnerabily. Party leaders pulled back from the most provocative of their initiatives, and made visible efforts to respond at least in part to the requirements of the IFIs. These efforts to mend relations with the international community met with at least partial success. In mid-2002 the World Bank approved resumption of structural adjustment funding to Moldova. This decision was absolutely critical, as Moldova was by that point facing default on $75 million of Eurobond debt. With conditional support from the World Bank and the IMF, Tarlev was able to negotiate a restructuring agreement with the country's main creditors and stave off the financial disaster that would have followed default. In the longer term, however, his government continues to face daunting financial difficulties.

Further brightening the general outlook, Moldova's economy showed steady improvement, growing by 6.2 per cent in 2001 and about 7 per cent in 2002. In part this dramatic turn-around was attributable to Russia's recovery following the economic collapse of 1998. Moldovan economic growth also resulted from the positive effects of reforms undertaken during the late 1990s, and improvements in fiscal policy following 1998. Whatever their source, better economic conditions clearly benefitted the CPRM. The Communists were credited not only with the economic upturn, but also the improvement in governance that resulted from its control over both the executive and legislative branches. As public perception of conditions improved, support for the Communist Party and its leader increased as well. In the period following the elections support for the Communists increased among nearly all sectors of the population. Most striking were the inroads that the CPRM made among ethnic Moldovans and the rural population. Despite the disruptions that marred the country's politics in early 2002, more and more Romanian-speakers supported the CPRM regime, seeing it as the only one able to govern the country. As the government moved to repay pension arrears and halt the decline in living standards in Moldovan villages, rural support shifted sharply in the direction of the government. Coming in the wake of a decade marked by political turbulence, growing poverty and increasingly blatant corruption, the restoration of communist rule has been met by many Moldovans, at least initially, as a potential deliverance from a failed transition.

Conclusions

Moldova's post-communist transition began under markedly unfavourable circumstances. While a weak and poorly-organised democratic opposition pressed for an end to Soviet rule, conservatives within the Communist Party worked to retain what was possible of the status quo. Extremists in the majority Romanian-speaking community espoused unification with neighbouring Romania, and ethnic minorities resorted to separatism, seeking to establish independent political entities in order to defend their interests. These competing forces drove the country into civil conflict even as it struggled to establish its independence.

In sharp contrast to a number of other countries, however, in Moldova the cycle of ethnic conflict was broken. Following a relatively brief period of active conflict in 1992 the country succeeded in stepping back from civil war. Particularly within the Romanian-speaking population, moderate opinion predominated, and a serious dispute over their own national identity (Romanian vs. Moldovan) arose among Romanian-speakers, complicating the course of intra-communal politics.

While the development of multiple divisions within the elite played a positive role in moderating ethnic conflict during the early transition, elite conflict was unfortunately prominent among the factors that led to the debacle that followed. Rival factions battled for control of the country as the economy crumbled and the population sank into poverty. Elite conflict was aggravated by weak constitutionalism and an institutional structure that left lines of authority unclear, leaving politicians free to act, if not at will, at least with minimal constraint. The nearly continuous factional conflict both hindered reform and frustrated efforts to establish stable patterns of administration. In conjunction with Moldova's admittedly difficult circumstances, this failure of governance utterly devastated the economy, casting a large proportion of the population into poverty and discrediting the democratic transition.

With no acceptable alternative on the horizon, the revived Moldovan Communist Party became heir to the faltering state, largely because the party's leaders could claim to have had no role in the failed transition.

As they seek to navigate a way through a second decade of independence, two crucial issues face Moldova's leaders. First, the integrity of the CPRM itself has come under increasing strain it its role as a governing party. While pragmatists within its ranks see the necessity of reform and cooperation with Europe, party conservatives remain hostile to market capitalism, loyal to Moscow, and highly suspicious of Western intentions. Thus far President Voronin has been successful in maintaining overall control, but ultimately escape from the economic crisis besetting the country will require decisive reform. Either the necessary steps will be taken, at the expense of party unity, or reform will be eschewed, with the likely consequence of limiting Moldova's access to Western support and committing the country to a course more in line with the authoritarian politics of Belarus and Ukraine. Second, the issue of Transdniestria continues to forestall Moldova's development efforts. Each of the republic's three presidents has endeavoured to resolve the separatist crisis, as yet to no avail. Staking his hopes on support from the Kremlin, President Voronin has committed his government to the reintegration of Transdniestria into a federalised Republic of Moldova with substantial guarantees of rights for Russian-speaking minorities. This outcome, however reasonable, can only be achieved if decision-makers in Moscow are willing to impose it on a reluctant Transdniestrian leadership. Hence President Voronin's Transdniestrian initiative, while potentially crucial to Moldova's further development, represents a high-risk/high-gain strategy which increases his own vulnerability and his government's dependence on the Russian Federation.

Struggling towards Law? Human Rights and Legislative Reform in Moldova

Peter B. Maggs

Moldova has made considerable progress in developing the rule of law and human rights since the fall of the Soviet Union. However, a number of serious problems remain. The central government has no control over the region between the Dniester River and Ukraine. This area, Transdniestria, with 17 per cent of the population, is controlled by the 'Dniester Republic', where separatists have been in power since 1991 with the support of the Russian army. The 'Dniester Republic' has kept most of the bad features of Soviet law and policy, including arbitrary arrests, restrictions on free speech, and rigged elections. In the rest of Moldova, human rights have been much better, though not perfectly respected. Elections have been free and fair. Citizens, political parties, newspapers, radio, and television have enjoyed far broader freedom of speech than was allowed under the Soviet regime. There is freedom of religion and freedom of movement within the country and abroad. New, modern legislation has slowly replaced Soviet-era laws. The linguistic rights of the Romanian-speaking majority, which were restricted under Soviet rule, have been restored, though occasionally at the expense of restrictions of the rights of the Russian-speaking minority. However, some actions of the Communist Party in power since 2001 have alarmed human rights advocates.

The Constitution of the Republic of Moldova was adopted in 1994 and has been significantly amended since then. It provides for a unicameral parliament, a president chosen by parliament, a judicial system headed by a Supreme Court, and a separate Constitutional Court. Constitutional amendments suppressing basic rights and freedoms are not allowed.

Constitutional amendments involving the sovereignty, independence and unity of the state may be passed only by vote of a majority of registered voters in a referendum. Thus, for instance, any decision to grant independence to Transdniestria, to cede Transdniestria to Russia, or to merge Moldova with Romania would require a referendum. Other constitutional amendments require a petition with a substantial number of signatories, approval by at least four judges of the Constitutional Court, a six-months' waiting period and a two-thirds majority in Parliament. The Constitution lists a set of important matters on which parliament may legislate only by majority vote of all its members. Parliament may legislate on all other matters by a majority vote of those present. The Constitution contains an extensive bill of rights, and indicates that international human rights treaties should be considered in interpreting and applying the bill of rights. The Constitutional Court has generally acted to enforce these provisions.

Moldova has been slow to replace the outmoded legislation of the Soviet era. With the fall of the Soviet system, laws were hastily drafted to provide the basis for a market economy until more comprehensive legislation was ready. Considerable progress has been made in codification with the adoption of new codes on Auditing and Accounting Ethics (2001), Automotive Transport (1998), Constitutional Jurisdiction (1995), Criminal Punishment (1993), Customs (2000), Elections (1997), Family (2000), Forests (1996) Land (1991), Merchant Shipping (1999), Subsoil Resources (1993), Tax (1997, 2001), and Water (1993). And, not surprisingly, given the importance of viticulture in Moldova, Parliament has adopted a Code on the Practical Conduct of Winemaking (2002). New Criminal and Criminal Procedure Codes effective in 2003 introduce major reforms. Other areas of modernisation of the legal system include laws which came into effect in 2003 on the Procuracy (the public prosecutor), the bar, and notaries (who play an important role in Moldova as in other civil law countries). A new modern Civil Code was adopted in 2002, but it will not replace the 1964 Civil Code until the implementation of the new Civil Procedure Code now being drafted. Parliament has considered a draft of a new labour code.

The new Criminal and Criminal Procedure Codes are a major improvement on their Soviet predecessors. However, the Criminal Code contains a few provisions that have caused concern to human rights advocates, in particular those allowing criminal prosecution for abuses by religious organisations and for defamation: the Soviet regime used similar provisions on religious abuses to persecute evangelical religions. Many countries have used threats of criminal defamation penalties to suppress free speech. In civil cases, the Moldovan courts have generally ruled in favour of journalists sued for defamation, so criminal prosecution for defamation appears at present to be more of a theoretical than an actual problem. The new Criminal Procedure Code reforms the investigative process to reduce the role of the prosecution. It reduces the maximum length of pre-trial detention. It provides for a form of plea bargaining, which might alleviate the serious problem of overcrowding of pre-trial detention facilities. The Code was prepared in the light of recommendations of the Council of Europe and the OSCE.

The new Civil Code draws upon civil codes already enacted in other former Soviet republics. It also incorporates provisions drawn from EU Directives. While the Code suffers from technical drafting problems, partly due to unfortunate rivalries between competing foreign aid organisations and partly due to translation back and forth between Romanian and Russian, it can provide a sound basis for the property and contract rights necessary to a market economy. Further reform is needed, however, to other legislation dealing with business entities and economic regulation. The new Civil Procedure Code is expected to introduce a more adversarial procedure which will give private parties and their lawyers greater rights and responsibilities in presenting their positions.

Much more important than the technical language of the codes are the quality and integrity of the judiciary. Efforts have been made to improve the quality, by requiring judges to undergo training and testing as a condition of reappointment. However, the gross inadequacy of judicial salaries inevitably tempts corruption. The wide disparity between judicial salaries and the earnings of private lawyers makes it very difficult to attract and retain high-quality judges. Formal rights, such as the right to a defence lawyer and the rights of members of the Russian-speaking minority to use their own language and to have the services of interpreters during trials, are respected. However, the judicial system has not gained the confidence of the public or of prospective foreign investors.

The situation in prisons all over Moldova, including Transdniestria, falls far below international standards. Prisons are crowded and AIDS and tuberculosis are common. Moldova has continued the Soviet practice of keeping a large percentage of those being investigated for crimes in detention facilities. Lack of funds prevents modernisation or expansion of these facilities. Some improvement may come with the planned new Criminal Procedure Code, which may reduce the numbers detained by shortening terms of preliminary detention and by allowing plea bargaining.

Moldova has made important institutional reforms in the enforcement of constitutional and human rights. It has created a Constitutional Court and has acceded to the jurisdiction of the European Court of Human Rights. The Constitutional Court has been quite active in protecting constitutional rights. It has declared well over 100 laws and regulations unconstitutional in whole or in part. A number of cases are now pending before the European Court of Human Rights. Only one case has been finally decided, that of the Metropolitan Church of Bessarabia. Moldovan legislation, much criticised by European organisations, denied unrecognised churches the right to own property and operate normally. Because of political issues involving a struggle between the Orthodox church authorities in Russia and Romania for control of Orthodox churches in Moldova, the government denied recognition to the Metropolitan Church of Bessarabia. The European Court of Human Rights ruled that Moldova had wrongly denied this church the rights given to other churches. Moldova bowed to the decision of the European Court and granted registration to the Metropolitan Church of Bessarabia.

Moldovans are free to travel both within the country and abroad. However, most cannot afford extensive foreign trips and some countries are reluctant to issue visas because of the high percentage of Moldovans who overstay their visas. While freedom to travel is a welcome change from the Soviet system, there has been one unfortunate consequence. Because of poverty and lack of employment opportunities in Moldova, many young women have fallen victim to international trafficking and have been enslaved and subjected to forced prostitution in Western Europe. Government attempts to stop this traffic have been ineffective.

In 2000, Parliament amended the 1994 Constitution (using the simplified amendment procedures then in effect) to provide for election of the president by parliament rather than by a direct popular vote. The Communist Party won the 2001 parliamentary elections (which were free and fair) and since then has controlled both parliament and the presidency. Under the Communists there has been further progress toward technical modernisation of the legal system, but there have been some disquieting developments with respect to human rights. After coming to power, the Communist passed legislation that would have replaced elected local leaders (most of whom were from other parties) with new local leaders chosen by local councils (where the Communists had better representation). The cutting short of the terms of office was, however, held unconstitutional by the Constitutional Court, and the Communists respected this decision. Legislation and other government actions of dubious legality led to the replacement of the popularly-elected non-Communist leadership in the semi-autonomous Găgăuz region with Communist Party members. The Communist government initially suspended the main opposition party's right to operate, but relented under pressure from the Council of Europe and the

EU. OSCE observers complained that state radio and television were heavily biased toward Communist candidates in the May 2003 election.

Unfortunately, the regime in Transdniestria does not respect human rights. Since neither the Moldovan Constitution nor decisions of the Moldovan Constitutional Court can be enforced in Transdniestria, there is no effective legal check on these authorities. They have arbitrarily imprisoned opponents of their regime. They have restricted the activities of evangelical religions. They have harassed the press and restricted assemblies and meetings. Elections have not been fairly conducted. There have been ballot-box stuffing and restrictions on campaigning. The regime in Transdniestria has discriminated in various ways against Romanian-speakers, including requiring the use of the Soviet-imposed Cyrillic alphabet in public schools rather than the Latin alphabet preferred by Romanian-speakers. Cases are currently before the European Court of Human Rights on behalf of some individuals imprisoned in Transdniestria. These cases have been brought both against the Moldovan government, which has theoretical but not practical control of Transdniestria, and against the Russian government, whose troops have kept the separatist regime in power. Enforcement of customs legislation on the border between Transdniestria and Ukraine has been a particular problem, since the Moldovan authorities cannot and the Transdniestrian and Ukrainian authorities choose not to control the Transdniestria side of the border. The result has been widespread smuggling of both ordinary and illicit goods.

With the exception of Transdniestria, Moldova has made slow but substantial progress in reforming its legal system. Its human rights record is imperfect, but far better than that of most of the newly independent states of the former Soviet Union. While Moldova was one of the last of the former Soviet states to adopt new legislation, the overall quality of the legislation is quite good. This legislation can form the basis for the further development of a market economy and respect for human rights. There are however hard tasks remaining, particularly strengthening the judicial system and public administration, eliminating corruption, and consolidating institutional protection for human rights.

Note

There are a number of sources for following new developments in the Moldovan legal system. A good English translation of the Moldovan Constitution may be found at http://www.ifes.md/constitution. Radio Free Europe/Radio Liberty provides daily reports on political, legal and economic events at http://www.rferl.org. The same website offers free subscription to a daily e-mail newsletter on developments in Moldova and other Central European countries. The United States Department of State publishes a detailed annual report on human rights at http://www.state.gov. The Moldovan Parliament maintains an official website, with some parts in English, at http://parlament.moldova.md/en.html. Cases involving Moldova before the European Court of Human Rights are reported at http://www.echr.coe.int. There is information on corruption problems and anti-corruption measures at http://www.transparency.md. Readers of Russian or Romanian can access legal databanks at http://www.lex.md (excellent, but requires registration and payment), http://www.lexinfosys.de (free) or http://www.docs.md (free).

The Media: Struggling to Break Free from Old Soviet Habits

Petru Clej and Alexandru Canţîr

The media in Moldova is a reflection of society as a whole: fragmented and underdeveloped when compared with other former communist countries, its freedom threatened by the state, often in subtle ways. The Moldovan press also reflects the crisis of identity in this post-Soviet country: torn between Romanian and Russian, between a closer relationship with Moscow and a pro-Romanian, implicitly pro-Western orientation. The accession in 2001 of the first communist government in history to be elected through free and fair elections has created new challenges to the fledgling Moldovan press.

Romanian vs Russian: an unequal competition

The free press in Moldova does not have a very long tradition. In fact, its beginnings date back to the mid 1980s when, with the advent of glasnost and perestroika, a certain amount of freedom of expression was encouraged. In the late 1980s this newly-acquired freedom was being channelled mainly into reclaiming Moldova's national identity, which had been suppressed after 1944 with the advent of the Soviet regime. The high point in the whole process was the reinstatement of the Romanian language with its Latin script as the official language of the then Moldavian SSR, which took place on 31 August 1989. Until then, the 'Moldovan' language had used the Cyrillic script, imposed by the Soviet authorities, to show its alleged difference from Romanian, which used the Latin script.

The early 1990s were a boom period for the Romanian-language media. It saw not only a mushrooming of newspapers but also the development of electronic media in Romanian, sometimes with help from neighbouring Romania. But shortly after independence (proclaimed on 27 August 1991) and the civil war of 1992 in the breakaway region of Transdniestria, the revival of the Romanian-language media began to stall. Following a steep economic decline, the country reverted to more cautious policies, often favourable to Moscow. Following parliamentary elections in 1994, overwhelmingly won by forces generally sympathetic to Russian interests in Moldova, the Russian-language media made a strong comeback.

Today Russian is by far the dominant language in Moldova's media. Not only is the language spoken and understood by an overwhelming majority of the population, but the superior power of attraction of the media from Russia, backed by greater financial muscle than that of neighbouring Romania (which was meant to be a model for the Romanian-language press in Moldova), makes competition between the two languages a rather unequal one.

Television: the struggle to break free from state control

As in most post-communist societies, state-run television channels occupy a pivotal role in the media in Moldova. Thus, the state TV channel is the only media outlet with national coverage, making it a potentially vital propaganda tool in the hands of the government. The number of TV sets, 250 per 1000 inhabitants, is about the European average. Private channels coexist alongside public channels, though outright foreign ownership of a TV station is not allowed, except for joint ventures.

One of the main demands of the anti-communist demonstrators in early 2002 was the transformation of Teleradio Moldova, the state-owned company, into a national public service modelled on Western public broadcasters like the BBC. This was also one of the demands of the Parliamentary Assembly of the Council of Europe (PACE), which was acting as mediator between the Communist government and the opposition, in its Resolution 1280 of 2002: '...the revision of radio and television legislation and amendment of the status of Teleradio Moldova to make it an independent public corporation; an immediate start of work by the relevant parliamentary committee; the possible resumption of consideration of the draft legislation examined by the previous legislature; and assistance of Council of Europe experts in defining the public service status of the Moldovan radio and television corporation. This work should be completed by the end of the current parliamentary session, on 31 July 2002...'

The Communist authorities duly addressed this issue, amending the law governing state television and radio. However, a few months later, after monitoring the situation on the ground, PACE adopted another resolution stating: '*However, it is unable to consider that the authorities have fully satisfied their commitments as the content of these laws continues to draw comment and controversy.*' It invites the authorities to '*revise, during the autumn of 2002, the law on the national public broadcasting company Teleradio Moldova, by genuinely involving civil society, associations representing the media and the political opposition in discussion, and by taking on board the recommendations made by the Council of Europe's experts. In particular, it requests that revision of the provisions on the composition, appointment and powers of the observers' council be the subject of the widest possible consultation;...*'. Again the authorities complied, but the political opposition and NGOs were still not happy with the degree of independence of state television. The appointment during the summer of 2003 of Artur Efremov, a young journalist with a business background, as chairman of Teleradio Moldova has gone some way to address these concerns. The opposition is still sceptical and is waiting to see if the new chairman will keep his promises of balanced coverage of the political scene.

As with all other media outlets, television in Moldova is very much Russian-oriented. Anyone zapping through Chişinău TV channels will immediately observe the greater number of Russian-language channels, be they domestic or from Russia. TV programmes in Russian are often more professional than their Romanian-language counterparts, and Moscow-based TV channels are far more popular than those based in Romania. Also, Romania-based channels like TVR1 have great difficulty penetrating the Moldovan airwaves, especially since the cooling of relations between Bucharest and Chişinău following the election of a communist government in Moldova. The Romanian public TVR1 resumed transmission in Moldova in March 2003 after being taken off the air for more than six months, officially for 'financial' reasons (an unresolved dispute over transmission costs).

TV channels in Moldova are more often than not politically biased, as they tend to represent the views of their owners. They are restricted in their coverage by scant resources and sometimes a sheer lack of professionalism among journalists. Reports about former collective farms have in a way become a trademark of Moldovan television, as has the wooden language used by many journalists.

Radio: Russian language domination

Moldovans are keen radio listeners, judging by the number of sets, 550 per 1000 inhabitants. As with TV stations, radio frequencies are awarded by the Audio Visual Council (CCA) through a process of public auction. The CCA was long criticised for not enforcing the 1995 law requiring that broadcasters respect the linguistic proportions within the population, ie two thirds in Romanian, and for tolerating Russian-language dominance in radio broadcasting. The courts ordered the CCA to redress the imbalance, but this decision was never put into practice because parliament changed the law abolishing the linguistic quota requirement in radio broadcasting on 29 September 2000. The lawmakers' initial stated intention had been to protect the Romanian language in broadcasting after half a century of sustained russification.

As with state TV, state-owned radio has a dominant position, albeit less obviously than its TV counterpart. The landscape is more diverse: FM frequencies are inundated by commercial stations broadcasting mainly in Russian and to a lesser extent in Romanian, plus international broadcasters like Radio Free Europe/Radio Liberty, BBC, Deutsche Welle, Radio France Internationale and Voice of America, all of which are rebroadcast on these FM frequencies.

Print media: partisanship, polemical tone and political masters

The print media in Moldova is far less buoyant than the audiovisual media. In just 3 years, between 1997 and 2000, the number of dailies, weeklies and other publications fell from 460 to 180. This is in part a reflection of the deepening economic crisis. Moldova does not have viable mass circulation newspapers like other former communist countries. Its papers are often political propaganda outlets in disguise. The government daily *Moldova Suverană,* one of the last of its kind in Europe, peddles the ruling party line, often aggressively criticising the opposition. Romanian speakers, many of whom live in the countryside, are not great newspaper readers. It is scarcely possible for a mass circulation independent newspaper in Romanian to exist, let alone thrive in these circumstances. Most of the newspapers have party political affiliation and rarely survive the demise of their parties. Some, like *Ţara,* the newspaper of the opposition Christian Democrats, have folded even though their sponsors are represented in parliament.

As in radio and television, Russian is dominant in the print media. A stroll along Chişinău's main boulevard is enough to demonstrate this: at the media stands, Russian-language titles make up 80 per cent of the newspapers on display. Moscow papers, unlike their Bucharest counterparts, have Chişinău editions, sometimes enjoying financial help from the Russian government.

Moldovan journalists often adopt a polemical tone, their language sometimes bordering on insulting. Many newspapers often give precedence to opinion over news, reflecting their political leanings, though a few serious, reliable news agencies became well established in the nineties.

Internet: a fledgling hope

In the last few years, many internet news-sites have been developed in Moldova. They tend to be more trustworthy and independent than the rest of the media and are often trilingual (Romanian, Russian, English). Some TV, radio stations, newspapers and agencies have created their own sites, though internet access is as yet rather limited and expensive in Moldova.

Transdniestria: a media black hole

A peculiar situation has arisen in the breakaway region of Transdniestria, where the media is under the strict control of the authoritarian regime in Tiraspol. Radio, television, news agencies and even newspapers tend to be mouthpieces of the regime. Most media outlets use the Russian language and seem to be leftovers from the Soviet era. Most of the time, the tone is critical of the Chişinău authorities, playing on the Russian-speaking population's fears of reunification with Romania.

Freedom of expression in the media: Soviet habits die hard

Moldova is not in the same (bad) league as Russia or Belarus, or even Ukraine, when it comes to freedom of the press. In Moldova journalists are not killed or kidnapped for the views they express in the media. However, in its 2002 report Freedom House classified the Moldovan media as 'partly free', like that of Romania, whereas the media in the EU accession countries was categorised as 'free'. Freedom House cited restrictive legislation and political and economic pressure on the media as the main reasons for this 'partly free' status.

Although the constitution provides for freedom of expression, some of the laws passed since 2001 have, according to human rights watchdogs, limited this freedom. For example, Article 19, the NGO which runs a global campaign for freedom of expression, has criticised a law on the prevention of terrorism which included provisions to restrict freedom of the press on anti-terrorism grounds. Article 19 also pointed out that the new Penal Code, in force as of 1 January 2003, provides for prison sentences of up to 5 years for libel, which contravenes Council of Europe provisions incorporated into law in Moldova, under which prison sentences for journalistic activity are deemed inappropriate.

Moldova also has a Freedom of Information Act dating from 11 May 2000. But, as in other former communist countries, the authorities resist many requests from journalists to release legitimate information, as provided by the law. The law is not specifically aimed at journalists, but as few ordinary citizens are aware of their rights, the media often tries to fill the gap, only to be confronted with a lack of transparency on the part of the authorities, central or local. In March 2003 parliament watered down the Access to Information Law by inserting an article relating to ecological accidents which allows information to be withheld '... *if announcing that information might negatively influence the environment to which that information relates (such as places where rare species multiply or nest) or may be erroneously interpreted by a public not familiar with the issue and may cause panic or other actions that can hinder measures to liquidate the consequences of human activities (evacuating wastes into the environment, industrial emergencies etc.)*'

Further limitations on press freedom may come from political pressure. Although journalists have not been killed in Moldova for doing their job, some have been threatened or even physically abused. The best-known recent case is that of Sergiu Afanasiu, editor of the *Accente* weekly newspaper, arrested in 2002 for taking bribes but eventually released. Afanasiu, who is known for his articles unmasking high-level corruption, has accused the communist authorities of framing him. Other journalists have been severely beaten, and their attackers never apprehended.

Another form of pressure on the electronic media is the withdrawal of broadcasting licences by the CCA. *Vocea Basarabiei* had its licence withdrawn for failing to pay its dues for using the airwaves. The station did not deny that it had arrears, but alleged that since many other stations were in the same situation, CCA's decision was selective for political reasons. Radio Free Europe and Voice of America, which alongside the BBC are rebroadcast by *Vocea Basarabiei*, lodged a protest with the Moldovan authorities. Following a public auction in early February 2003, CCA re-awarded the broadcasting licence to *Vocea Basarabiei*. This shows that the Moldovan authorities are still sensitive to criticism coming from the West.

A more recent case involved a programme called 'Hyde Park', a midnight talk show broadcast by *Antena-C*, the municipal radio station in Chişinău. The talk-show host, Oleg Brega, and some of the callers who spoke on air were interviewed by the Special Intelligence Service and the Municipal Prosecutor.

Some of their remarks were deemed offensive to the Moldovan authorities and CIS states like Russia and Belarus; some of those in favour of reunification with Romania were alleged to 'endanger the integrity of the Moldovan state'. In the summer of 2003 the show was taken off the air by *Antena-C*'s management.

In one highly-publicised case, the Canadian-Moldovan businessman Boris Birştein sued the opposition-supporting newspaper *Flux* and the leader of the opposition Christian Democrats, Iurie Roşca. Roşca's People's Party Christian Democrat was briefly part of the government from April 1998 to March 1999, and is the strongest supporter of reunification with Romania. The opposition, who consider Birştein to be a go-between between the Kremlin and the Chişinău leadership, had accused him of large-scale corruption. Both *Flux* and Roşca risk financial ruin if convicted of libel, since Birstein is seeking damages running into tens of thousands of dollars, in a country where the monthly average salary is just $50. They see this as an attempt to silence opposition.

Finally, press freedom in Moldova is threatened by economic pressures. The opposition newspaper *Ţara* has folded, and many other opposition media outlets are struggling to make ends meet. Selective law enforcement by the tax authorities seems to be one of the main ways of exerting pressure on the media.

Looking to the future: Moldova torn between East and West

The Moldovan media has come a long way since the dark days of Soviet repression. But many of the Soviet inhibitions and habits survive. The communist government elected in 2001 seems much more intent on controlling the news agenda than its predecessors, encouraging and supporting those who back official policies while viewing opponents as 'wreckers'.

One cannot avoid questions about what the future will hold if, as seems to be happening, Moldova moves towards closer ties with Russia. The Communists promised in their election manifesto to make Russian a second state language and to move towards integration with the Russia-Belarus Union. Since winning the election, President Voronin has avoided bringing up these issues, though other Communist leaders mention them from time to time. Lately the leadership has stated that EU integration is a 'strategic goal'.

What would a tilt towards Moscow mean for the Romanian-language media? What would happen to journalists representing the strong strand of opinion opposed to such a move? In May 2003 Moldova took over the chairmanship of the Council of Europe and moves to crack down on press freedom were less visible. But as a general election approaches (in February 2005), there is a danger that the Communist Party will resort to less subtle moves against those deemed to be 'hostile'.

The Moldovan press will undoubtedly be influenced by Romania's accession to NATO and the EU. The River Prut will in all likelihood become the new eastern border of 'Europe' or 'the West'. This will put many journalists who see Romania as 'the West' in an awkward position. Younger journalists, like many other Moldovans, are already attracted by 'the West' and might well find a move to Romania or elsewhere quite tempting.

In the end, the Moldovan media cannot avoid the dilemma in which the country is entangled: move closer to Russia, jeopardising links with Romania and the Moldovans' common identity and to some extent links with the West, or 'doing a Baltic' and cutting links with Moscow, which in the past has proved to be much easier said than done.

Minority Rights in Moldova: Consolidating a Multiethnic Society

Angelina Zaporojan-Pirgari

Introduction

The process of change in the Soviet Republics at the end of the 1980s arose from claims to self-determination by groups representing the titular nations, and posed serious challenges to the minority protection systems throughout the region. It not only necessitated the introduction of measures for the protection and promotion of minority rights, but fundamentally changed the relationship between majorities struggling to redeem their national identity, and communities, formerly dominant, which became the new minorities.

The situation in Moldova after the break-up of the Soviet Union was no exception. However, compared with other former Soviet Republics the quest for the national identity of the Moldovan majority proved controversial, involving a never-ending debate between 'pro-Romanians', who claimed that there was only one Romanian nation which included those living in the Republic of Moldova, and 'pro-Moldovans', who claimed that Romanians and Moldovans were two distinct nations. No wonder the Moldovan majority was confused about its national identity. This situation resulted partly from Moldova's chequered history, as described elsewhere in this book, but also from Soviet attempts to create a new identity for Moldovans by introducing the Cyrillic alphabet for the Romanian (Moldovan) language, re-writing history and forbidding any relations with neighbouring Romania. So it is not surprising that the national liberation movement which emerged in Moldova at the end of the 1980s was motivated by a wish to return to historical truth, national identity and the Romanian language based on the Latin alphabet. On 27 August 1989 about 500,000 people gathered in Chişinău calling for the reintroduction of the Latin script and the adoption of Romanian (Moldovan) as the state language. This was achieved when parliament adopted the Law on the Functioning of Languages on the Territory of Moldova on 31 August 1989. This stipulated in Article 1 that the Moldovan language based on the Latin alphabet was the official language of the Republic of Moldova. (Linguists generally agree that Moldovan is the same language as Romanian. For political reasons current practice in Moldova is for 'Moldovan' to be used in legal and formal contexts, while 'Romanian' is common usage. This article follows this practice.)

The rebirth of the Moldovan national identity coincided with the rebirth of the national identity of the minorities which had been suppressed under the Soviet policy of assimilation. After independence and the establishment of democracy, it became possible for the minorities to enjoy their national identity on the basis of a legal framework in line with the international instruments to which Moldova acceded. However some members of the 'new' Russian minority feared both losing their dominant social and political status under the new regime, and Moldova's possible reunion with Romania. They fought for the preservation of the Soviet Union as the main guarantee for their minority rights through an anti-independence movement. Members of other minorities which felt threatened did likewise. These movements acquired secessionist connotations in the south of the country, mainly inhabited by Găgăuz, and in the east (Transdniestria), inhabited preponderantly by Russians and Ukrainians.

Under these circumstances, the Moldovan authorities faced a dilemma: how to secure the rights of national minorities in accordance with international standards, preserve and promote the national identity of the majority population, and put an end to the secessionist movements.

Transdniestria is dealt with elsewhere in this book. This chapter focuses on the legal framework covering the rights of national minorities, and measures taken by the Moldovan authorities to accommodate the minorities in general, and the Russian minority in particular, by granting the right of citizenship to all those living in Moldova before independence, adopting a liberal language policy and supporting education in a variety of languages.

The minorities

According to the 1989 (and latest) census[1], Moldova's then population of 4,335,733 included about 100 different nationalities. Ethnic Moldovans accounted for 64.3 per cent; Ukrainians 13.8 per cent; Russians 13 per cent; Găgăuz 3.5 per cent; Bulgarians 2 per cent; Jews 1.5 per cent, and Roma 12,000. There were also smaller 'historical' communities of Belorusians, Poles, Armenians, Greeks, Germans, Turks etc, and 'newly-established' communities of Africans, Chechens, Arabs, etc.

The Ukrainian minority, though the largest in Moldova, was the least active in reclaiming its national identity after independence. This is partly because it was the most assimilated minority under the Soviet regime, but also because the Ukrainian communities were not compact in composition, being spread along the north-eastern border with Ukraine. According to the 1989 census, only 61.6 per cent of Ukrainians said Ukrainian was their mother-tongue; 37 per cent gave their mother-tongue as Russian. Also, after independence the Moldovan authorities made special efforts to promote the rights of the Ukrainian minority through the 1992 Treaty with Ukraine and by introducing education in the Ukrainian language in the regions inhabited by Ukrainians. Thus, according to Ministry of Education[2] data for 2001/2002, Ukrainian language as a subject was studied in 71 secondary schools and 7 high schools, and 374 children (out of a total of 589,679) studied all subjects in Ukrainian. For the same academic year 175 scholarships were offered by the Ukrainian government for students wishing to continue their education in Ukrainian universities.

The Russian minority is mainly concentrated in the big cities (about 27 per cent of them) and Transdniestria (about 25.5 per cent)[3], having migrated from Russia mainly after 1945 as part of the Soviet policy of industrialisation. Although numerically only the second largest in Moldova, members of this minority posed most challenges to the Moldovan authorities after independence, when their status and influence were threatened. The Russian minority was the most active politically, organising the *Interfront* movement at the end of the 1980s advocating the preservation of the Soviet Union. This movement became especially strong in 1989–1991 when reunification with Romania was increasingly being discussed, fuelled by nationalistic statements directed against the Russian minority as 'invaders' in Moldova. Subsequent events, culminating in the declaration of independence, and the radical policies and nationalist agenda of the Moldovan authorities, led to the escalation of the Transdniestrian conflict and the alienation of the Russian minority in that area. After 1992, as government leaders became more moderate, policy towards the Russian minority became more accommodating. The 1989 Law on the Functioning of Languages conferred special status on the Russian language as the 'language of inter-ethnic communication', and during the nineties the Moldovan authorities concluded a number of cooperation agreements with

Russia designed to promote and preserve the identity of the Russian minority. One landmark was the Framework Agreement between the Republic of Moldova and the Russian Federation concluded in November 2001, in which, among other things, Moldova undertook to *secure adequate conditions to fulfil the need for education in Russian within the education system of Moldova.* Moreover, in 2002 the Moldovan government concluded a treaty with Russia on educational matters under which 100 scholarships were offered by the Russian government to Moldovan citizens to study in Russian universities. In the same year the Russian government donated some 200,000 books to the 263 Russian schools in Moldova. In 2001–2002, within the general education system of Moldova, 124,899 children (21.1 per cent) received their education in Russian.

The Găgăuz minority. The Găgăuz are a Christian-Orthodox Turkic people which, according to one ethno-genesis theory, arrived on the current territory of Moldova during the Russo-Turkish wars. The Găgăuz were granted territorial autonomy under the Law on the Special Legal Status of Găgăuzia in 1994, enabling the local authorities to legislate on political, economic and cultural issues. Moreover, the Law also provides for the right of self-determination should Moldova lose its independence (ie by joining Romania). The Law also stipulated that the official languages of Găgăuzia were Moldovan, Găgăuz and Russian, although only the last is used in most official communications. In the 1989 census, 91 per cent of the Găgăuz stated that their mother tongue was Găgăuz, and 7.4 per cent Russian; 73 per cent of the Găgăuz considered Russian their second language and only 4 per cent said they were fluent in Romanian. Although in 49 schools[4] in the region lessons are conducted partly in Găgăuz, there is no school that teaches the entire curriculum in this language. One reason for this is that the Găgăuz language has not yet developed a sufficiently refined grammar and vocabulary. Also, the vast majority of media output is in Russian, whether from state-owned or private TV stations. Some analysts argue that although Găgăuz autonomy can be regarded as a successful model of conflict resolution, there are still power-sharing issues to address relating to the relationship between central government and the local authorities.

The Bulgarian minority, although relatively small, is territorially concentrated in the Taraclia district in the south of Moldova, where it constitutes 64 per cent of the population. In 1998–99 there was a bid to secure special autonomous status for the district like that enjoyed by neighbouring Găgăuzia. A compromise was finally reached during the reform of local government under which Taraclia district was offered the status of county with the range of self-governing powers enjoyed by other counties in Moldova.

The Bulgarian minority was also subject to massive assimilation under the Soviet regime and most therefore prefer to use Russian schools, although some favour the gradual introduction of education in Romanian. In the 1989 census, 70 per cent of Bulgarians gave Russian as their second language and only 7 per cent said they were fluent in Romanian. In 2001–2002, Bulgarian language was taught as a subject in 26 schools, and 171 students were learning all subjects in Bulgarian. In the 1990s the Moldovan government adopted a number of special measures for the protection and development of the Bulgarian identity as well as signing agreements with the Bulgarian government. For example, the Bulgarian Government offered 72 scholarships for 2001–2 to students interested in continuing their education in Bulgarian universities.

The Jewish minority. The Jews settled on the current territory of Moldova at the end of the 19th century and in 1897 comprised about 11.8 per cent[5] of the entire population. They were mostly concentrated in the big cities, making up about 45.9 per cent of the population in Chişinău and 55.9 per cent in Bălţi. A pogrom was organised against the Jews of Chişinău in April 1903, with devastating consequences (45 Jews killed, 1350 houses and 571 shops destroyed). Currently the Jewish minority is one of the smallest in Moldova due to massive emigration after independence. This minority was subject to severe russification as a result of policies directed against the Jewish communities throughout the USSR during the 1940s. Thus, in the 1989 census 73 per cent of Jews gave Russian as their mother tongue, against 26 per cent Yiddish. Two Jewish schools and one kindergarten were opened in Chişinău in the 1990s. The Jewish community has several organisations, including a library, several associations and a university, and the local authorities are taking steps to rebuild the synagogue in Chişinău.

The Roma community. The 1998 census put the Roma community at around 12,000, but experts believe it is much larger, perhaps around 100,000. However this is hard to assess due to frequent migration both within and beyond Moldova. Much of the Roma community is concentrated in the north of Moldova, where they are the majority in several villages and towns. The Roma community was less russified than other minorities, and in the 1989 census 82 per cent said their mother tongue was Roma and only 3.5 per cent Russian. As the Roma community is neither very large nor very well-organised (although there are some associations), little attention has been paid to promoting the Roma culture and language. Thus, the Roma language is not taught in schools, even as a subject. At the same time there have been claims that members of the Roma community are discriminated against through social stereotyping. The government has introduced a number of measures to preserve the Roma culture, and one of the Roma associations is a member of the

Advisory Board to the Department of Interethnic Relations (which includes representatives of a total of 18 associations of national minorities).

Legal framework[6]

Moldova has ratified and acceded to a number of international human rights instruments, including the Universal Declaration of Human Rights, International Covenant on Civil and Political Rights, International Covenant on Social, Economic and Cultural Rights, and documents adopted in the framework of the CSCE, undertaking to guarantee basic human rights, including prohibition of discrimination and the protection of minority rights. The legal framework has been gradually strengthened since Moldova became a member of the Council of Europe in 1995, with the entry into force of the Framework Convention for the Protection of National Minorities (October 1996) and the European Convention for the Protection of Human Rights and Fundamental Freedoms (September 1997). The Charter of Regional and Minority Languages was under discussion in parliament in 2003.

The first law regulating *inter alia* minority rights adopted after independence was the 1989 Law on the Functioning of Languages, which, besides defining Moldovan in the Latin script as the state language, guaranteed people belonging to ethnic and linguistic minorities the free use of their mother tongue in private and public as well as the opportunity to choose, as their language of communication with public servants, between Moldovan, Russian and other languages in localities where the majority population speaks a minority language. The 1991 Law on Citizenship extended the right to apply for citizenship to all those registered as permanently living on the territory of Moldova before the proclamation of sovereignty (23 June 1990), thus creating favourable conditions for the national minorities to obtain the status of citizen and enjoy all consequent rights.

The Constitution of the Republic of Moldova (29 July 1994) laid down that the provisions of human rights treaties take precedence if there is a contradiction between them and national legislation. The Constitution also stipulates (Article 10) that *the state recognises and guarantees the right of all citizens to the preservation, development and expression of their ethnic, cultural, linguistic and religious identity.* The Law on Education (1995) lays down the right of every person to choose their language of education.

One great achievement was the adoption of the Law on National Minorities and the Legal Status of their Organisations in July 2001. This Law for the first time introduced the definition of persons belonging to national minorities as *'persons who reside on the territory of the Republic of Moldova, are citizens thereof, have ethnic, cultural, linguistic and religious characteristics which make them different from the majority of the population – Moldovans – and consider themselves of a different ethnic origin'.* The Law not only guarantees fundamental human rights to the national minorities and prohibits discrimination, but also lays a positive obligation on the state to create the necessary conditions for the preservation, development and expression of the ethnic, cultural, linguistic and religious identity of persons belonging to national minorities.

Right to national identity. The Law on National Minorities provides that persons belonging to national minorities can freely choose to belong to a national minority or not, and that this choice cannot put the person in an unfavorable position. Also, it stipulates that they can write their names, including in official documents, in the form used in their mother tongue. Moreover, the legislation regulating registration and identity documents, unlike in Soviet times, no longer requires the registration of ethnicity. Thus the notion of 'nationality' now refers entirely to 'citizenship'. Persons belonging to national minorities are also entitled to celebrate their national holidays and historically important dates and to use their national symbols. Moreover, the national minorities can create various kinds of organisation and associate in political parties. The Law on Political Parties de facto prevents the creation of parties based on ethnic origin by requiring for the registration of a party a minimum of 5,000 signatures of support from at least half the districts in Moldova, with no less than 600 signatures from each district. Minorities are nevertheless proportionally represented in parliament. Thus, the number of non-Moldovan parliamentarians increased from 16 per cent in 1998 to 30 per cent in 2001[7]. At the same time, the Law on National Minorities introduced as mandatory the proportional representation of minorities in decision-making bodies at all levels, including the army, judiciary and law enforcement bodies.

Right to freedom of religion. In Moldova the predominant religion is Christian Orthodox, and around 90 per cent of the population belong to the two Orthodox denominations (the Moldovan Church under the Russian Patriarchate and the Bessarabian Church under the Romanian Patriarchate).

The right to freedom of religion is a universal right under the Moldovan Constitution, to be enjoyed equally by all people. The Law on National Minorities specifically lays down the right of persons belonging to national minorities to adhere to a religion and to undertake religious activities alone or in community with others. According to the Law on Religions (1992), religious denominations are entitled to establish associations and foundations, and the government may not interfere with their activities. But the Law also states that in order to function, religious organisations must be registered by the government, enabling them to own property, hire personnel, etc, though the government may not refuse registration arbitrarily. There was an attempt (in 2000) to introduce religious education in primary schools, but this was not pursued due to the difficulty of establishing the content of such religious education, as well as a lack of financial resources. The only exception is the Jewish community, which has established a private school for girls and boys. According to Ministry of Justice data, 20 religious organisations (among them Roman Catholic, Baptist, Pentecostal, Seventh Day Adventist, Muslim and others) have been officially registered, and there are a number of theological faculties and other places for religious education.

Language rights. The language legislation adopted in 1989, as well as proclaiming Moldovan as the state language and offering special status to the Russian language, introduced a requirement that public servants take a Moldovan language proficiency test, allowing a period of 5 years for learning. The led to an odd situation: national minorities felt threatened by these new measures and by the declining role of the Russian language, yet successive governments, though not cancelling the language tests, did not enforce them and so failed to fulfil the original intention of transforming Moldova in a truly bilingual country (Moldovan/minority language).

This brings us to the debate on the status of the Russian language in Moldova. Although the Constitution recognises only one state language, Moldovan, it lays on the state the obligation to preserve and develop the Russian language as well as other languages, and according to the Law on the Functioning of Languages, Russian serves as the 'language of inter-ethnic communication'. Furthermore, the Law on National Minorities gives Russian equal status to Moldovan in some respects. For instance, the state undertakes to guarantee education (pre-school, primary, secondary, graduate and post-graduate) in Moldovan and Russian, but only to create conditions for the enforcement of the right to education in the mother tongue for Ukrainians, Găgăuz, Bulgarians, etc. Moreover, the Law on National Minorities also guarantees the publication of legislation, official communiqués and other important information in both Moldovan and Russian. It could be argued that the authorities are implicitly recognising the quasi-equal status of Russian, thus ignoring the interests of the majority and the constitutional provision for only one state language. Moreover it could be considered discrimination compared with other minority languages, which enjoy a lower status than Russian.

In the field of education, the children of national minorities face the need to learn four languages at the same time: their mother tongue, Moldovan (state language), Russian, and one foreign language, each language playing an important role. So it is understandable that some parents choose education for their children not in their mother tongue (eg Găgăuz) but Russian, both to avoid over-burdening their children and in the belief that they will thus be better equipped for higher education.

Conclusions

This short analysis of events before independence and the legal framework regulating the rights of national minorities shows that except for a short period in 1989–1991 marked by an outburst of nationalism, the authorities have attempted to provide a fair climate for the development and protection of minority rights. This is also shown in Moldova's accession to the major human rights documents prohibiting discrimination and enforcing the rights of national minorities. Moreover, Moldova has never suffered from wide-spread inter-ethnic hostility, and ordinary Moldovans, Ukrainians, Găgăuz and Bulgarians have long co-existed peacefully. While some hostility was expressed towards the more recently-arrived Russian community, people's resentment was primarily directed at the Russian political elite and not the general population, aggravated by the presence of the Russian army in Transdniestria and the claims for independence of the secessionist region.

While the adoption of international norms on minority rights is an important accomplishment, more practical steps are needed in order to secure cohesion within Moldova's multicultural society. While the state should respect all members of national minorities, they in turn should be loyal to the state in which they live. For example, in such a society the government should not only take steps to protect and support minority languages but also promote and strengthen the position of the state language. In this context, moves by the Moldovan authorities and international organisations to offer adult courses in the state language and to promote new methods of teaching it in minority schools should be continued and enhanced. Only by being able to speak the state language and understand better the culture of the country where they live, will the national minorities be able fully to integrate and take part in the social, economic and political life of the country.

Since the national authorities consider diversity and multiculturality to be assets to the Moldovan state, the national minorities should be encouraged to integrate and to develop a sense of belonging to and inclusion in Moldovan society. Policy-makers should focus not on differences but on common problems, such as growing poverty, the slow pace of economic reform, and environmental matters. In order to achieve cohesion and avoid conflict, both government and civil society should encourage and stimulate debate on matters such as integration into the European family and raising living standards for all.

The author would like to thank Claus Neukirch for his valuable guidance.

Notes

[1] Data from the *Basic Study of the Human Rights Protection Situation in the Republic of Moldova*, UNDP 2002 p.67

[2] Data from the *Basic Study of the Human Rights Protection Situation in the Republic of Moldova*, UNDP 2002 p.71

[3] Charles King: *Moldovenii – Romania, Rusia si politica culturala, Chișinău 2002, p.176*

[4] Data from a report by T. Stoyanova, Director of the Department of Inter-ethnic Relations, 2000

[5] Moraru Anton: *100 de ani de la pogromul evreiesc, provocat de _ovinismul ruses la Chișinău*, published in *Literatura _i Arta Nr.15(3007), April10, 2003*

[6] It should be noted that the legislation adopted by the Moldovan parliament, though theoretically applicable throughout the country, is not in practice applied in Transdniestria, where the old Soviet legislation is still in force.

[7] Data from the OSCE/ODIHR Election Observation Final Report on the 2001 Parliamentary Elections in Moldova.

Not a Happy One: Woman's Lot in Moldova

Ala Mîndîcanu

Gorbachev's perestroika saw an explosion not only of the Soviet empire, but also of the Soviet social conscience. Like many Moldovans, I remember the period 1985–1991 as the best part of my life: years of hope, trust in the future and optimism. Now it seems we were not ready for real freedom and democracy.

Transition found the people of Moldova psychologically and morally unprepared for such radical change. During the Soviet period people did not need to think about their future, enduring poverty as something pre-destined and thankful for their wages, however low. But after the fall of the system, which had seemed so permanent and imperturbable, people found themselves at the mercy of destiny.

Restructuring processes were unleashed without well-established plans, without clear mechanisms for implementing structural changes, without a planned system of social, economic and psychological protection, without skilled staff and without any inherited memory of private ownership and independent leadership, the result of over 50 years of totalitarian dictatorship. Overnight, the entire population found itself in a strange new society, in which totally different rules and laws operated.

Unfortunately, during such unstable transition periods the ugliest social patterns come to the fore. We are now witnessing more corruption than we ever had before, the promotion of false values, a lack of culture in all areas of economic, political and social life, and processes affecting the whole of society such as unemployment, social stress and a drastic decline in living standards.

Today Moldova is one of the poorest and most corrupt countries in Europe. In 1994 the UN Human Development Report had Moldova in 75th place, in 1995 in 81st place, and in 2002 in 105th place. The national economy is in a mess, GDP has been falling steadily, the shadow economy is 60 per cent higher than GDP, and external debt is about 80 per cent of GDP.

More than 50 per cent of young Moldovans surveyed wish to go abroad, citing rising unemployment and miserable wages as their main reasons. Women constitute 68 per cent of the unemployed and are exposed to longer periods of unemployment than men. Although they are educated to the same level as men, they make up three-quarters of the unskilled labour force and are paid 70-80 per cent of men's salaries (while doing a double work-load since their working day continues in the home). As a result, women's pensions are smaller than men's. That is why they wish to go abroad and find jobs that would pay more than $35–50 per month (the average wage in Moldova), even though they know a lot about the possible risks.

Today most families in Moldova have 1 or 2 children. But the birth-rate is causing concern, and there were actually twice as many deaths as births in 2002–2003. This trend stems from the fact that most women of 30–45 are either migrating or restricting themselves to one child because of poverty.

Survival is one of the biggest issues for Moldovan families. During Soviet times, women used to work, making up 50.1 per cent of the labour force. Today thousands of them cannot find a job at home and go abroad to work illegally, without social protection or insurance, leaving their children with elderly parents or relatives.

Despite international support in combating poverty, Moldovan society does not provide very effective help to families with children. There are more than 25,000 large (three or more children) families in Moldova, amounting to 2 per cent of all families. Child-care legislation lays down various payments, but leave and other benefits for child care are too small: $3–10 per month for each child from big or one-parent families, and for handicapped children. This minimal payment cannot ensure normal development and education for the younger generation. That is why desperate parents look for other means of survival.

Another problem confronting women in Moldova today is family violence. In 2002, 129 persons died as a result of family conflicts, most of them women. Rape, beating and psychological aggression are common, but the state does not consider them a high priority. As a result, there are more and more cases of suicide, drug addiction, prostitution, alcoholism, and the abandonment of babies. In 1998, 27 women killed their partners, claiming to have been unable to endure their suffering any longer. Violence generates violence: two-thirds of children educated in such conditions become criminals.

The divorce rate is very high in Moldova, three times that of marriage. Usually, children remain in the care of their mothers and grandparents. Very often the only hope for this kind of family is to have a relative working abroad.

More than 20,000 women of fertile age leave Moldova every year. Women working abroad are mostly active in the caring professions or services (nursing, hospital orderlies, seasonal agricultural work) and are paid a half or a quarter of the pay-rate for locals. One of the most painful features of migration is women's involvement in prostitution and trafficking. According to national statistics, more than 100,000 Moldovan women have been trafficked to countries such as Turkey, Israel, Spain, Portugal, Greece, Germany, Italy, Cyprus etc. over the last ten years. But nobody is keeping track of how many Moldovans are missing from their homes or what they do in the West.

Every year Moldovans abroad send home to their families over $400 million, almost equal to the annual budget. Qualified doctors, engineers and teachers are working very hard overseas in jobs for which they are overqualified, separated for years from their children and parents, paying the price of the state's insolvency. They are working without social security, without medical care, without holidays, without trade unions or normal labour rights. Does anyone care what happens to them?

Official statistics show a massive number of Moldovan women in Kosovo during the conflict period, accounting for 61 per cent of all the trafficked persons there. Most of them were brought by force and many sold to various owners, without recourse to any legal assistance or any psychological or material support. International organisations have been unable to track down more than a few of them, and according to the press and official reports, many have been forced by traffickers to change their citizenship, maltreated, beaten or even killed.

I have met a few trafficked girls who have returned to Moldova. Young and pretty, they speak like old women. They have returned from the 'hell' of Kosovo and live now in small villages. 'I have lost my innocence', said one of them, Tatiana, 18, during our conversation filmed by a CNN team in March 2001. 'I believed that life was wonderful, but it is not true. My life is full of cruel suffering. My parents do not understand me. Maybe the wounds to my soul will heal as time goes by. I do not know. Today I am a person without wishes, without hope, without a future.'

Women living in the countryside (where 65 per cent of Moldovans live) have little hope of moving to the cities. The two big cities, Chişinău and Bălţi, cannot offer jobs, having thousands of unemployed citizens of their own. Both industry and services remain undeveloped. Agriculture, the mainstay of the Moldovan economy, is still outdated and does not offer women an adequate livelihood. Private enterprise is most developed in Chişinău: the flea market offers hundreds of women every day the opportunity to buy and sell goods (clothes, shoes etc), and thus survive on a minimal income. Moldovan children are dressed entirely in second-hand clothes.

Since Soviet times Moldovan women have been in a worse job situation than men (no women in decision-making positions, higher unemployment, lower salaries and pensions etc). Moldovan women are also in a worse situation than those in neighbouring countries. Comparing women in Moldova and Romania, the latter fare better because the social sphere (education, health care etc) is better paid in Romania. In Moldova, for example, the median salary for a teacher is $30–35 per month, in Romania more than $150. In health care, it is $40– 45 in Moldova, $200–250 in Romania. In both countries women make up 80–90 per cent of the workforce in these sectors. The pension system in the two countries reflects the same gap.

Moldovan women perform an enormous volume of work at the social level (family, health, education, etc) and play a determining role in the social development of the community. At the same time they are absent from decision-making, partly because of the lack of a coherent and supportive state framework, partly because of the patriarchal mentality which still affects the whole of society, including women themselves.

In the last few years the growth of the women's movement in Moldova (with more than 50 NGOs dealing with gender issues) shows that things have started to change. International assistance in developing women's studies and raising the level of women's self-esteem and civic activism is beginning to show results. More and more women are no longer afraid to say no to those who treat them as second-rate. They are helping to bring to court traffickers, rapists, and private entrepreneurs who are guilty of sexual harassment or not giving women their due rights. Women are a growing presence in the lists of candidates for election at every level. All this is a sign of a new understanding by women of their rights and power. They are applying for higher positions (even if not yet selected by men), they are more active in political life, and some parties (Liberals and Social Liberals) have, under female pressure, introduced a gender equality provision in their regulations.

It is difficult to change people's mentality. Difficult, but not imposible. A wind of change is blowing through the House of Moldova as the younger generation open the doors and windows. The wind will blow away inhuman, outdated values.

European integration is the only way to achieve freedom for the women of Moldova. European integration means first of all respect for human rights, the rule of law, and the responsibility of the state for the citizen's life, liberty and security. In addition, Moldova citizens working illegally today would become legal workers with social protection, law-abiding tax-payers of the countries where they live. For women, that would give them the opportunity to look after their children and bring them up in love and security. Of course all this would require a major shift in mentality. But it would give the younger generation hope of becoming part of the European family, sharing our common values in culture, history and civilisation.

The 'Dniester Moldovan Republic': Building an Authoritarian State

Gottfried Hanne

On 2 September 2003, the 'Dniester Moldovan Republic' (DMR) celebrated the 13th anniversary of its proclamation. Ten years of internationally mediated negotiations have not led to a political settlement of the conflict between the central Moldovan authorities in Chişinău and the separatist authorities in the DMR's 'capital' Tiraspol. On the contrary: protected by an ineffective Russian-led peacekeeping mechanism, sustained by all kinds of legal and illegal economic activities, supported and used by different political and economic groups in Russia, Ukraine and Moldova itself, and aided by the absence of serious outside pressure from the international community, the unrecognised mini-republic has stabilised over the years and embarked on a separate state-building process.

The DMR authorities today control nearly all of Moldova's tiny eastern landstrip between the River Dniester and the Ukrainian border (Transdniestria) – a territory that historically never belonged to any Moldovan state and was incorporated into the newly-established Moldavian Soviet Socialist Republic (MSSR) only in 1940 – as well as the west-bank city of Bendery with a few surrounding villages, altogether about 4,000 km^2 or 11 per cent of Moldova's state territory. After an influx of tens of thousands of Russian (and fewer Ukrainian) functionaries and workers during the 1950s and 1960s, in 1989 39.9 per cent of Transdniestria's then roughly 750,000 inhabitants (17 per cent of the MSSR population) were Moldovans, 28.3 per cent Ukrainians, and 25.4 per cent Russians. Thanks to a greater degree of urbanisation and industrialisation, the region is more socially sovietised and linguistically russified than the rest of Moldova.

In Soviet times, Transdniestria produced more than a third of Moldova's GDP. Political elites from Transdniestria occupied many key positions in the nomenklatura of the MSSR and, together with cadres from Russia and Ukraine, dominated MSSR politics and the economy (with the exception of agriculture). This political and economic domination, as well as the constant russification, were resented by the younger Moldovan cultural, political and economic elites on the right (west) bank of the Dniester, many of whom were not able to rise higher than the second grade in the nomenklatura.

In the late 1980s, Gorbachev's policies of glasnost and perestroika enabled these Moldovan elites to challenge openly both russification and the political domination of the MSSR by non-Moldovans. Moldovan cultural, economic and political elites joined a nationalist movement led by the Popular Front, demanding that Moldovan (Romanian) should be the sole state language and that its use be made obligatory in public life. The aim was not only to stop russification and to develop the national language, but also to exclude non-Moldovans, most of whom did not speak any Moldovan/Romanian, from competition for political and economic leadership positions. When the MSSR Supreme Soviet in autumn 1989 adopted new language legislation to that effect, the Transdniestrian political and economic elites – predominantly ethnic Russian and Ukrainian directors and other leading personnel from state enterprises, plus local government and party functionaries – feared for their positions and career opportunities and mobilised the Russian and Ukrainian population of Transdniestria's cities and Bendery behind plans to establish an Autonomous Republic. However, when the new Moldovan government elected in spring 1990 implemented comprehensive cadre changes in the executive and judicial organs, resulting in a 90 per cent dominance of Moldovans, when the newly-elected MSSR Supreme Soviet adopted new state symbols and a declaration of sovereignty, and when the Popular Front announced that union with Romania was its political goal, local Transdniestrian politicians, with support from conservative political forces in Moscow, proclaimed a separate 'Dniester Moldovan SSR' on 2 September 1990. During 1991 and early 1992 the Transdniestrian local authorities, with the help of personnel and equipment from the Soviet 14th Army, evicted the Moldovan executive and judicial authorities from most of Transdniestria's towns and villages. Trying to avoid bloodshed, the Moldovans gave in to the pressure and left most of Transdniestria. When, however, the Moldovan authorities refused to leave the cities of Dubasari and Bendery, Transdniestrian guardsmen attacked Moldovan police stations and provoked a military response from the Moldovan central government. The resulting clashes peaked in brief but intense fighting around Bendery and Dubasari, which the Moldovan armed units lost against the better trained and equipped Transdniestrian armed formations and their allies from the 14th Army under General Lebed.

Under the Moldovan-Russian Agreement of July 1992 a Russian-led peacekeeping mechanism was installed comprising Russian, Moldovan and Transdniestrian units. The inclusion of the warring parties and the adoption of decision-making by consensus for a long time hindered any serious demilitarisation of the established security zone and any confidence-building between the sides. In effect, the mechanism allowed the Transdniestrian authorities, with tacit Russian acquiescence, to use the consensus principle to block most decisions and at the same time develop and stabilise their quasi-state structures. Protected by the peacekeeping mechanism, the Transdniestrian authorities expanded their administrative base, silenced or expelled any serious internal opponents, and developed their own political, economic, financial, judicial, social and educational systems.

The leadership of the DMR today consists of a core group who emerged from among the directors and other leading personnel of Transdniestrian state enterprises, as well as local government and party officials who joined the autonomist and then separatist movement of 1989 and 1990. While Ukrainians are represented roughly according to their share of the population, Russians are heavily over-represented and Moldovans heavily under-represented in the executive, legislative and judicial organs, as well as in leading economic functions. Many in this core group, such as large parts of Transdniestria's urban population, came to Moldova from Russia or Ukraine during Soviet times or even later, and are thus not native to the region (unlike the region's Moldovan and Ukrainian rural population) and are often Russian or Ukrainian citizens. Over the years, however, Russian-speakers dismissed from positions elsewhere in Moldova, as well as younger people born in Transdniestria, have also been co-opted into leadership positions.

The head of the DMR authorities is 'president' Igor Smirnov, a Russian citizen and former director of one of Tiraspol's biggest state enterprises, who came to Moldova in 1987, only 2 years before becoming the leading personality in Transdniestria's autonomist and separatist movement. The most influential person apart from Smirnov is security 'minister' Vadim Antyufeev, a Russian citizen and ruthless former officer of the Soviet internal forces in Latvia, who came to Transdniestria in early 1992. His notorious and widely-feared security service is the most important instrument through which the Transdniestrian leadership has stabilised its authoritarian regime by expelling (in the early years even murdering), harassing and silencing any internal opponents. Other influential politicians are the heads of the Transdniestrian city and *raion* administrations installed by Smirnov, and a few key ministers who enjoy the Smirnov group's confidence. One of the few ethnic Moldovans in leadership positions is the Chairman of the Transdniestrian Supreme Soviet ('parliament'), Grigori Marakuţa. However, political observers consider him to be isolated in the leadership and totally dependent on Smirnov.

In their political leanings and attitudes, the DMR leadership look towards Russia and, to some extent, Ukraine. Soviet nostalgia, panslavism and Russian and Ukrainian nationalism are used by the regime to mobilise and stabilise their support among the politically more active older generation (up to 50 per cent of the DMR population), who have kept much of their Soviet mentality. Russia and Ukraine are considered ethnic brethren and geo-politically interested neighbouring states which could 'protect' the DMR against Moldova and serve as examples for political, economic, financial, legal (Russian laws are often adapted for DMR legislation), social, educational and cultural development, while Romania, Moldova and the West (especially the US, EU and NATO) are seen as adversaries.

Popular elections for the DMR 'presidency' (1991, 1996, 2001), Supreme Soviet and local councils (both 1990, 1995, 2000) have not met international standards and have regularly suffered from fierce media and security service campaigns against potentially disloyal candidates. As candidates not approved by the regime are often denied registration, and face dirty campaigns, harassment or the annulment of election results by the courts, only candidates supported by the regime have any chance of being elected. A few well-known opposition candidates on the extreme left, orthodox communists in their critique of the regime's social and economic policies and thus not attracting much internal or external support, have been tolerated by the regime for some years as a fig-leaf opposition. In 2001–2002, however, when this opposition started to co-operate with the communists in power in Chişinău, the three main radical left-wing organisations and their extremely regime-critical newspaper were eventually banned by the Transdniestrian 'Supreme Court'. More serious internal opposition and discontent have come periodically from within the group of influential state enterprise directors, but always been suppressed immediately.

Under this presidential regime, Transdniestria's legislative and judicial organs (including the 'Supreme Court' and 'Constitutional Court') are not independent but used mainly to disguise the authoritarian nature of the regime. The Supreme Soviet and local councils, as well as the courts, willingly follow the regime's policies and do not risk serious confrontation. The few instances of disagreement or resistance to the regime's social, economic and financial policies have been suppressed. To enable Smirnov to run for a third term, further strengthen his powers and diminish the weak criticism from within the Supreme Soviet, constitutional changes were pushed through against the will of many deputies in 2000. The bicameral Supreme Soviet established by the 1991 'constitution' was transformed into a much smaller unicameral legislature with even fewer powers.

The media in the DMR are under the almost total control of the regime. Most of the media are either instruments for regime propaganda or exercise pre-emptive loyalty and self-censorship. The two independent newspapers are regularly harassed and intimidated by the security service or taken to court for various 'violations'. Furthermore, the political opposition and civil society lack freedom of association. All political and social organisations must express support for the 'independence and sovereignty' of the DMR. The very few NGOs that neither have close relations with the regime nor accept its control are constantly harassed, intimidated, and prevented from co-operating with Moldovan NGOs. Democratisation and the development of civil society are actively hindered by a regime which fears potential opposition behind any independent political and social activity.

Three (formerly four) members of the 'Ilaşcu Group', sentenced to long prison terms for alleged terrorist crimes during the 1992 armed conflict, remain in prison. International experts have found serious violations during the 1993 show trial of this group, so the three prisoners can be considered (the DMR's only) political prisoners.

The linguistic and educational rights of Moldovans are also breached in the DMR. Although the regime stresses that there are no majorities or minorities in Transdniestria, since no nationality makes up more than about 30 per cent of the population, policies towards ethnic Moldovans perpetuate Soviet nationality policies, under which Moldovans were considered a different nation from Romanians, and Moldovan a separate language which, under pain of legal sanctions, must be written in the Cyrillic script. Parents, pupils and teachers in many Moldovan schools in Trandniestria want to be allowed to write Moldovan in the Latin script and to use the curriculum of the Moldovan Ministry of Education. The DMR authorities regularly react to these demands with harassment and intimidation, as well as threatening to close down those few schools that managed to retain the Latin script after 1992. Although the DMR officially has three 'state' languages (Moldovan, Ukrainian, Russian), only Russian is used in the public sphere.

Most other human rights violations in the DMR occur also in Moldova proper (eg torture and inhuman treatment, violations of social and economic rights) but are more pronounced in the DMR because of the lack of effective and independent political, legal and civil control mechanisms, as well as the lack of will (as well as knowledge and experience) on the part of the Transdniestrian executive, legislative and judicial authorities to disseminate, train for and implement international human rights standards.

Some political observers have described the DMR authorities as 'Moscow's puppets', incapable of surviving in the long run. The last decade, however, has shown that the DMR is much more stable than predicted. Externally, the DMR authorities have learned to exploit political friction within Russia, Ukraine, Moldova and the international community, as well as between them, to mobilise political support especially from Russian communists and nationalists, or at least to ensure the tacit acquiescence of the Russian authorities with their geo-political interests in Moldova, and the absence of interest or interference from the rest of the international community. The DMR authorities are today less dependent on material support from Russia and Ukraine than earlier, and have on occasion been able to take political decisions against the express wish of the Russian authorities, which are hampered in their ability to punish the DMR authorities by their very need of these authorities' collaboration on other Russian (geo-political) interests in Moldova and the region.

The DMR authorities and enterprises today maintain economic relations with a good number of Russian and Ukrainian regions, as well as state and private enterprises in these and even Western countries. In addition, the DMR has become an unrecognised 'free economic zone' for all kinds of smuggling. Russian, Ukrainian, Moldovan and international organised criminal gangs use the DMR to smuggle alcohol, cigarettes, fuel, foodstuffs and other items in various directions. Trafficking in human beings (though no more than in Moldova proper) and (limited) export of small weapons are other illegal activities that occur from and through Transdniestria. The DMR leadership profits immensely from such illegal business. While the legal economy has long been able to cover the mini-republic's 'state' budget, the profits of these illegal economic activities flow into the private accounts of the DMR leaders. Only in 2002, after the Moldovan authorities issued new customs stamps and documents in 2001 but refused to share them with the DMR as was done before, did the DMR's budget come under severe strain, shrinking by half in a single year. While the DMR's budget per capita was largely comparable with Moldova's in 2001, expenditure had to be cut dramatically from 2002. However, after the first shock the DMR economy seems to have somewhat stabilised again in 2002 and 2003 though at a lower level. The fact that the most important Transdniestrian enterprises were registered in Chişinău, and thus able to receive the necessary legalisation and customs documentation, has helped to limit the first economic shock. How long this will last remains to be seen.

In the political as well as economic sphere the regime has become in part a family business. While Smirnov figures as 'president' of the DMR, one of his sons is chief of customs, channeling the income from smuggling in the 'correct' direction. Security 'minister' Antyufeev is responsible for the stability of the regime, while his wife chairs the human rights commission of the Supreme Soviet. And former 'minister' of information Akulov heads the profitable Transdniestrian mobile telephone company *Interdniestrcom* while his wife succeeded him as information 'minister'. The original causes of conflict with Moldova have been superceded by the personal material interests of a small, oligarchic leadership group which uses the pretext of protecting the interests of the region's population to gain legitimacy. However, the material interests of the regime are pursued in conjunction with influential circles in Moldova proper, who, in the absence of any political will for compromise and the resulting stalemate in negotiations, use their contacts with the DMR authorities and economic groups to participate in smuggling and other illegal activities and their rewards. Some political observers consider that the desire of certain Moldovan circles to benefit from the unresolved conflict is not the result but the very cause of the noticeable lack of political will for compromise.

In the meantime, the DMR authorities have managed to stabilise their regime not only economically but also politically. The ruthless security service and regime propaganda play an important role, but so does the mentality of the population. As in other parts of the former Soviet Union, democracy is popularly associated with a lack of social and economic security, outright poverty, rising criminality and the absence of legal protection. The call for a strong leader and more authoritarian rule to fight crime and poverty and to give the population the impression of protection and stability can be heard in Transdniestria too. Given the regime's information monopoly and the lack of alternative and comparative sources, many Transdniestrians are inclined to trust Smirnov, the epitome of the strong leader. The authoritarian nature of the regime is regarded as a necessary evil and only criticised when it affects someone's personal circle. Based on this assessment, some political observers consider that Smirnov might be elected even in democratic, free and fair elections. Some tentative opinion polls in Transdniestria, carried out jointly by Western and Russian specialists, seem to indicate that the regime's propaganda, the absence of an open information space, the regime's institutional and ideological state-building, especially educational policies, together with the unattractiveness (especially economic) of Moldova proper, have led a growing number of Transdniestrians to support separate statehood for the region.

As politics are ultimately determined by political elites, who can to a critical degree structure popular beliefs and attitudes, this process is not irreversible. However, if the vicious circle of mutually sustaining political and economic interests of the DMR and certain Russian, Ukrainian and Moldovan interest groups in blocking a political settlement cannot be broken through outside political and economic influence, the existing stalemate and the state-building process in the DMR will continue.

It was this vicious circle of interests, and the absence of any serious Western interest in the conflict and its resolution (which might have helped a decade ago to avoid the very development of such intertwined interests), that hindered the OSCE for more than ten years in trying to help the sides find a political solution. With the recent growing EU interest in Moldovan affairs, Western influence in the conflict settlement process both inside and outside the OSCE framework might have a chance of breaking the artificial stalemate. In current discussions the two sides are trying forcefully to maintain their positions. This might be a sign that they are becoming aware that political negotiations could be reaching a decisive phase. If the sides fail to grasp this opportunity and if Western states, especially the US and leading EU countries, miss this chance of promoting a breakthrough in negotiations, the stalemate might become permanent. In that case the reintegration of Transdniestria into the Moldovan state could become a utopian dream.

Part 2
The Economy

Moldova's Economic Transition: Slow and Contradictory

Stuart Hensel and Anatol Gudîm

The extent of Moldova's economic collapse exceeded that of all the other former Soviet republics following the break-up of the Soviet Union. This reflected not only dislocation related to the secession of Transdniestria shortly after independence, but also the unusually severe terms-of-trade shock suffered by Moldova at that time. During the communist era, Moldova had sent its agriculture-related output to markets throughout the Soviet Union and had received subsidised energy imports in return. This arrangement collapsed spectacularly with independence, when Moldova found itself cut off from export markets and, as Russian energy prices adjusted to world levels, faced with an exponential increase in import costs. By the late 1990s Moldova's official economy had shrunk to around two-fifths of its late-Soviet size, in contrast to most of the former communist economies in Central Europe, which had managed to return to 1990 levels. Among the former Soviet republics, only Georgia and Tadjikistan approached the scale of decline experienced in Moldova.

This poor showing belies a number of policy successes achieved in the early years of the transition period, when Moldova earned a reputation as one of the leading reformers in the region. By the mid-1990s, Moldova's policy-makers had successfully tackled a number of first-generation reforms, such as freeing up the vast majority of prices and liberalising domestic trade. Similarly, responsible monetary policies had brought a relatively quick end to the hyperinflation experienced in the early 1990s, while liberalised trade policies (on paper at least) paved the way for Moldova to become one of the first CIS countries to join the WTO. In terms of privatisation, a mass voucher scheme launched in mid-1994 relatively quickly sold off the state-run small and medium-sized enterprise sector. As a result, Moldova's private sector now accounts for 80 per cent of official GDP, dominating not only the nascent services sector but also agriculture, following the break-up of collective farms in the late 1990s, and industry, following the post-privatisation restructuring of two-thirds of the country's manufacturing enterprises.

These achievements in moving towards a market, or at least a hybrid, economy have nevertheless failed to bring any significant improvements to the lives of most Moldovans. Despite the relatively strong economic growth recorded since 2000, Moldova still ranks as the poorest country in Europe. Malnourishment and disease have proliferated since independence, life expectancy has fallen, and per capita GDP is now equivalent to that of many third-world countries. Even though average wages rose by almost 50 per cent in real terms in 2000–2001, they remained under $2 per day and well below Romanian or Russian levels. As wages cover less than two-thirds of the minimum consumer budget, many Moldovans are forced to rely on the shadow economy or household garden plots to survive, and have yet to feel economically any more secure. According to an opinion poll conducted in early 2003, as much as 60 per cent of the population claimed that their personal situation had either not improved or had actually deteriorated over the previous year, despite the strong economic growth and rising real wages reported by official data.

The fall in Moldova's living standards since independence has produced a remarkable exodus of somewhere between one-fifth and one-quarter of the workforce in search of jobs abroad, primarily in Western Europe and Russia. The remittances that these workers send home through official channels amount to 15–17 per cent of the country's total GDP. Adding in the sums sent through unofficial channels (legal and illegal) would double that figure. Although this helps to stabilise the currency and to sustain family members left in Moldova, it underlines the extent of Moldova's brain drain, which has deprived the Moldovan economy of many of its youngest, most skilled and most entrepreneurial workers.

A narrow economic base

The scale of labour migration since independence, and of the country's poverty more generally, underlines the failure of elites and institutions to transcend Moldova's unfortunate Soviet inheritance. Notwithstanding the relative success of first-generation reforms, Moldova's leadership has for the most part dragged its feet in implementing the structural reforms needed to protect the country from economic shocks. The break-up of the Soviet Union left Moldova even more susceptible to these sorts of shock than most of the other republics. Unlike many of the Central Asian countries, for instance, Moldova lacked a readily exploitable fuel resource to drive economic growth, export earnings or investment inflows. Instead, Moldova entered the transition dependent on fuel imports and reliant on the sort of agriculture-related exports that struggle to penetrate hard-currency markets.

Moldova's narrow agricultural economy is partly a function of geography, which endowed it with a favourable climate and the fertile 'black earth' that covers more than three-quarters of its agricultural land. It is also a function of the extreme economic concentration favoured by Soviet economic planners. For decades, Moldova acted as a major supplier of food and beverages to the other republics, providing almost 20 per cent of the Soviet Union's grapes and wine, 30 per cent of its tobacco, and 10–15 per cent of its fruit and vegetables. This economic concentration intensified even further after independence, when Transdniestria's secession from the rest of the country deprived Moldova of much of its industrial capacity, since Soviet planners had situated most of the country's heavy industry and electricity-generating capacity in Transdniestria. The importance of the farming sector in the rest of Moldova rose sharply as a result, and the industrial sector become disproportionately reliant on agro-processing plants. These plants now account for over half of total industrial output, with wine alone responsible for one quarter of total manufacturing sales. In terms of exports, the economic concentration is even more extreme, with agriculture and agro-processing accounting for nearly two-thirds of export revenue. (Please note that all the statistics in this article, with the exception of the section on Transdniestria, refer to Moldova *excluding* Transdniestria.)

Moldova's unusually narrow economic base has rendered the need for meaningful structural reform that much more urgent. In order to reduce the serious risks posed by bad weather, Moldova needs to encourage the expansion of industries and services not related to the agricultural sector. Even then, as agriculture and agro-processing will inevitably remain of undeniable economic importance, Moldova also needs to boost competitiveness in these traditional sectors. Without greater competitiveness, these sectors will find it difficult to penetrate the EU market, which offers no concessions to key Moldovan exports such as wine, fruit or vegetables, yet appears to be the most obvious alternative to the less predictable Russian market. Shifts in Russian trade policies and import demands have repeatedly underlined the need to diversify into new markets, most notably following the collapse in exports to Russia during the rouble crisis in 1998, and more recently Russia's decision to introduce quotas for key Moldovan exports such as sugar, tobacco and liquor.

During the early transition period (the first 5–7 years), successive governments delayed the reform of the agricultural sector and the privatisation of key sectors such as wine production, in spite of the urgent need to address the economy's structural shortcomings. At the time of independence, Moldova inherited collectivised farms accustomed to operating in a centrally-planned environment in which market signals did not apply. Enterprises had responded to administrative targets rather than consumer preferences, and benefited from favourable procurement prices and subsidised inputs. Easy access to credit and soft budget constraints had obviated the need to consider profitability or efficiency. The agro-processing sector in Soviet times featured similar distortions, as it could rely on a centralised production and distribution system, captive markets within the Soviet Union and protection from competitors abroad.

Both the agro-processing and agricultural sectors were therefore woefully ill-suited to compete in a more market-oriented environment. They lacked efficient distribution and supply channels, expertise in packaging and marketing, and effective means of controlling quality. Not least, distorted Soviet energy prices had resulted in massively inefficient production techniques. Not needing to account for input costs, Moldovan producers had largely ignored efficiency concerns and consumed several times more energy per unit of production than Western producers.

On paper at least, Moldova's first attempts to tackle these structural issues came shortly after independence. As early as December 1991, Moldova approved a Land Code and began the process of transferring land from state to private ownership. However, these reforms sought only to restructure collective farms into joint-stock companies and ignored the need to reinvigorate the agricultural sector by breaking up collective structures. Moreover, for the next few years, the resistance of powerful vested interests among collective farm managers, who were well connected politically at both regional and national levels, effectively blocked consideration of more substantial sectoral reforms. Vested interests in wine and tobacco, two of the most important processing sectors, prevented any significant restructuring there as well, with parliament waiting until 2000 to approve at long last the legislation needed to privatise the large enterprises that the state still controlled in these sectors.

Meaningful reform in the agricultural sector began only slightly before the decision to privatise the large state-owned wine and tobacco enterprises. Attempts to break up collective farms picked up moderately during the second half of the 1990s, but only really began with the launch of the National Land Programme in 1998. This USAID-supported programme was designed to reduce the unwieldy scale of Moldova's inherited agricultural enterprises by turning collectivised holdings over to individual farmers and business-like corporate farms. By the end of 2000, the National Land Programme had emerged as one of the most successful projects of its type in the former Soviet Union. Over a relatively short period of time, it liquidated almost 900 collective farms, creating more than a 1000 debt-free agricultural enterprises and hundreds of thousands of individual landowners. These new owners formed peasant farms and rural household farms, and now account for over 80 per cent of agricultural output. Despite concerns about excessive fragmentation in the newly-reformed sector, preliminary evidence suggests that newly-created small and medium-sized private farms are proving more productive than larger holdings.

The post-privatisation reforms under way in the agricultural sector since 2000 have proved more difficult than the initial privatisation programme. These follow-on reforms are needed to ensure effective regulation of the various new relationships that have emerged within the sector and to establish a market infrastructure, including networks of agro-stores and machinery stations, Western-style service co-operatives and an efficient commodity exchange. Farmers also need improved access to advice and expertise on legal, technical and marketing issues. Not least, the new private farmers require financial institutions able to serve their needs, including through mortgage lending and savings and credit associations.

The creation of viable market-based structures has proceeded only slowly. Although the process of transferring land from less efficient to more efficient agricultural producers is under way, it still occurs primarily through leasing arrangements due to limited progress in developing a viable land market. Similarly, the commodity exchange in operation since 2002 remains for the most part experimental, and has yet to result in a fully developed wholesale market for agricultural products. As a result, powerful local actors continue to capture sizeable rents through their local-level dominance, and show little interest in permitting the transparency which would be possible through more effective price signals and liberalised commodity trade.

Moldova's slow progress on post-privatisation reforms has precluded anything but limited progress towards addressing the negative trends apparent in the agricultural sector in recent years. These include a reduction in the area planted to high-value crops (such as peaches and apricots) and an increase in the area devoted to low-value crops (such as cereals and potatoes). There is also a continuing problem with low productivity of both land and labour. This is likely to have worsened over the last decade, as displaced industrial workers have gravitated towards the safety net offered by the agricultural sector. The government has lacked the means to invest in the irrigation system, and hardening budget constraints have sparked a sharp drop in investment in key inputs such as fertiliser.

A sustainable basis for growth

The agricultural sector's productivity problems, coupled with the slow pace of economic diversification, raise questions over the sustainability of the economic recovery under way in Moldova since 2000. At first glance this recovery seems impressive. The cumulative 16 per cent GDP growth recorded in 2000–2002 has drawn a line under the protracted decline of the preceding years. Annual inflation fell to a record low during this period, and the currency remained relatively stable, in contrast to the high inflation and extreme currency collapse of the late 1990s. This in turn allowed the central bank to boost liquidity and encourage lending by aggressively lowering interest rates and remonetising the economy.

The government, for its part, has achieved a remarkable fiscal correction. For years, Moldova's political elites resisted adjusting their unrealistic expenditure commitments to fit a shrinking revenue base. In particular, they proved unwilling or unable to tackle rent-seeking by vested interests eager to secure preferential treatment or subsidies. Only once external funding dried up during the financial crisis of the late 1990s did the government finally accept the need for fiscal consolidation. By 2002, it had narrowed its budget deficit to under 1 per cent, from as much as 10 per cent in the mid-1990s, and reduced expenditure to below 25 per cent of GDP, from almost 40 per cent in 1996. This proved possible only through a steep reduction in net lending to the enterprise sector, better targeting of social assistance, and the almost complete elimination of quasi-fiscal subsidies, including directed bank credits to favoured sectors.

However it is by no means clear that these impressive achievements will suffice to sustain the 6–7 per cent annual growth rates promised by the government over the medium term. Most importantly, the optimistic official forecasts ignore the extent to which a number of unusually fortuitous circumstances have converged to drive economic recovery. Not least, Moldova has benefited from favourable weather conditions. The importance of this should not be underestimated in an economy as concentrated as Moldova's, or with a similar past history of crises sparked by bad weather. An unusually strong recovery in three key export markets, Russia, Ukraine and Romania, has also proved crucial. Just as plummeting demand in these countries had catastrophic effects in Moldova in the late 1990s, so their robust recovery has buttressed Moldova's macroeconomic stability since 2000. Finally, Moldova has capitalised on a significant shift in relative exchange rates, caused by the leu's collapse during the regional financial crisis of the late 1990s. Faced with a sudden rise in the local-currency price of imports, and a corresponding improvement in the price competitiveness of exports, Moldova has succeeded at least in reducing the external imbalances that impeded growth in the 1990s.

Lagging investment

These favourable one-off factors cannot be counted upon to converge again in a similar fashion over the medium term. Instead, the economy still appears vulnerable. Most importantly, investment since independence has fallen well below what is needed to ensure the steady technological improvements needed to build a productive and broadly-based economy. Consumption, rather than investment, proved instrumental in achieving the economic recovery of 2000–2002, with the rise in consumption in 2002, for instance, considerably outpacing GDP growth. This reflects in part the increase in wages and pensions achieved by the communist government, which fuelled a surge in consumption-related imports. As a result, net exports remain a considerable drag on growth despite the currency's real depreciation and the export sector's recovery.

The moderate 4 per cent rise in investment reported in 2002 should therefore be viewed against a very low base. At under 17 per cent of GDP, fixed capital investment in Moldova remains extremely low even by regional standards. Neither the government nor the enterprise sector appears able to invest to the extent required, while inflows of foreign direct investment, let alone portfolio investment, are negligible compared with the more dynamic transition economies in the region. A total of only around $725m in FDI has flowed into Moldova since independence. This translates into around $200 per head, compared with around $1000 in Poland and $2000 in Hungary.

Even Russian investors, who are most familiar with Moldova and relatively cash-rich after several years of high oil prices, have only belatedly begun to compensate for the limited interest showed by their Western counterparts. Russian companies have only recently begun to consolidate their presence in Moldova, which lies across key routes for Russian exports to South-Eastern Europe. In the last few years, Russian investment has begun to flow into infrastructure projects, including gas transportation, the production and distribution of electricity, rail transport, Danube port facilities, fuel storage and petrol stations. The presence of Russian companies is growing in Moldova's wine and machinery sectors.

However, without more interest from Western investors, investment inflows into Moldova remain insufficient. In theory, at least, the communist administration is open to Western investment. The government's programme acknowledges the importance of FDI, particularly in the light of Moldova's inadequate natural resources and low personal and corporate incomes. A series of conflicts between the Moldova authorities and foreign investors has nevertheless sent opposite signals. The government decided in early 2002 to review the list of foreign investors benefiting from income tax exemption (shortly after unveiling its 'Investment Strategy for the Republic of Moldova') and has presided over some controversial renationalisation plans since coming to power. Some of the worst publicity has involved the largest Western investor, Union Fenosa, which has seen the legality of its purchase of three of Moldova's five electricity distributors in 2000 questioned in court.

Reforming the business environment

Even without these high-profile cases, Moldova would still struggle to attract significant inflows of Western FDI. Not least, the country is handicapped by its less than ideal endowment, which includes a small domestic market and the unresolved issue of Transdniestria. Neither the current administration nor its predecessor has done much to compensate for this. To a large extent, this reflects the power of vested sectoral interests, and of state officials unwilling to surrender the prerogatives left over from their Soviet-era role in running the economy.

The continued power of these groups has helped to deter potential investors, and the expansion of the SME sector more generally, by perpetuating an unpredictable legal environment and convoluted procedures for obtaining licenses, permits, and certificates. For instance, the system of licensing businesses has changed little since the establishment of a chamber to licence most types of business activity in early 2002. The new chamber still needs to co-ordinate its decisions with the almost two dozen ministries and departments that it has theoretically replaced. Similarly, registration procedures remain costly and time-consuming. Entrepreneurs complain that it takes months to start a business, or that they are discouraged even before registering, due to the range of permits and authorisations required from local authorities. In a significant number of cases, this either precludes entrepreneurial activity completely or else drives it underground.

Investors are further put off by the unstable and opaque tax system, which remains hostile towards enterprises, and by problems of excessive inspections of enterprises. Although the authorities have reduced the number of inspecting bodies, the process has yet to become any more efficient. The various inspecting bodies are still not subject to legal limits on the number of times they can inspect a given enterprise, nor are they required to co-ordinate their activities with each other. Enterprises continue to complain about excessive controls and the lack of professionalism of the inspecting authorities, and generally avoid legal action in the knowledge that most court decisions favour the inspectors. Finally, pervasive corruption remains a major concern. On most major scales of corruption, Moldova continues to rank at or near the top for the region, generally ahead of countries such as Russia and Ukraine. Despite vowing to fight corruption on coming to power in 2001, the current communist leadership has so far done little to address the problem.

Moldova is not alone among transition countries in failing to address the shortcomings of its business environment. In line with most other former Soviet republics, Moldova has struggled to establish transparent and accountable institutions. As a result, powerful vested interests have become entrenched both in key economic sectors and within the bureaucracy. They have benefited from the country's weak and unaccountable political structures, which encourage rent-seeking rather than entrepreneurship, and have succeeded in slowing the structural reforms that might otherwise endanger their rents.

The reform process under the Communist Party of Moldova (CPRM)

Unlike much of Central Europe, Moldova's efforts to redress its skewed incentive structures and accelerate reforms have not benefited from any credible promise of imminent EU membership. In the more advanced transition countries, the promise of EU accession presented an effective means for constraining policy options and forcing through tough decisions, while at the same time providing a coherent framework for reform and technical assistance. Although Moldova has long sought closer integration, including through a PCA agreed in 1994, the EU has never been able to suggest that accession is anything more than a distant, abstract possibility.

In the absence of a broad consensus united behind the goal of EU accession, the progress of reform in Moldova has had to depend on the occasional appointment of reformers to key positions, as in the case of the reformist government in 1999, or on the harsh realities created by Moldova's financing constraints. The crisis in emerging markets in the late 1990s was a case in point. By putting an end to most external financing inflows, it forced the government to work more closely with multilateral organisations and to contemplate the sort of expenditure rationalisation it had long postponed.

The state's depleted financial resources have probably also helped to prevent a lurch away from reform since 2001, when the CPRM won decisive control of parliament and subsequently the presidency. The communists came to power on an anti-reform platform and with a long-standing antipathy towards the multilaterals. They tried initially to use their control of both executive and legislative branches to roll back reforms passed by previous centre-right administrations. In particular, the CPRM hoped to undo in part the break-up of collective farms, re-assert state control over the allocation of agricultural inputs and outputs, and reinstate a range of price controls. It is likely that financial constraints played a major role in forcing the CPRM to retreat, however unwillingly, from this agenda.

Unfortunately for Moldova, the constraints imposed by depleted government coffers or the promise of multilateral financing are hardly the same as a credible promise of imminent EU membership. The CPRM has only partially retreated from its state-centred economic agenda, and still hopes to achieve many of its goals not through radical reforms but through administrative methods, such as strengthened tax administration, increased domestic borrowing, and legislating minimum wage increases. Although some of these measures have helped to raise incomes and contributed to economic expansion since the CPRM came to power, the party's continued resistance to real reform is worrisome, and several of the most important structural reforms have slowed noticeably since 2001.

The CPRM authorities appear reluctant to admit this, and in 2003 were still rejecting IMF criticism of their slow progress in reform (reducing subsidies to agriculture, dismantling restrictions on exports and privatising key sectors). In the end, the IMF and World Bank decided to suspend credit to the Moldovan government due to its failure to comply with the co-ordinated terms. The government's attitude underlines the ongoing internal debate within the CPRM over the need to accept reforms, a debate that has resulted in considerable policy confusion. The results for 2003 are quite contradictory. While the country's GDP continued to expand, inflation intensified, the trade balance worsened, and state external and internal debts increased. Most importantly, the CPRM has been unable to develop clear answers to several basic questions, including how to improve the entrepreneurial and investment climate, how to bring the shadow economy into the open, and how to deal with the pervasive problems of corruption. Until the government finds answers to these questions, Moldova will struggle to establish a sustainable basis for growth.

Transdniestria as a 'parallel' developing region

The unresolved question of Transdniestria's political status has compounded this policy confusion. Despite more concerted efforts since 2002 to address the Transdniestria issue, the integration of the two economies remains a distant prospect. To some extent, the reintegration process will benefit from the range of economic links that have survived despite the protracted political stand-off. The rest of Moldova takes around a quarter of Transdniestria's exports, while the interests of private foreign investors have ensured that some links have been re-established in a number of key sectors. However, over more than 10 years of quasi-independence, Transdniestria has built up a full range of parallel structures and a legislative basis for its own banking sector, currency, tax system, trade regime and system of property rights. Even with international assistance, the alignment of two separate financial, economic and social systems promises to be a complicated and politically charged process.

Moreover, the process of reintegration will bring considerable short and medium-term costs for Moldova, due to the poor state of Transdniestria's economy. This has seen far fewer structural changes than in the rest of Moldova since the break-up of the Soviet Union. Although reform has speeded up somewhat over the last two years, Transdniestria's leaders still retain considerable economic control. They play a leading role in the joint-stock companies established in the industrial sector, and have only recently begun the process of reforming the agricultural sector, which has required significant government subsidies and directed credits to avoid complete collapse. Although the Transdniestrian government finally approved a Land Code in 2002, in order to begin reducing its role in the agricultural sector, a referendum on private land ownership in April 2003 failed to secure the turnout needed for approval.

Delays in the structural reform process have brought similar problems to those experienced in the rest of Moldova during the first decade of independence. These include extremely low levels of investment and productivity, insufficient working capital, and widespread non-payment or barter transactions between enterprises. Transdniestria has relied on only around a dozen exporting industrial enterprises to supply more than two-thirds of GDP and the bulk of budget revenue, and has needed easy credits and cheap energy imports from Russia to disguise the uncompetitiveness of these enterprises. Forced to loosen monetary and credit policies in order to compensate for the slow pace of reform and chronic external imbalances, the Transdniestrian leadership precipitated soaring inflation and a sharp currency decline in the second half of the 1990s, as well as a considerable contraction in output. Although Transdniestria's economy recovered briefly during the first three-quarters of 2001, the Moldovan government cut this short by introducing new customs procedures in September of that year as part of the country's WTO accession requirements. The introduction of new Moldovan customs seals, to which Transdniestrian exporters were denied access, precipitated a collapse in Transdniestria's exports.

Transdniestria's dire economic situation since late 2001 has at least helped to convince the region's leadership of the need for some reforms, in the hope of securing the investment inflows needed to stabilise the economy and shore up the public finances. In addition to approving a new Land Code, the Transdniestrian government has begun cash privatisation sales of major industrial enterprises, including the region's fixed-line telephone monopoly sold in January 2003. Other planned sales include stakes in major strategic enterprises, including in the metallurgy and electricity sectors. Perhaps even more importantly, the dislocation caused by the introduction of the new Moldovan customs seals in 2001 might also have spurred a greater interest in economic co-operation. Although Transdniestria denounced the Moldovan government for imposing what it considered to be an economic blockade, the region's leadership subsequently appeared more open to expanding bilateral ties. Transdniestria is more reliant on exports than the rest of Moldova, and recognises that increased co-operation could help to overcome its uncertain international status, which has impeded the investment and exports needed to ensure macroeconomic and social stability.

*****

For the whole of Moldova, closer economic co-operation and eventual reintegration promise obvious benefits. Resolution of the Transdniestria issue would eliminate a major source of distraction and permit greater investment and political stability. It would also help to broaden the country's narrow economy, through access to the machine-building, light industry, electricity and metal sectors that are at the core of Transdniestria's economy. However, reintegration on its own is unlikely to solve Moldova's problems. In order to tackle its considerable economic difficulties, Moldova will above all need to improve its administrative capacity and strengthen its existing institutions. In particular, Moldova needs a more effective state administration in order to tackle widespread tax evasion and exemptions, and to ensure the allocation of resources based on more strategic priorities. More generally, it needs administrative reforms to ensure a government responsive to citizens and less beholden to the powerful interests currently entrenched within state structures and atop key sectors. Reforms of this kind will prove critical if Moldova is to achieve the robust long-term growth needed to address problems of widespread impoverishment, declining provision of even basic government services, and the continuing exodus of much of the workforce.

Moldova's Main Macroeconomic Indicators

	1994	1995	1996	1997	1998	1999	2000	2001	2002
"Real GDP (% change, year on year) "	-30.9	-1.4	-5.9	1.6	-6.5	-3.4	2.1	6.1	7.2
as % of 1993	-30.9	-31.9	-35.9	-34.8	-39.1	-41.1	-39.9	-36.2	-31.6
Nominal GDP (Lei million)	"4,737"	"6,479"	"7,798"	"8,917"	"9,122"	"12,322"	"16,020"	"19,052"	"22,040"
Nominal GDP (USD million)	"1,165"	"1,441"	"1,694"	"1,929"	"1,698"	"1,171"	"1,288"	"1,481"	"1,624"
GDP per head (USD)	323	400	471	537	473	327	354	408	448
"Industrial output (% real change, year on year)"	-27.8	-3.9	-6.5	0.0	-15.0	-11.6	7.7	13.7	10.6
as % of 1993	-27.8	-30.5	-35.0	-35.0	-44.8	-51.2	-47.4	-40.2	-33.9
"Agricultural output (% real change, year on year)"	-24.6	1.9	-11.9	11.4	-11.6	-8.4	-3.3	6.4	3.0
as % of 1993	-24.6	-23.2	-32.3	-24.6	-33.3	-38.9	-41.0	-37.2	-35.3
"Investments in fixed capital (% real change, year on year)"	-51.0	-16.0	-8.0	-8.0	10.0	-22.0	-15.0	11.0	4.1
as % of 1993	-51.0	-58.8	-62.1	-65.2	-61.7	-70.1	-74.6	-71.8	-70.6
Exports of goods (fob; USD million)	618	739	823	890	644	474	477	567	660
Imports of goods (fob; USD million)	672	794	"1,075"	"1,238"	"1,032"	611	770	879	"1,038"
Trade balance (USD million)	-54	-55	-252	-348	-388	-137	-294	-311	-378
as % GDP	-4.6	-3.8	-14.9	-18.0	-22.9	-11.7	-22.8	-21.0	-23.3
Current-account balance (USD million)	-82	-98	-191	-275	-335	-69	-97	-95	-103
as % GDP	-7.0	-6.8	-11.3	-14.2	-19.7	-5.8	-7.5	-6.4	-6.4
Foreign direct investment (net yearly flows; USD million)	18	73	23	78	76	38	129	156	110
State external debt (USD million)	506	659	766	"1,004"	"1,003"	935	997	930	971
as % GDP	43.4	45.7	45.2	52.1	59.1	79.8	77.4	62.8	59.8
State internal debt (Lei million)	270	477	737	984	"1,572"	"1,910"	"2,022"	"2,400"	"2,821"
Consolidated budget deficit (% of GDP)	-5.8	-5.8	-9.7	-7.5	-3.3	-3.2	-1.0	0.0	-0.5
Nominal wage (monthly average; USD)	26.7	31.9	40.7	47.5	46.6	28.9	32.8	42.3	51.0
"Real wage (monthly average; % change, year on year)"	-40.8	1.6	5.4	4.9	5.5	-12.5	2.0	21.6	21.0
Consumer price inflation (end-period; %)	104.6	23.8	15.1	11.2	18.3	43.7	18.4	6.3	4.4
Consumer price inflation (annual average; %)	487.0	30.0	24.0	12.0	8.0	39.0	31.1	9.6	5.2
Exchange rate (end-period; Lei/ USD)	4.27	4.50	4.65	4.66	8.32	11.59	12.38	13.09	13.82
Exchange rate (annual average; Lei/ USD)	4.07	4.50	4.60	4.62	5.37	10.52	12.43	12.87	13.57

"Source: National Bank of Moldova, Department of Statistics and Sociology, CISR"
"All figures exclude Transdniestria, for which no suitable figures are available."
The data start from 1994 because previous years' statistics are unreliable.

Why is Moldova Poor and Economically Volatile?

Vlad Spanu

The transition to a market economy in Eastern Europe and the former Soviet Union proved to be more difficult and lengthy than many economists predicted. In Moldova, the 'side effects' of the reforms had the worst impact on the quality of life of the population. After more than 10 years of economic experiments, the country is much poorer and more volatile than in 1991, when it gained its independence from the Soviet Union.

Although Moldova has been an obedient follower of the international financial institutions' (IFI) guidelines since 1992, its government consistently failed to implement sound economic changes. Why this underperformance? Lack of institutional capacity, leading to an inability to analyse critically and understand the advice given by Ifis; and a lack of political will to implement tough policies fully. Ironically, it was the Sangheli government, the most anti-reform of all post-independence Moldovan governments, which launched the major reform programme in 1994, including large-scale privatisation of small and medium-sized enterprises and agricultural land. The promoters of the 'Washington Consensus'[1] used a stick and carrot approach in persuading Moldova to transform its economy by providing loans in return for promises of reform. Moldovan officials paid less attention to the stick while gobbling up the carrots. Otherwise how can one explain Moldova's accumulated debt to the IMF and the World Bank of $621 million (over 50 per cent of total debt) and the fact that the country is one step from default? Moreover, IMF monitoring reports affirm that Moldova meets most of its targets. Looking at the state of the country today, a question arises: are the targets set by the IMF in consultation with the Moldovan government real? Do they contribute to the country's development? Or are they deliberately set low?

Moldova failed to be creative in the search for its own path of transition. Governments, due to their weak capacity, blindly accepted the recipes of the IFIs and donor countries without taking a lead in crafting a policy for Moldova that would incorporate local needs, particularities and differences.

Today, the communist-controlled government and parliament are doing no better than their predecessors. Populist policies oriented towards short-term electoral goals just camouflage the real problems the country faces without touching the roots of Moldova's poor economic development. While real GDP has risen in the last few years, since the communists won the parliamentary vote, this economic growth in no way reflects sound policies. Two effects, both unrelated to government policies, contributed to the first signs of economic activity since the 1990s: (i) growth in Moldova mirrored the economic boom in Russia, Moldova's main partner and investor, and (ii) Moldova's GDP rose because it had no further to fall. From 1990 to 2001 output declined steadily at 8.4 per cent per year, resulting in a 60 per cent cumulative loss of its 1991 value by 2001.[2]

Level of development

Moldova is labelled 'the poorest country in Europe'. The World Bank classifies Moldova in the group of low-income economies. Indeed, its GDP per capita, as measured in 2001 at purchasing power parity, was $2150, putting Moldova at the bottom of the list of countries in Central and Eastern Europe and the western former Soviet republics. Even Armenia, Azerbaijan and Georgia, three Caucasian countries that face war and ethnic conflict, have left Moldova behind. Moldova's GDP per capita in constant 1995 prices was $678 in 2001, so that Moldovans were even worse off when travelling abroad.

In order to gain a deep understanding of Moldova's quality of life and development, knowing its GDP per capita is not enough. Income is unevenly distributed among different social groups, regions, and ethnic groups. The inequality index (Gini) in Moldova is 40.6 points. The country's Gini has increased more than in other countries in the region. In Hungary, for example, the inequality index has increased by 1.6 points in the last decade compared with 13.6 points in Moldova. This growing inequality makes things worse for the many who live below the poverty line. According to the World Development Report 2003, 38.4 per cent of people in Moldova live on less than $2 a day.

Due to the poor performance of the economy, Moldovans are forced to seek jobs abroad, children drop out of school and farmers continue to work at subsistence level. The economic decline of the last decade is the main cause of the poverty. This weak performance stems from three main factors: institutions, geography and demography.

Institutions and structural reforms. Bad governance and high levels of corruption are the main causes of the weakness of Moldova's institutions. Low wages in government jobs (monthly average of $53 as of 2003) and party-based rather than merit-based job promotion are the main factors keeping highly-qualified professionals out of the system. The low salaries of public officials and the excessive regulation of public services and economic activities cause corruption to flourish. The government shifts the blame for poor performance onto external shocks: adverse weather conditions for scarce agricultural output, or Russia's 1998 crisis for weak Moldovan exports and volatile financial conditions. The authorities are not focused on smoothing the effects of inevitable shocks through diversification of export markets and reducing dependence on agricultural production for the country's main exports. Thus, during the last decade little has been done to reduce the country's vulnerability. The IFIs, the country's main foreign advisers, concentrate primarily on structural reform and financial stability policies, which, while important in the short run, do little to address the country's long-term problem of vulnerability to external shocks.

Nobody is to blame for the delays in privatisation but the government. Since the communists took full control of all branches of the body politic in 2001, privatisation has slowed down. Implementation of the last stage of the privatisation programme for large enterprises (the two remaining energy distribution networks, Moldtelecom, wineries and distilleries) has been postponed. 20 per cent of Moldova's industrial sector is still owned by the state. These enterprises drag down industrial growth. In 2002, their output declined by 10 per cent, while the sector grew 11 per cent overall thanks to the strong performance of privatised companies and those with foreign capital.

Although the appropriate legal framework was created, it failed to ensure a favourable environment for attracting foreign direct investment (FDI). Since 1991, cumulative FDI has reached just $414 million, or $125 per capita. Moldova is far behind Poland ($920) and Hungary ($1970), and even behind Belarus with its $128 per capita.

Trade amounts to 125 per cent of Moldova's GDP, so the country had no choice but to embrace openness in trade policy. But trade liberalisation and accession to the WTO in 2001 had no immediate positive effect on economic growth. Both of the country's main partners, Russia and Ukraine, are non-WTO members and they impose tariff barriers against Moldova's exports.

Thus Moldova, unlike other countries in the region, has been unable to secure a sound process of structural reform over the last decade. Reforms were not backed up by efficient enforcement of the law and regulations.

Geography. Almost every second government official in Chişinău will say proudly that Moldova's geopolitical location means that it can become a second Swiss haven or bridge between East and West. Even speeches by heads of state or government refer to Moldova's 'treasures': 'fertile black earth which is the best in the world, along with famous Moldovan wines and brandies, sweets and beautiful women'. In reality, the country is more likely to become a second Kaliningrad, dominated by Russian interests, unless Moldova turns to the West, implements sound reforms, and is lucky enough to engage the interest of the EU and US in its political and security concerns.

In the case of Moldova, I cannot but agree with Harvard Professor of Economics Dani Rodrik, who believes that geography has a significant impact on a country's economic performance: it affects both trade and institutions. Geography is not Moldova's ally. Invaded, occupied and divided over centuries, what we now know as the Republic of Moldova always lacked natural resources and relied on agriculture as the mainstay of its economy.

The structure of the economy has not changed much in 21st century Moldova, with agriculture still the dominant sector. Since 1998, weather conditions have affected agricultural output. Draught and frost have hit crops almost every year.

Unlike its neighbours, Moldova has not used its proximity to EU markets to its advantage, in part due to the EU's restrictive policies towards agricultural products from non-members or non-associate members. Neither has it developed new markets outside the former Soviet Union. Thus, Moldova remains heavily dependent on the CIS market, mainly Russia and Ukraine, for its agriculture-dominated exports (which make up over 50 per cent of all exports) and fuel imports (which account for 20 per cent of all imports). There are recent signs of exports to the EU picking up, mainly thanks to German and Italian investment in the textile industry and the use of their distribution channels throughout Europe. Trade with Romania is significant – its western neighbour is Moldova's number three trade partner – but investment from that country is very low due to lack of interest from both the Romanian business community and the Bucharest government. Relations between the two countries have deteriorated since the communists won the elections in

Moldova. In any case the Romanians are preoccupied with their country's accession to NATO and the EU, and Moldova is no longer on Romania's priority list.

Demography. Moldova's population of 4.3 million is ethnically diverse due to Russia's 150-year occupation, which stimulated migration by different groups, leading eventually to the creation of the quasi-state of Transdniestria, which is *de facto* independent of Moldova. Transdniestria used to be the most industrialised part of Moldova in its Soviet period. Special arrangements for the Găgăuz and the Bulgarians also had nothing to do with the economic interests of Moldova as a whole or of the ethnic groups concerned.

From 1993 to 2003, population growth was negative and fluctuated between -0.07 and -0.35 per cent annually. But these are official statistics or estimates that do not reflect emigration. Since 1996 about one million Moldovans are believed to have left the country in search of better jobs. Mainly, these are temporary workers, in most cases illegal migrants. Since the vast majority of emigrants are aged 25–45, Moldova is short of about half its labour force. Also, these people are voters who are not able to participate in the electoral process in Moldova.

The efficient education system inherited from Soviet times has been preserved and developed since independence. The illiteracy rate is just 1 per cent. Private education competes with public institutions. Unfortunately, due to the lack of job opportunities in Moldova, this resource is wasted. In most cases, Moldovan emigrants with first and masters degrees or even doctorates work abroad as unqualified workers in construction, retail or, even worse, as prostitutes on the streets of Western Europe. There are estimated to be 200,000 Moldovans in Italy alone. Thus, Moldova has failed to make proper use of its most valuable resource, its educated people.

Moldova's economic volatility

The main causes of Moldova's volatility lie in the structure of the economy, high external debt, dependence on CIS export markets, and dependence on CIS fuel imports.

Agriculture employs the largest share of the labour force and also accounts for the largest share of GDP, 21 per cent. Its importance is slowly decreasing, making room for growth in the service industries. Between 1995 and 2002, the share of services grew from one third to almost a half of GDP. Now, trade accounts for 11.5 per cent, transport and communications 10.2 per cent and construction 2.9 per cent.

Moldova's main exports are food, alcoholic beverages and vegetables, which together account for over 50 per cent of total sales. All these exports are highly dependent on variable climate conditions. High-technology products do not exceed 3 per cent of exports of manufactures. Sales to Russia and other CIS countries dominate Moldova's exports; these are vulnerable to the stability of these transition economies and dependent on political relations between Moldova and the other countries, especially Russia. For instance, Russia uses trade barriers as leverage in its policies towards the 'near abroad' (former Soviet republics), and Moldova is often a victim of such policies. On the positive site, the flexible exchange rate system efficiently promoted by Moldova's Central Bank helps to alleviate the negative impact on the currency caused by fluctuations on the foreign exchange market.

Dependence on gas, oil and electricity imports from one main supplier increases the volatility of Moldova's economy. The natural gas price for Moldova is also used for political leverage. Moldova pays $80 per 1000 cubic meters for imported gas from Russia, while Belarus and Armenia pay about half that. The more obedient a country is towards Russia, the better its chances of getting an advantageous price and facing fewer trade barriers to its exports. Thus, using economic leverage, Russia is able to keep Moldova in its sphere of influence and prevent the country adopting a pro-Western orientation in its foreign policy. While the EU and NATO are moving their borders further east, Moldova will not be included in the enlargement process anytime soon. Under pressure from Moscow, the government in Chişinău almost abandoned GUUAM, a regional grouping that aims to enhance economic co-operation through the development of a Europe-Caucusus-Asia transport corridor.[3] This organisation caught the attention of the US and West European countries, but it is not welcomed by Russia, which sees it as an attempt to break out of the Russia-dominated CIS.

Annual trade deficits are over 20 per cent of GDP, while annual current-account deficits are in the region of 8–9 per cent of GDP. The difference is made up by remittances from Moldovan workers abroad, estimated at $250–260 million annually (15 per cent of GDP), more than foreign aid and investment combined.

Moldova has done little to diversify its fuel imports. Central Asia, the Caucasus and the Gulf would be alternative oil and gas sources, if it were not for the strong political and business interest of Moldova's decision-makers in running things in the old way.

Moldova's total external debt exceeds $1.2 billion. The external debt/GNI ratio is extremely high: 84 per cent. Moldova has used most of its loans for consumption rather than for infrastructure development which would increase the country's capacity for growth. Moldova owes $289 million (as of 2002) just to Gazprom, the Russian supplier of natural gas, $114 million in payments for gas and $175 million in penalties for late payment. Most of the gas debt is due to non-payments by inefficient state-owned industrial enterprises. Once these debts have grown to significant proportions, the government transforms them into government loans and pays them from tax-payers' pockets. When these pockets are empty, under an agreement between Gazprom and the Moldovan government, the Russian concern can take shares in profitable enterprises in lieu of debt. This debt-for-equity swap has made Russia the largest investor in Moldova.

The only way for Moldova to reduce the burden of gas debt is to stop subsidising failed enterprises and put them in the hands of private owners. Then, with less debt for gas, Moldova would strengthen its negotiating position with Gazprom when the fee is set for gas transit through Moldova to the Balkans. In 2003, Gazprom was pressing Moldova to lower the gas transit tariff from $2.5 per 1000 cubic meters per 100 km to $1.5.

What is the way out?

Does the Republic of Moldova have any chance of preserving its political and economic independence? How can the country achieve sustainable economic development?

I remember that when Zbigniew Brzezinski, former US National Security Adviser, was asked in 1998 about the future of Moldova, he said he thought that the only way for the country to survive was to become part of the Euro-Atlantic political and security structures. Brzezinski also believed then that the only vehicle by which Moldova might join the EU and NATO was Romania. Five years have passed since that discussion and Brzezinski's words have been proved right. Romania is already in NATO and will join the EU in the near future. Moldova's western neighbour is now in a good position to support the country's integration into Europe. Unfortunately, Chişinău has missed this chance by letting its relations with official Bucharest deteriorate. Fear of unification between the two countries has kept all post-independence governments in Moldova from building friendly relations with Romania. And, of course, pro-Russian communists have even more acute feelings in this respect towards Romania.

From the economic standpoint, joining the EU would indeed be Moldova's only chance of improving the life of its people. The economic and social development achieved by the Baltic states and the countries of Central and Eastern Europe since 1991, when they made their choice between Moscow and Brussels, are irrefutable arguments showing the Moldovans which path they should take.

Moldova needs to reduce its economic volatility in order to prevent the damage caused by frequent external shocks. It must increase the share in GDP of high-value-added products and services, thereby reducing its dependence on agricultural exports prone to severe weather conditions, fluctuating world prices and demand, and restrictive import policies for food and beverages. High-tech industries are one of Moldova's still unexplored avenues. Once known as a supplier of electronic components for the Soviet military complex, Moldova has an abandoned electronic sector today. Its whole army of engineers have nowhere to use their skills. While software programming is booming in other countries in the region (especially Russia and Romania), programmers in Moldova have no jobs.

By providing more opportunities for Moldovan businesses to cooperate with companies in the EU through transparent policies and trade and investment promotion campaigns, the government would address another problem that makes the country vulnerable: dependence on one market to the east and a single large investor, Russia. Instead, the only major Western investor, the Spanish Union Fenosa, was harassed in 2002 by the Moldovan Audit Court, which claimed that the electricity distribution infrastructures privatised by this firm were undervalued, and that the deal should therefore be considered null and void. Intervention by the IFIs was required to avoid an embarrassing scandal.

Diversification is what Moldova needs most in both export and import markets. In order to improve the quality of its products and their competitiveness on external markets, the country needs technology transfers from the industrialised countries. Government intervention to lower or eliminate import tariffs for technological equipment and machinery would play a crucial role in this regard.

To reduce its external debt/GNI ratio, Moldova must take bold steps to end its subsidies to industries that are not economically viable and constitute a burden on the state budget. Free from the pressure of gas debt, Moldova could be more selective in choosing investment in its economy. Diversification of foreign interests would also be to Moldova's advantage.

Finally, the country must create a favourable environment for local and foreign investors. Moldova's institutions must do their best to reduce the political risk that now keeps investment low. Re-nationalisations carried out by the communist government since 2001, such as those of Eurofarm, a US-Romanian joint venture, and Air Moldova, a firm with significant German capital, do no good to the country's image. The Transdniestrian conflict, until resolved completely, will be a threat to Moldova's national security and increase the risk premium demanded by foreign investors. Also, the Russian army stationed in Moldova will continue to deter western investors. In sum, Moldova needs to realise that it is not only high rates of return that attract foreign investment; it is equally important to ensure that investors have confidence in the country's institutions.

Notes

[1] A term invented by John Williamson from the US Institute for International Economics for the liberalising economic policies of the past two decades that were imposed on emerging countries by Washington-based institutions like the World Bank and the IMF.

[2] In this article, most of the data for the Republic of Moldova does not include data for Transdniestria; although official Chişinău considers the break-away region part of Moldova, governmental institutions do not provide statistical data for Transdniestria, nor are estimates available.

[3] GUUAM also became a forum for discussing common security concerns and for promoting conflict resolution, in particular in Azerbaijan's Nagorno-Karabakh, Georgia's Abkhazia and Moldova's Transdniestria.

Foreign Aid, Trade and Investment: Inconsistent Policies

Ion Sturza and Veaceslav Negruţa

The appearance of a new state on the world map presents new and interesting challenges not only to its citizens but also to its neighbours and the whole world. The period of affirmation, consolidation and development, including economic, is the most turbulent period in the growth of any new state. The success of these processes depends mostly on its own society and on the world which surrounds it. Its economic, social, cultural and educational integration with other states and international institutions is vital to its success, and contributes to the image which the country creates for itself.

Historically, the Republic of Moldova inherited an economic system which was bankrupt from the very start. Moldova had no integral economic system, only components and fragments of the old system left on this new territory. Moreover, a large share of its industrial potential (about 60 per cent) and energy sector was situated in Transdniestria. Once Moldovan independence had been achieved in the political, economic and other areas, it became obvious that these components had been torn apart from the integral system. Building new and prosperous economic agents in a shattered system has been difficult: sales outlets were restricted or even cut off, limited to a local market which was both small and poor. To create the foundations of a new economy required liberalisation, structural reorganisation and privatisation, and the introduction of a national currency. The financial system, including the banking system, had to be created almost from zero.

The key sector for Moldova was and remains agro-industry, which offers employment to more than half the population. Great hopes were placed on the development of this sector for the resurrection and rapid development of the national economy as a whole. Other South-East European countries have almost the same production profile. But while Moldova had and still has some advantages in manufacturing certain types of products, it yields to its neighbours in sales due to its slow pace of reform, inadequate foreign and local investment and lack of assertiveness in penetrating new markets. At the same time, Moldova is recognised as having an open economy, with a low level of internal market protection. This makes local producers, especially of agricultural products, less competitive even on the domestic market. This is partly due to the large inflow of counterfeit and smuggled products through the uncontrolled eastern border.

Moldova's adherence to the WTO in 2001 contributed to its integration into international trade on new principles, including well-established and clear rules of external trade. Both internal and external subjects of foreign trade are treated equally, without discrimination or preference in terms of access to the market. There is also less scope for smuggling imported goods through the eastern border. Many international bodies exerted pressure on the Ukrainian authorities to recognise only Moldovan customs stamps and to introduce tougher controls on all import-export transactions with economic agents from Transdniestria.

Foreign aid

Many international organisations and institutions became active in Moldova in the early 1990s. Over the years the country has benefited from technical and financial assistance from many bilateral and multilateral aid agencies. And since 1992 Moldova has been a member of the IMF, World Bank and EBRD.

The role of the donors and their technical assistance has varied over the years. A great deal of help had been accorded by USAID (financial sector reform, land reform, reorganisation of agricultural enterprises, post-privatisation assistance in developing agro-services infrastructures in rural areas, fiscal reform). Another important donor is Tacis (local territorial reform, trans-border cooperation, democratic institutions and economic reforms).

Many analyses of technical and financial assistance from the donors' side point to frequent parallelism and duplication. In some cases, the same subjects and beneficiaries have been funded by two or even three different donors, without any co-ordination. This has resulted in a low level of efficiency in some projects implemented in Moldova. Often Moldova, in comparison with other countries in the region, has been offered consultants with poorer competences and qualifications.

Moldova's experience of technical and financial assistance suggests some major defects:

1. Lack of clearly formulated priorities and a balanced reform strategy. This led to difficulties in determining the areas in which technical assistance (TA) was needed.

2. Insufficient co-ordination of TA by the recipient. The role of the Ministry of Economy (which is in charge of this) has long been reduced to the simple compilation of consolidated information on TA, without any real ability to influence the 'spontaneous actions' of ministries and departments. Attempts to create a Project and Programme Implementation Centre came to an end with the cessation of UNDP financial support for this specific project.

3. Spontaneous actions by ministries, departments and state agencies (there are about 50 of these) wanting TA. With departmental squabbles and insufficient analysis and clarification of issues requiring TA, this generated errors during the selection of goals, duplication of activities, or rivalry for TA. For instance, in the 1990s a variety of donors helped to prepare the Law on Foreign Investments, Bankruptcy Law (GTZ, World Bank), elaboration of agricultural sector strategy (Tacis, World Bank, USAID), export promotion (UNDP, GTZ, Tacis). The relay race to work out a new market-oriented Civil Code lasted for seven years, using the resources by turns of Tacis, GTZ and USAID. The Code was approved in 2002, but according to some assessments its applicability in practice is problematic. It seems that additional work will be required.

4. Inadequate monitoring of implementation of TA projects.

5. Insufficient transparency in the elaboration and implementation of projects. The government neglects the opinions of NGOs and media signals.

Trade

The structural and functional weaknesses of Moldova's economy damaged external trade a great deal at first. The lack of contractual relations, dominance of barter in business with FSU partners and new customs barriers brought considerable distortions into external trade. At the same time, only 5 per cent of Moldovan exports went outside the CIS.

In the early nineties there were no credible foreign trade statistics for Moldova. The 'transparency' of the border (the eastern border is not controlled by the Moldovan authorities even today), as well as the institutional and functional weaknesses of the fledgling state structures and a financial market characterised by hyperinflation and massive depreciation of the currency, introduced distortions in the volume and value of external trade. As a result, by the end of 1998 the current account deficit to GDP ratio was reaching dangerous proportions (about 23 per cent) for the further development of Moldova's economy. The balance of trade deficit was more than 20 per cent at that time.

1998 was a turning-point in Moldova's external trade, with the external shock of Russia's economic crisis seriously affecting traditional exports to Russia and the CIS and imports becoming more expensive after the depreciation of the Moldovan leu. Lack of diversification in markets and products led to a reduction in export volumes by the end of 1998 and in 1999. Only from 2000 did Moldova again experience an upward trend in exports and imports.

Many believe that the 1998 regional financial crisis had only negative effects on the Moldovan economy. However, it should be noted that the crisis also helped identify and eliminate certain deficiencies in the functioning of the economy. The depreciation of the national currency created new incentives for exporters, while imports (especially of goods which could be produced in Moldova) were less in demand on the local market. After the 1998 crisis, the economic reforms implemented over the years began to show results. Economic agents started to recover, and to pay attention to exports. As a result, many producers which were inefficient and loss-prone before the crisis became profitable after it.

One might expect that economic recovery and higher incomes would lead to faster growth of imports than exports. However, in 2001–2002 the opposite was true: the growth in exports of goods and services outpaced that of imports. Although the trade deficit grew, with a slightly lower value in 2002 compared with the financial crisis year of 1998, its relative value (compared to trade volume and GDP) fell over the period 2000–2002.

Nevertheless, the trade structure has not changed. Agriculture, food-processing and textile products account for more than half of all exports. On the import side, energy resources still account for the greatest share of total imports, despite their continuous decline in volume.

Traditionally, thanks to bilateral free trade agreements, the CIS countries were the main importers of Moldovan products and Moldova had a trade surplus with them. However, in 2002 the trade balance with the CIS region turned negative. This occurred on account of a sharp increase in imports from Ukraine, which overshadowed the simultaneous increase in Moldovan exports to Russia. As a result of the reduction in the share of energy resources in the total volume of imports, the position of leading import market passed from

Export Structure by category, 2002

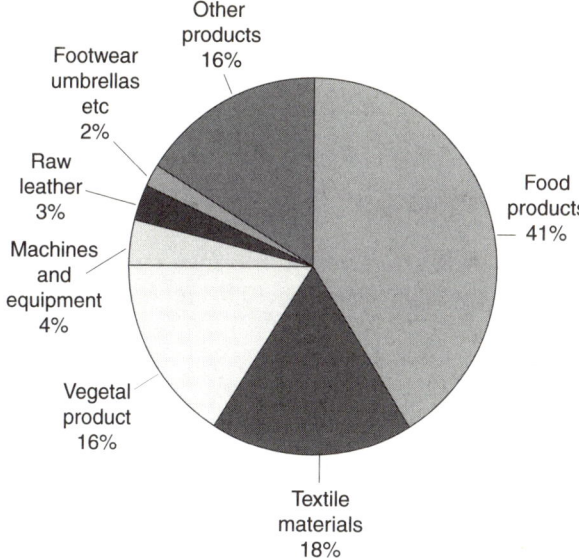

Imports Structure by category, 2002

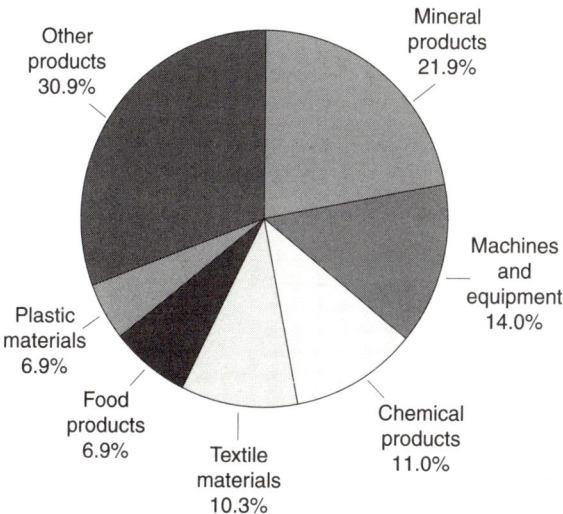

Russia to Ukraine. At the same time, Moldova had trade deficits (in both goods and services) with the EU and with the rest of the world. The geographical concentration of external trade shows Moldova's continuing economic dependence on Russia and vulnerability to changes in Russia's import preferences.

Export Structure by selected country, 2002

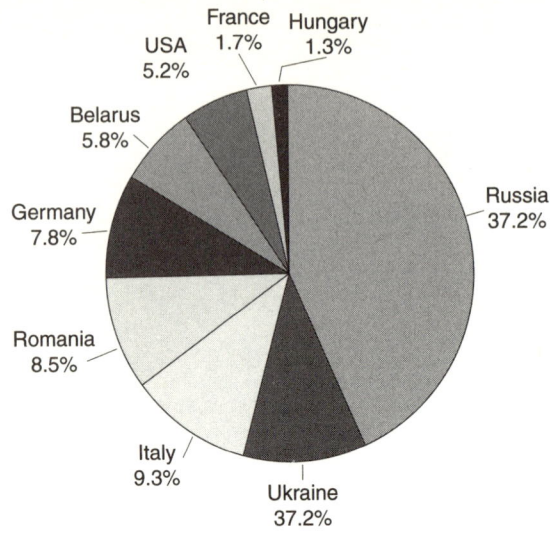

Imports Structure by selected country, 2002

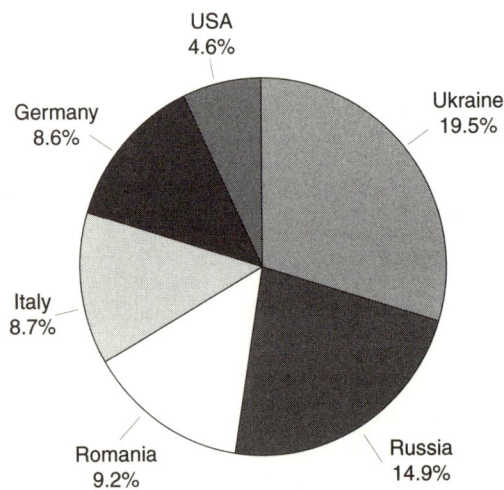

In spite of better terms of trade with the EU (compared to those with the CIS), Moldova's exports to this region are still modest. This may be due to the large agricultural and textile component in Moldova's exports to the EU, which come up against EU protectionism in these sectors. In other cases, access to this market is hampered by the poorer quality of exported goods. Nevertheless, there have been some positive signs since 2000. Both improved

Development of Foreign Trade 1998–2002

competitiveness on the part of some industries and preferential schemes offered by the EU for a number of products have increased the share of Moldovan exports to this region.

Currently there are some positive trends in Moldova's foreign trade relations. The volume of exports is increasing with a higher growth rate and improved structure of exports, and more diversified export markets. However, a radical diversification of export markets and significant reduction in the trade deficit are not likely to be achieved in the short term. Moldova's accession to the WTO and the Stability Pact free trade area are expected to stimulate foreign trade in the long run. The initiation of bilateral talks with the EU on free trade is also a step in this direction. Combined with structural reforms, these actions are likely to improve market access for Moldovan goods.

Exports and imports require specialised banking services, such as letters of credit (LCs), confirmation of LCs, quick and low-cost facilities for the international transfer of funds and currency exchange, and a variety of guarantees. Moldovan banks provide limited services due to their small size and lack of international reputation. This problem was solved for three banks through a guarantee facility provided by EBRD. This scheme, operating in many CIS countries, will guarantee LCs issued by one of the three participating local banks to a foreign bank, with exposure limits of $2–2.5 million per participating bank. With time, and increased demand, the exposure limits per bank may also limit the system's ability to support economic relations with Western Europe, where international trade is done through LCs and confirmations.

However, it seems that importers from CIS countries are unable to use LCs as a means of guaranteeing import orders until the goods are received. In many cases CIS exporters demand full payment in advance for goods, whereas Moldovan exporters are required to send their products and then wait for payment. Thus, Moldovans dealing with CIS countries are required to pay for imports in advance while receiving payment for exports after delivery, all without the benefit of quick settlements and guaranteed payments provided by LCs.

Efforts to liberalise foreign trade gained momentum in 2001. Accession to the WTO triggered a radical change in trade policy. For the first time in many years state policy became transparent and predictable. It included concrete commitments to the liberalisation of trade in goods and services, as well as to the adjustment of national legislation to WTO provisions.

However, businesses continued to receive mixed messages because state policy remained static, reducing the benefits of accession. The government proposed to introduce discretionary excise duties on some imported goods, and attempted to stabilise target prices for some products and restrict some exports (especially wheat). This led to a lengthy dispute between the Moldovan government and international financial institutions like the IMF and World Bank, which resulted in there being no financing from these institutions. Now the government accepts the elimination of barriers and restrictions, and relations with these institutions will be unblocked in the near future, probably in 2004.

Investment

In Moldova's current situation, investment will be the most important factor in economic revival. The investment environment is the key to both domestic and foreign investment. Most technological capacity was already outdated at the time of independence. In Moldova many people speak of 'productive capacity', or 'activity below the level of productive capacity', when talking about activities based on old technologies which cannot actually be considered capacities at all.

Technical and technological renovation has begun under the new owners. But though there has been some economic growth in recent years, it is unlikely that current economic growth will be sustainable without improvement in the investment environment. In recent years Moldova's fixed capital formation has declined, with its share in GDP falling from 22.1 per cent in 1998 to 16.6 per cent in 2002.

The main cash investors have come from the US, Great Britain, France and Luxembourg. Although Russia remained Moldova's main strategic partner in 2001, Russian investment consisted mainly of the conversion of gas debt into shares. There are, however, several Moldovan-Russian projects under way. The ratification by the Russian parliament of the Russia/Moldova Treaty on Partnership and Cooperation in April 2002 and the results of the CIS Summit in October 2002 have served as a 'political umbrella', reducing investment risks for Russian investors.

The energy, transport, communications, trade and manufacturing sectors continue to attract most investment. While the actual number of companies with foreign investment within these sectors is fairly small, they account for most of the FDI in both absolute and relative value.

Many international, including financial, institutions have commented on the business environment in Moldova. Their reports show that business risks in Moldova have grown in recent years. There have been some striking cases of re-nationalisation of previously privately-owned companies. The revision of the law on privatisation to introduce provisions allowing for re-nationalisation aroused uncertainty among economic agents and investors (including foreign investors) already working in Moldova or planning to do so. This move will

FDI: Moldova's position among South-East European countries

Indicators	South-East Europe	Moldova	Moldova's FDI as per cent of the whole region's
FDI, US$ million			
2000	22.700	143	0.63
2001	25.500	160	0.63
2002	33.700	98	0.29
per cent year on year			
2001/2000	112.3	111.9	
2002/2001	132.2	61.3	

naturally worry foreign businessmen and IFIs running technical assistance programmes in Moldova.

The investment environment in Moldova is less favourable than that in other South-East European countries (Romania, Bulgaria and the Western Balkans). Generally, over the last few years, investors' perceptions of this region have improved, with eight countries given higher ratings than before. Moldova's situation, however, is deteriorating, as shown in the FDI statistics, because of the high level of risk.

Despite government efforts to improve legislation on and create incentives for foreign investment, the investment climate has deteriorated considerably over the past few years. While a certain stability and predictability were imposed by Moldova's accession to the WTO, the economic and political environment is still sending mixed messages to business people.

The political climate in Moldova has not been supportive of economic relations over the past few years and has driven investors into adopting a conservative approach. Foreign companies have moved from purchasing ownership capital in Moldovan companies to extending short and medium term loans to their own businesses in order to minimise the potential risk. In 2002, for the first time, FDI in the form of loans was greater than that in ownership capital.

Conclusions

Even a very superficial look at the experience in terms of growth of other transition countries shows that output recovery, following a fall in output during the period of change, will not last for ever unless it is supported by continuous structural and institutional reform. Otherwise, simple reserves for growth (mostly reallocation of existing resources, without major investment) will be quickly exhausted. The next growth push must come, first of all, from large-scale investment. This is possible given a substantial improvement in the business and investment climate. In the case of Moldova, which has a very small and open economy, external economic relations will also play a very important role, and liberal export and import policies are vitally needed.

Foreign investors, those who are already in Moldova and those who are considering coming in, will observe closely the government's privatisation and regulatory policies. Any attempt at reversing past privatisation transactions (in effect, re-nationalisation) will send out a warning signal to the whole business community. The same goes for any regulatory measures which seek to favour some market players at the expense of others.

Moldova also needs to rebuild its close cooperation with the IMF and World Bank, damaged recently by failure to meet the policy conditionality of both organisations or circumvent agreed steps. The support of the IFIs is necessary not only because of their direct financial support but also because their approval of the government's programme (a kind of certificate of good practice) will open the door to debt restructuring negotiations with Moldova's creditors.

Part 3
The International Scene

Moldova between East and West: a Paradigm of Foreign Affairs

Ion Stăvilă

The Republic of Moldova is situated at the confluence of three geographic and political regions: Central Europe, South-Eastern Europe and Eastern Europe. Moldova may have been geographically placed in the centre of Europe, but this has not stopped people traditionally including it in their minds in the East European area, along with Ukraine, Belarus and Russia. The main geo-strategic characteristic of Moldova is its 'buffer' position between two political-military blocks – NATO and the military alliance of the CIS. Even if the rivalry between the two is not declared, it is clear that they are in a latently antagonistic relationship, Russia's reaction to NATO's eastward enlargement being a case in point. Another important characteristic lies in the strategic and political interest of another power, the Russian Federation, in Moldova, and Russia's effective military presence on its territory. This fact predisposes Russia's potential opponents, the USA, the EU and Turkey, to take a negative position vis-à-vis Chişinău.

Besides these two important factors, there are two other specific military and political features to note. Moldova is close geographically both to an emerging regional power, Ukraine, and to another region of tension, the Balkans. These points cannot be ignored by political analysts or the military when evaluating the strategic importance of Moldova.

One of Moldova's geo-strategic disadvantages is its relative distance from every important military-geographic point in Europe, above all the mouth of the Danube and Odessa (although they cannot be considered prime strategic objectives). Moldova also suffers from a lack of direct geo-economic interest in the country. The intensive 'economisation' of international relations means that, regrettably, the main power centres have little interest in Moldova. The lack of any 'positive' incentives for foreign interest makes the country even more vulnerable given the existence of multiple negative factors – the hostility of some Moldovans to the West, local conflicts within the country, and Moldova's involvement in illegal arms trafficking.

The dissolution of the Soviet Union into independent political entities aiming for a sovereign affirmation of their individual political, economic and cultural identity has led to a change in both the content and form of the relationship between the big international actors and the newly-independent states, including Moldova. At the same time, the new states faced unexpected political and economic problems. Moldova was no exception in this respect, as it had to find an answer to the key question regarding its foreign orientation: East or West? One tradition, with its particular way of thinking and its economic links as they existed at the end of 1980s, urged us to keep to the 'Euro-Asian way'. At the same time, our history and aspirations inclined us to start our journey back to Europe. The difficulty of this choice was accentuated by the fact that the EU was not ready to respond properly to our expectations. The events of 1988–91 surprised the West and revealed the lack of an 'Ostpolitik'. Also, the implosion of the Soviet Union brought chaos to the Euro-Asian region, and there were few, if any, ready to come up with a viable scenario of cooperation in the post-soviet area. The EU was a major economic power when the USSR collapsed, yet it continued to play the role of a satellite of the United States in international relations and politics. But, for the first time in post-war history, the EU saw unique prospects for its emergence as the second world power on the global scene, in some way taking the place of the Soviet colossus after its fall. In order to achieve this, the EU had to answer the following two questions: what kind of Europe did the member states wish to build (and by this I mean the *finalité politique* of the European integration process) and what kind of accession process was to be undertaken.

Unfortunately, Moldova did not react wisely to Europe's opening towards the East because of its 'dual option'. Along with Ukraine and Belarus, it had a choice: East or West. Despite the fact that Moldova made some considerable progress in preparing for negotiations for a Partnership and Cooperation Agreement (PCA) with the EU, it was only in 1994 that the first formal steps were taken on this matter. Among the reasons for this delay one can count the lack of a clear foreign and domestic policy concept in Moldova, the outbreak of a secessionist conflict in the east of the country, a deficient strengthening of Moldova's sovereignty and, more importantly, a political elite that was overtaken by events and in any case narrow-minded in its conception of a world that it thought started in Bucharest and finished in Moscow. On 28 January 1994, President Snegur requested the Council of the EU and the European

Commission to start negotiations for a PCA. This was seen in Moldova as the first step in the European integration process, though a large majority of the new democracies of East-Central Europe were already associated to the EU at that time. The PCA aimed to establish favourable conditions for the diversification of economic and trade links, as well as facilitating the political reforms needed in Moldova. On 23 February, the Council of Foreign Ministers of the EU decided to give a green light to the PCA, after a report by the EU delegation to Moldova concluded that the country was in a transition stage on its road to a democratic society and market-oriented economy. The negotiations ended on 26 July after only two rounds with the conclusion of the text of the future PCA. The Agreement was signed on 28 November the same year, and a new phase was opened in the development of relations between the EU and Moldova. Moldova's foreign affairs policy position, approved by Parliament in 1995, described the PCA as the first step in Moldova's integration into the European Union.

However, the Agrarian government interpreted the PCA in the context of its efforts to strengthen Moldova's statehood, rather than as a real opportunity for EU membership. Despite the formal attitude of the leadership in Chişinău during 1994–1998 toward the question of European integration, Moldova did improve its image and credibility at the international level through the PCA. From the EU's side, the conclusion of the Agreement with Moldova acknowledged the country's efforts to democratise society and implement reforms. The Agreement reflects the commitment of the two sides to democratic values, and demonstrates the EU's wish to support Moldova in its democratisation process and its transition to a market economy. Further, the PCA introduced a political dimension to the EU-Moldova relationship, going beyond the purely economic objectives of the EU's Trade and Cooperation Agreement with the Soviet Union. The establishment of economic links is not really the heart of the document, but rather a way to bring symmetry to all the fields of interaction between the EU and Moldova. However, despite the advantages of the PCA, it was far less generous than the Europe Agreements signed by Brussels with the Central and East European countries which expected to join the EU at some stage.

The PCA takes its inspiration from the Europe Agreements, in terms of structure and even content. Yet the two documents represent two different regional approaches by the EU as far as its final goals and territorial limits are concerned. The Europe Agreements offer the real prospect of EU membership, in contrast to the PCAs, which envisage only partnership with the CIS member states and not a gradual rapprochement and integration into the EU. In addition, the financial assistance given under the Europe Agreements through the Phare programme is far more substantial than financial assistance through the PCA programme, Tacis. Hence, the present agreement does not open the path to Moldova's accession to the EU, especially since the country is bounded by another regional organisation, the CIS, to which the EU does not aim to offer any prospect of integration. The fact that the European Commission emphasises the need to implement the PCA underlines the lack of a differentiated strategy toward the Newly Independent States and the lack of any will to treat each country on its merits. Nevertheless, neither the European Commission nor the EU member states exclude the prospect of a gradual evolution in relations between the EU and Moldova, though only after the expiry of the PCA in 2008.

The tragic consequences of the Russian financial crisis of August 1998 came like a cold shower to the Moldovan authorities, and especially to people in trade and business, who took huge losses in their eastern markets. This shattered many of the dreams linked to Moldova's pro-Eastern orientation, underlining the need for deeper and more intensive relations with EU member states. European integration started to be perceived more and more as an essential element to ensure the country's security, stability and prosperity. As a result, for the first time the 1999–2002 government programme put an emphasis on European integration as the primary goal of Moldova's foreign policy. Yet the East-West dilemma is still present in Moldova's domestic and foreign affairs, and many observers point to the country's CIS membership as an obstacle to its future integration into the EU. It is, however, hard to say how far this is a valid argument in practice as opposed to theory.

Although Moldova has been *de facto* a member of the CIS since 21 December 1991, its *de jure* adhesion was possible only after the election of a new parliament in 1994, which ratified the constituent agreements. Officially, Moldova has limited its participation in the CIS to economic cooperation, since military-political cooperation was seen as conflicting with Moldova's sovereignty and independence. Still, given the political realities, the leadership in Chişinău has signed up to various political, social, cultural and environmental agreements. Moreover, in 2002, parliament dropped Moldova's reserves vis-à-vis the CIS in the fields of foreign policy and migration.

The CIS's role was, however, diluted in Moldova's new 2001 foreign affairs concept, since the Eastern orientation appears there as a 'marginal concern' of foreign policy in contrast to the importance given to integration within the EU. Facing profound political, economic and social transformations (like other former Soviet states) and confronted with a lack of reliable energy resources, Moldova is in poor state at the moment. Yet one cannot say that this is due exclusively to Moldova's membership of the CIS. The economic and political failure of the CIS, acknowledged even in its tenth anniversary reports, is confirmed indirectly by the re-groupings that have occurred lately within the organisation: the Russia-Belarus Union, the Eurasian Economic Community (serving as a pole of attraction to the Central Asian countries), GUUAM, and the newly-created European Economic Space between Russia, Belarus, Ukraine and Kazakhstan.

Another frequent argument from those who denounce Moldova's membership of the CIS is that there is an inherent contradiction between simultaneous integration into the EU and the CIS. So far this is not a well-researched subject, but rather one dominated to a large extent by emotions. Judicially speaking, there is no direct connection between Moldova's membership of the CIS and its future relations with the EU. However, politically and psychologically, Moldova continues to be associated by the West with the former Soviet Union, and to be treated as such. That is not the case with the Baltic States, which cut all their links with the Soviet past and oriented themselves strongly towards Europe. It seems that even the authorities in Brussels and other European capitals have not yet come to a clear idea regarding the foreign orientation that Moldova could embrace in the future. Some European politicians see Moldova's place as lying in the CIS and suggest it has no alternative, at the moment, to its Eastern orientation. But there are, obviously, other politicians who consider that Moldova's chances of integration into the EU are directly linked to its degree of integration in the CIS, ie that membership of the CIS is a serious obstacle in the process of Moldova's European integration.

The official position in Chişinău in respect to this problem is the following: European integration is a medium to long-term goal, an inevitable process which is being embraced slowly due to local opposition and traditional inertia. In the short run, Moldova will remain in the CIS, given its lack of room for manoeuvre, understanding that this will preserve stable relations with its main economic and political partner, the Russian Federation. Moldova's participation in the CIS is the result of a political decision that takes into account the geo-political situation, rather than a long-lasting and fundamental decision taken at the national level. Nevertheless, any precipitate exit from CIS membership would probably have negative consequences for Moldova, given its extensive economic dependence on Russia, which remains its most important economic and trade partner, and also the most serious voice in the complicated process of seeking a political settlement to the Transdniestria conflict. But this fact does not constitute a policy of capitulation by Moldova, which maintains the long-term option of a Western orientation.

The CIS was conceived as a way of limiting the painful dissolution of the Soviet Union, rather than as an integrationist structure. Twelve years after its establishment, the CIS continues rather as a mechanism of gradual disintegration. Its evolution has been ambiguous and its composition heterogeneous. None of the leaders said 'No' to certain projects, but at the same time nobody took clear steps to ensure the viability and dynamism of CIS activity. Paradoxically, Russia did not ratify the free trade agreement, which frustrated the other members economically; evidently it was more interested in the political-military aspect. The 'common historic past' of the CIS states is losing ground in the face of a harsh and pragmatic present, and each member state has interests of its own which are perceived as being potentially successful only outside the CIS.

The current Moldovan situation is a case in point. The number of politicians and diplomats who acknowledge the experience of the Baltic States as a successful path towards the EU is increasing. Even the President is convinced that European integration is the only alternative for Moldova's future. Even if it has taken Moldova a decade to come to this conclusion, it is our conviction that is not too late to catch the 'European train'. Moldova will face severe risks once it is engaged on the journey to Europe, but this gordian knot of 'East or West' has to be cut. The European option will allow Moldova to overcome its historic syndrome of being, as a historian once said, at the cross-roads of all the bad influences, and will offer Moldova a better future among other European nations.

Moldova's Eastern Dimension

Claus Neukirch

European integration has become, at least on paper, the main vector of
Moldova's foreign policy in 2003. But the Communist government which
came to power in Moldova in early 2001 has long believed this orientation
towards Europe to be compatible with the country's strategic partnership with
Russia and Moldova's participation in the Commonwealth of Independent
States (CIS). Thus, its relations with Russia and the CIS have in practice not
declined in recent years. In fact, Moldova's orientation towards Russia and its
dedication to the CIS have even become stronger. The current government in
Chişinău prefers co-operation within the framework of the CIS to co-operation
within other organisations and groups in the post-Soviet area; and aims to
consolidate bilateral relations with CIS member states in order to achieve
stronger integration and partnership in the framework of the CIS. This is
particularly true for Moldova's relations with the Russian Federation, which
has been declared Moldova's 'strategic partner' by President Vladimir Voronin.
As will be shown below, relations with Russia and the CIS have nevertheless
always been and remain ambivalent as Moldova's foreign policy has tried to
balance western and eastern leanings since independence.

Moldova and the CIS – starting on the wrong foot

On 8 December 1991, the presidents of Russia, Belarus and Ukraine signed
an agreement on the establishment of a Commonwealth of Independent
States, a move which finally made the Soviet Union history. On 21 December
1991 a protocol to this agreement was signed by the presidents of eleven former
republics of the Soviet Union. In this protocol these presidents, including
Moldova's Mircea Snegur, agreed to establish the CIS on a basis of equality.
Only the Baltic states and Georgia, the last of which finally adhered in 1993,

did not join. On 22 January 1993 the eleven heads of state agreed the CIS Charter.

However, the Moldovan parliament, elected in early 1990 in semi-free and semi-competitive elections, failed to ratify Moldova's accession to the CIS. The deputies elected in 1990 on behalf of the Popular Front opposed the country's integration into a structure which they perceived as a successor to the Soviet Union and a tool of Russian control over the post-Soviet space. The Popular Front, and the political parties which are rooted in this movement, favoured Moldova's integration into West European structures; some right-wing politicians even called, and still call, for unification with Romania. Those Moldovans who, like Snegur and others, were deeply rooted in the Communist Party of Moldova, were more cautious about their country's integration into the West and were definitely opposed to a union with Romania. And for the Russian-speakers, almost 35 per cent of Moldova's population, integration in the CIS and close relations with Russia and Ukraine were a clear priority over relations with the West. Since the deputies elected in the Transdniestrian and Găgăuz constituencies in eastern and southern Moldova boycotted the parliamentary sessions, the pro-Western deputies were able to block the ratification of accession to the CIS even though they represented only a minority in parliament.

The failure to ratify the documents resulted in a de facto economic blockade of Moldova by Moscow, which provoked a severe political crisis in Chişinău. This was finally resolved through the dissolution of parliament and the holding of early elections on 27 February 1994. These elections resulted in an absolute majority of seats for the Agrarian Democratic Party, formed by Moldovan members of the former nomenklatura, and in a crushing defeat for the pro-Western forces, which won only 20 out of the 104 seats. The Socialist Unity electoral bloc, which represented the Russian-speaking electorate, won 28 seats. Thus, the way was finally open for ratification of the CIS documents. But it has to be borne in mind that accession to the CIS was a decision not endorsed by the whole political spectrum. And even the centrist forces which opted for the CIS did not intend to focus their foreign policy solely on relations with the CIS and its member states. The foreign policy concept adopted on 8 February 1995, by the very parliament which had ratified Moldova's accession to the CIS, named relations with Russia, Ukraine and Belarus a priority and called for a deepening of co-operation within the CIS framework, but also identified co-operation with Romania as 'important' and called for the broadening and deepening of Moldova's relations with the states of Central and Western Europe.[1] After the centre-right parties gained a parliamentary majority in 1998, co-operation with the CIS lost its priority and relations with the EU and Romania became even more important. This partial re-orientation was revised again after the communist victory in the 2001 parliamentary elections. The new leadership declared Russia to be the strategic partner for Moldova and relations with the CIS also regained importance. But, as indicated above, relations with the EU nevertheless remained in the top half of the foreign policy agenda.

Military, no; trade, yes

Moldova concentrated its policy towards the CIS from the outset on economic relations and did not join all the treaties adopted in the CIS framework. For example, Moldova did not sign the June 2001 accord on the creation of a single CIS education space since its provisions would have contravened the country's national education policy. Most importantly, Moldova did not join the CIS Collective Security Treaty signed in 1992 in Tashkent, and even the pro-CIS communists are not considering Moldovan participation in the military structures of the CIS. Nor has Moldova turned to the CIS for a solution to the Transdniestrian conflict. In contrast to Abkhazia, where a nominally CIS but de facto Russian peacekeeping force was deployed after the civil war, the CIS plays no role in the trilateral peacekeeping force stationed since August 1992 in a security zone on both sides of the river Dniester. These troops consist of Russian, Moldovan and Transdniestrian forces plus Ukrainian military observers. The OSCE, which opened a civilian long-term Mission in Moldova in April 1993, also has observer status. When discussions began in the OSCE on replacing the trilateral peacekeeping operation with peacekeepers under the supervision of the OSCE, the CIS was not even considered. Only the OSCE itself, NATO, the NATO-Russia Council and above all the EU were mentioned in the corridors of Vienna and Brussels as possible sponsors of such an operation.

Moldova's main focus in its relationship with the CIS is economic. The CIS is still the most important market for Moldova. Although trade with western states had increased considerably over the previous decade, the CIS still accounted for 51.9 per cent of Moldova's exports and 39.4 per cent of its imports in 2002. Moreover, in contrast to Western countries, Chişinău has in recent years had a positive trade balance with the CIS. Moldova therefore has a special interest in concluding free trade agreements in the CIS area. A treaty establishing a CIS economic union was signed in September 1993, followed in April 1994 by an agreement on the establishment of a free economic zone. But neither agreement had come into effect by autumn 2003. Thus, Moldova's trade relations with the other CIS states are based solely on bilateral free trade agreements, and these agreements do not always satisfy the Moldovan side. Ukraine, for example, recently announced the exclusion of Moldovan sugar imports from its trade, and in 2001 Russia went so far as to exclude 14 categories of goods accounting for 47 per cent of Moldova's exports. Although an agreement was signed in summer 2003 gradually to abolish these exceptions, this process will be completed only in 2012. Thus, the free trade regime based on bilateral agreements excludes important Moldovan export goods. Moldova therefore hoped to get a better deal out of the final agreement on a CIS free trade zone to be signed at the CIS summit in Yalta on 26 September 2003. But no such an agreement was signed in Yalta and, even worse for Moldova, Kazakhstan, Russia, Belarus and Ukraine created a 'Common Economic Area' (CEA) without Moldova. Thus, Moldova's hopes turned to deep frustration, vividly expressed in President Voronin's statement on the results of the Yalta CIS summit: 'The event cannot indeed give cause for any particular optimism. I have always said that Moldova would never become a gravedigger for the CIS. After what happened in Yalta, the future of the Commonwealth has been buried for ever.'

Multilateralism in the CIS and the Russian factor

The CEA was not in fact the first sub-regional body formed within the framework of the CIS, and the practical implications of this step remain to be seen. The creation of the CEA was however another proof that economic and political co-operation embracing all CIS states is difficult. It is therefore important to touch upon the other economic and/or political forums which have developed within the CIS area and which are of relevance to Moldova.

In 1995 Russia, Belarus and Kazakhstan, later joined by Kyrgyzstan and Tajikistan, signed a treaty on a customs union, but neither Moldova nor the other CIS states were ready to join at that point.[2] In October 2000, the customs union was elevated to an institutionalised Eurasian Economic Community (EURASEC). Although President Voronin had spoken in favour of a CIS-wide free economic zone, since this would promote the consolidation of the CIS and reduce the need for other structures in the post-Soviet space, Moldova was nevertheless ready to join EURASEC so long as economic integration could not be achieved in the CIS. Since May 2002 Moldova has had observer status within EURASEC and the Moldovan president has repeatedly expressed his intention to join the union as a full member. But only when Ukraine also joins EURASEC will Moldova share a common border with the union, which is a pre-condition for joining. Ukraine remained cooler than Moldova towards the idea of joining EURASEC, but it did join the CEA in Yalta. Since neither

Moldova nor EURASEC members Kyrgyzstan and Tajikistan have been offered CEA membership, EURASEC membership can no longer even be regarded as an alternative to a CIS free trade agreement. As the CEA will also include a customs union, and as it will even have supra-national structures, the future of EURASEC as such is currently in doubt.

Another union which has emerged on the territory of the former Soviet Union is the Russia-Belarus Union (RBU). The Communists' electoral programme referred to Moldova's possible integration into the RBU. According to leading party officials this meant that a communist government would carefully study this issue, but only take steps in this direction if it were concluded that membership of the RBU would be advantageous from an economic point of view. President Voronin in fact concluded as early as October 2001 that it would not bring Moldova any great economic benefit. Thus, the RBU is not considered in Chişinău to be a real alternative to the CIS.

Since the Communists came to power in Moldova, Chişinău's interest in GUUAM has also cooled. GUAM (Georgia, Ukraine, Azerbaijan and Moldova) emerged under this name in October 1997 during the Council of Europe summit in Strasbourg. At this summit the presidents of these four countries issued a joint communiqué highlighting the importance of cooperation in order to establish a Eurasian Trans-Caucasian transport corridor. Moreover, they declared their intention to deepen political and economic ties and cooperation. As all four countries had had difficulties with Russian-sponsored secessionist movements in the early 1990s (Abkhazia and South Ossetia in Georgia, Crimea in Ukraine, Nagorny-Karabakh in Azerbaijan, Transdniestria in Moldova), the four countries had already co-operated closely over the years within the OSCE framework. In April 1999 Uzbekistan formally joined the group, making it GUUAM instead of GUAM. Although Uzbekistan had no separatist movement, the country had also had an uneasy relationship with Russia during that period. Thus, GUUAM united those CIS countries which had the most critical relationships with Russia. In addition they soon came to realise that they also had other important common goals. All these states were then striving to establish closer ties with the West and Western political and economical institutions. Although the Unites States promoted integration in this framework, GUUAM developed slowly. It was transformed from an informal group into an international organisation only on 7 June 2001, when the GUUAM Charter was signed in Yalta. The goals defined in the charter include, inter alia, the development of reciprocal trade and the creation of a GUUAM free trade zone. The creation of transit routes between Europe and Central Asia is another of its aims.

At the July 2003 GUUAM summit in Yalta, it became apparent that the organisation had lost rather than gained relevance since its formalisation in 2001. Only two of the five heads of states attended this meeting and no real progress was achieved on either the free trade regime or transit routes between Europe and Central Asia. Nor is the US's strong backing for GUUAM any longer, for Moldova, an incentive to engage more deeply with the organisation. While Moldova was keen on GUUAM as a counterbalance to Russia and the CIS when the country had moderate centre-left and centre-right governments between 1997 and 2001, the communist government has openly warned against turning GUUAM into an alternative to the CIS. Today the Moldovan government maintains that the entire spectrum of economic, social and cultural problems discussed within GUUAM is reflected just as fully and profoundly in the programmes developed in the CIS. In order to demonstrate Moldova's loyalty to Russia, President Voronin even suggested that Russia should be invited to be an observer in GUUAM. So while, in line with his pragmatic foreign policy concept, Voronin might be ready to participate in GUUAM economic projects if they are of benefit to Moldova, he is not ready to challenge the priority Moldova accords to CIS co-operation in the post-Soviet space nor its strategic partnership with Russia.

Relations with Russia are without doubt the most important factor in Chişinău's foreign and economic policy. The communists have made strenuous efforts since 2001 to develop their bilateral relationship with Russia, which has officially been designated a strategic partner. The Friendship and Co-operation Treaty between Moldova and Russia signed on 19 November 2001 mentioned explicitly the strategic partnership between the two countries and foresaw close co-operation on political, military, economic, scientific, environmental and other issues. The treaty even envisaged that the two countries would consult each other on their co-operation in the framework of the OSCE and the Council of Europe. Thus, the bilateral treaty binds Moldova much more closely to Russia than the multilateral treaties in the CIS framework.

By leaning more towards Russia, the new leadership in Chişinău hoped to solve the country's most pressing problems: social-economic decline and the Transdniestrian conflict. With respect to the first, it must be stressed that most of Moldova's trade with the CIS is actually trade with Russia. In 2000, 75 per cent of its exports to and 46 per cent of its imports from CIS countries were to and from Russia.[3] In the first seven months of 2003, Moldova exported to Russia goods and services worth $151.5 million. This represents an increase of 21.3 per cent compared with the same period in 2002. Although Moldova also increased its exports to the EU in 2003, Russia remains by far the most important export market for Moldovan goods. Moreover, Russian gas deliveries are crucial for Moldova, as they cannot be even partially replaced by other energy deliveries. Thus, Moldova's economy is heavily dependent on Russia. This dependence has become even greater as Moldova has been unable to pay for all the gas delivered in recent years. Moldova's debts for natural gas consumption, including penalties, amounted to $121.1 million as of 1 July 2003. In autumn 2003 Gazprom suggested that the Moldovan government cede 35 per cent of the shares held by Moldova in the Moldovan-Russian venture Moldova-Gaz in exchange for debts. Moreover, Gazprom is interested in shares in Moldova's three thermo-electric power stations as well as other strategic enterprises like wineries, the tobacco factory Tutun, former Soviet military industries, an important glass factory and textile factories. As Russia has become already the most important investor in Moldova and as the Moldovan government tends to prefer Russian companies in the current privatisation process, the influence of Russian companies on the Moldovan economy will most probably increase further in the coming years. Finally, Moldova needs Russian co-operation to restructure its foreign debts, which in June 2003 amounted to almost $1.7 billion, including debts for energy resources. Thus, Moldova's economic development is heavily dependent on its relations with Russia, which is not only Moldova's most important export market, its most important investor and its most important creditor, but also supplies most of its energy resources.

Moreover, Russia plays a key role with respect to the settlement of the Transdniestrian conflict. It is not only a mediator in the conflict settlement process, along with Ukraine and the OSCE, but also has potentially the greatest political and economic influence on the Transdniestrian leadership. Transdniestria also exports most of its goods to Russia, has accumulated even higher debts for gas than the rest of Moldova, and is also in other respects dependent on continued support from Moscow. Almost all Transdniestria's leaders hold Russian passports. Russia is also the main contributor to the trilateral Russian-Moldovan-Transdniestrian peacekeeping force operating in the former conflict zone and has a total of about 1,600 troops stationed in Transdniestria. Although the Russian military presence is not an important military factor in regional terms, it is seen as reassuring by the current leadership in Tiraspol. Accordingly, the Transdniestrian authorities have repeatedly blocked the withdrawal of Russian troops, ammunition and military equipment to which Russia committed itself at the 1999 OSCE Summit in Istanbul.

One of the key questions for Chişinău is whether Russia is really ready to use its potential economic and political power to overcome Transdniestrian resistance to the withdrawal process or use its influence on the Transdniestrian leadership to agree to a political settlement to the conflict brokered by the three mediators. Most opposition parties and representatives of Moldovan civil society fear that Russia actually intends to prolong its military presence in Moldova indefinitely and to use Transdniestria as additional leverage to prevent Moldova's integration in western structures. They are therefore afraid that Russia will only back a political settlement which would make it possible for Russia to influence Moldovan politics via the re-integrated Transdniestrian region. Thus, in economic as well as in political terms, Russia is seen in Moldova as as much as part of the problem as of the solution.

Russia's policy towards Moldova is shaped by a number of different actors: in the presidential administration, the foreign ministry, the ministry of defence, the parliament and the economic sphere. This makes it almost impossible to discern clearly Moscow's intentions in Moldova. Although there are some who argue for a continued military presence in Moldova and who would object to a CIS member like Moldova looking westwards, it does not mean that this is or will be official Russian policy towards the country. Military withdrawal from yet another country would not go down well in Russia, but whether the Kremlin will be ready to risk a deterioration in Russia's relations with the West over a couple of hundred soldiers in Moldova is another question. One should however bear in mind that Moldova was part of the Russian Empire between 1812 and 1918 and a Soviet republic between 1940 and 1991. Given this history, the fact that more than 30 per cent of the population are Russian-speakers, and the involvement of Russia in the economic sphere, Russia has an interest in very close relations with Moldova.

Conclusions

It is clear that Russia is by far the most important factor in Moldova's 'Eastern Dimension' and that it will continue to be the main vector of Moldova's foreign policy as a whole. Ukraine is also important to Moldova as a direct neighbour, transit country, economic partner and mediator in the Transdniestrian conflict, but it cannot be compared with Russia in any respect. The CIS is first of all a forum in which Moldova can conduct its relations with Russia in a multilateral setting, thus partially softening Russia's influence. Membership of EURASEC was not an aim in itself for Moldova, but rather seen as an option in case economic integration within the CIS did not develop at the same pace. With the creation of the CEA, from which Moldova is excluded, this option seems to be history. This is also true of the RBU, as participation in this union would not bring Moldova any advantages at all. Finally, GUUAM is not attractive for a Communist-led government because it excludes Russia. Although Chişinău's interest in GUUAM might change if the current leadership is replaced by a government more critical of Russia, the question remains whether this organisation has a future at all after the creation of the CEA.

At the end of 2003 the only forum for multilateral co-operation in the former post-Soviet space available to Moldova remains the CIS, and from this perspective it becomes clear that the negative line taken by President Voronin in the aftermath of the Yalta CIS summit has subsequently been softened. Moldova was one of the strongest promoters of the CIS until the Yalta summit, and has always emphasised that EURASEC, GUUAM and the RBU must be viewed through the prism of developing relations within the CIS. Moldova even tried to galvanise the CIS. However, it was obviously unable to do much to strengthen the CIS, and has now started to rethink its policy towards the organisation.

Moldova's orientation towards the EU seems to be gathering pace in the absence of any multilateral body in the post-soviet space offering a real alternative. As long as Moldova was still promoting the CIS, statements in favour of Moldova's European orientation sounded like pure lip-service. Both trends − towards Europe and the CIS − are in fact still seen more on paper than in action, but this will have to change at some point. Although Moldova might still profit from the CIS in the short and medium term, in the long term it will find more solutions to its problems in Brussels than in the CIS. Future governments, especially if they are supported by right-wing parties, might therefore turn away from the CIS in words and deeds. They might still depend on and need Russia, but not necessarily the CIS. In August 2003, the first signs of this appeared when deputy foreign minister Stratan declared that Moldova would consider leaving the CIS if and when it was officially accepted as a candidate for EU accession and if the union explicitly demanded such a move.[4] President Voronin's call to 'resort to more resolute action in the direction of the European Union' after the Yalta CIS summit was another strong signal. However, the idea that cooperation within the CIS would be no obstacle to EU membership still holds sway in Chişinău, though it seems to be fading. Giving the strong hints from Western Europe that EU membership is in fact not compatible with CIS membership, this attitude reflects either a denial of the realities or an attempt to calm down the pro-Russian and pro-CIS part of the Communist Party and its voters.

As of autumn 2003, the Moldovan leadership was in fact still saying different things to different audiences and apparently acting in ways that went against what it had previously said or written. Given that EU membership for Moldova is still a long way down the road and that trade relations with the CIS countries are still more important to Moldova's economy than relations with the EU, there are in fact good arguments for Moldova to maintain good bilateral relations with the member states of the CIS. Above all, it would be wrong to ask Moldova to choose between Russia and the EU. Moldova needs good relations with Russia especially in the economic field. However, if the Moldovan government does start to move from words to deeds with respect to its European integration policy, it might also need to re-think whether Russia should remain Moldova's only 'strategic partner'. It will certainly remain an important partner, but if the long-term goal really is closer integration with the EU, Moldova will gradually have to reorient its foreign policy from East to West.

Notes

[1] Conceptia politicii externe a Republicii Moldova, *Monitorul Oficial al Republicii Moldova*, 6 aprilie 1995, pos. 187.

[2] Manuela Troschke, Neue Wirtchaftsunionen oder doch nur Theater? Die GUUAM, die Eurasische und die Zentralasiatische Wirtschaftsgemeinschaft, in Olga Alexandrova/Roland Götz/Uwe Halbach (Eds.), *Rußland und der postsowjetische Raum*, Baden-Baden 2002, p. 388.

[3] See Comertul exterior al Republicii Moldova cu tarile CSI at http://www.statistica.md/statistics/?g=15&id=16.

[4] RFE/RL Newsline Vol. 7, No. 153, Part II, 13 August 2003.

Moldova and Ukraine: Pro-Western Guarantor to the East

Rostyslav Khotin

When the giant of the Soviet Empire collapsed in 1991, Ukrainian political elites were keen to gain state independence and preserve at least some superpower attributes. As former US president John Kennedy once put it, a state's weight is judged by its missiles and its Olympic medals. Ukraine was going to give up its nuclear arsenal, the third largest in the world; and there was no way the newly-established state could keep up the flow of Olympic gold which propped up the Soviet Union's political prestige. So the new Ukrainian state would have to find something else on which to rest its pride.

In order to fit into the new reality of 'missiles and Olympics', Ukraine aspired to become at least a regional leader, even though it would take on only a shadow of the former Soviet global leadership agenda. The claim to regional influence, taking into account Ukraine's size, population and economic potential, was justified. However, after decades of Kremlin rule, Ukraine's western neighbours – Poland, Hungary, and what was until 1993 Czechoslovakia – were themselves looking westwards for leadership and were reluctant to become a part of any regional structure run by influence-starved Ukrainians.

Post-Soviet territory was assumed to be a Russian sphere of influence, and Ukraine could only become leader of a grouping not worthy of Russian participation or else risk having its role overtaken by the former master.

The only natural smaller neighbour to be led was Moldova, which in the early 1990s faced the same problems: an influx of Russian 'investors' pouring in after independence and trying to buy up economic assets cheaply; and breakaway tendencies in the regions: in Ukraine's case Crimea and in Moldova's

Transdniestria and Găgăuzia. Both Kiev and Chişinău were struggling to climb out from under Russia's geopolitical umbrella.

Despite the similarities, it took more than half a decade for a formal structure to be set up which involved Ukraine and Moldova. Washington's blessing paved the way for Ukraine, Moldova, Azerbaijan, Uzbekistan and Georgia to set up GUUAM, a regional political and economic alliance established to protect its members' independence and territorial integrity, and to construct joint energy transportation routes bypassing Russia.

A second chance for Ukraine and Moldova to 'link up' came in 2001, when Britain and Sweden launched the 'New Neighbours' initiative, designed to grant a special status to new neighbours Ukraine, Moldova and Belarus after EU expansion to the east in 2004.

At first, some Ukrainian diplomats were sceptical about the idea. Kiev always made it clear that it aimed to join the EU. Pro-European Ukrainians found it hard to accept being put in the same category as Moldova and especially Belarus, run by maverick leader Alexander Lukashenko. But other diplomats and politicians thought that neighbour status was not a bad start to a process which could eventually lead to Ukraine's acceptance as a 'super-neighbour' and more powerful ally of the EU than the other two plain 'neighbours'.

The theory was that in this context Ukraine could try and realise its old ambition: regional leadership. The more optimistic observers saw the 'maximum task' for Ukraine as being not only to secure EU membership for itself in, say, 10 years, but also to bring along (as regional leader!) its protégés Moldova and, hopefully, Belarus. There was even talk of a 'western CIS' which would include Ukraine, Belarus and Moldova, or indeed of Ukraine's own (akin to Moscow's) 'near abroad' (the term used by Russia to refer to the other parts of the FSU).

Ukraine, unlike Russia, has no integrationist aspirations towards Moldova or Belarus which would deprive them of the least bit of their sovereignty, but, rather, special EU-related responsibilities for the two neighbours. Ukraine could become the driving-force to enable these countries, along with Kiev itself and in their own time, to join NATO and the EU. The main motive for this would be to prevent any renewal of Moscow's policy of reabsorbing the countries of the former Soviet Union.

This is especially true in the case of Ukraine's relationship with Moldova. Ukraine is a kind of guarantor of Moldova's independence because, unlike

Romania and Russia, Kiev has no unification agenda towards Moldova, but rather an interest in strengthening Moldovan statehood (though some observers suggest that if right-bank Moldova were to merge with Romania, Ukraine would have little choice but to absorb Transdniestria).

Moldovan-Ukrainian partnership has been nurtured by all the three Moldovan and two Ukrainian post-Soviet leaders. Kiev's natural partners of choice in Moldova would be pragmatic, centrist, pro-independence and pro-EU politicians who would maintain a safe distance from both Moscow and Bucharest. Of the three post-Soviet Moldovan leaders, the nationalist Mircea Snegur, the pragmatic former Soviet Politburo member Petru Lucinsci, and the Communist Vladimir Voronin, it was Lucinsci with whom Kiev was most keen to do business. This was not only because he came from the same *nomenklatura* as the majority of the Ukrainian elite, but also and not least because Lucinsci was perceived as 'pro-Moldovan, Chişinău-oriented', unlike Bucharest-leaning Snegur or Moscow-inspired Voronin.

Geography itself is a constant reminder of how natural an alliance between Ukraine and Moldova would be. It is not Russia but Ukraine which is Moldova's immediate neighbour to the east, and whoever runs Moldova cannot vault Ukraine to get closer to Russia in any kind of post-Soviet political, economic or military grouping. Moscow would have to 'swallow' Ukraine first in order to bring Moldova closer. In that sense Ukraine serves as a buffer for Moldova, guarding its independence. Geography also dictates that Moldova and Ukraine move in tandem in their pro-European orientation. As long as Kiev aims and slowly but surely moves towards eventual, albeit distant, EU membership, so will Chişinău, sandwiched as it is between the newly-expanded EU and Ukraine.

The 600,000 ethnic Ukrainians in Moldova also support co-operation with the EU. Unlike the pro-Romanian part of Moldovan society or the ethnic Russian community, the Ukrainians in Moldova would prefer their country to be in the EU, not least because Ukraine itself will be accelerating towards Europe in the decade to come. The overwhelming majority of Ukrainians in Moldova are not Ukrainian nationalists but rather loyal Moldovan citizens, interested in close ties between the two countries.

The same goes for NATO, with which Moldova is trying to establish close ties without alienating the Transdniestrian separatists. Ukraine's own active cooperation with the alliance, together with Romania's impending membership, give Chişinău a free hand in dealings with the alliance.

Ukraine has so far successfully managed to keep Moldova on a western path despite the communist president and government and the leftist-dominated parliament in its small neighbour. Kiev put enormous pressure on Chişinău not to join any post-Soviet Moscow-dominated alliances. It was, according to Ukrainian diplomats, President Kuchma who in 2002 persuaded Voronin to stay in GUUAM and not to join the loose Russian-Belarusian Union. (Some observers suggest that Moscow had made departure from GUUAM a condition for its support for Voronin and the Communists before the 2001 parliamentary election.). President Voronin nevertheless declared his wish to join the Russia-dominated Eurasian Economic Union and even called upon Ukraine to follow suit. Both have in fact joined (but only as observers), more to keep Moscow happy than to boost that organisation.

Moldova is probably the only country which Ukraine is in a position to influence but has never punished. The lion's share of Moldova's exports go through Ukrainian territory. For example, Moldovan exports of vegetables and fruit bound in the summer months for Russia and Belarus receive preferential speedy checks at the Ukrainian customs rather than being left to rot for days at the border.

Kiev and Chişinău have been working quietly to resolve the long-standing problem of Moldovan property on Ukrainian soil: more than a hundred sanatoriums, mostly by the Black Sea, in the Odessa region and in Crimea.

The two countries set a precedent in post-Soviet history by peacefully exchanging territory in 1999. Moldova received a 100 metre strip of land along the Danube and started construction of a small oil terminal, while Ukraine got a 7.7 kilometre stretch of the strategic Odessa-Reni highway.

Chişinău is also interested in constructing a spur from the Odessa-Brody pipeline which will carry Caspian oil via Ukraine to Poland and on to Western Europe. President Voronin once even attempted to blackmail Ukraine: either the pipeline was extended to Moldova or his country would leave pro-western GUUAM. Moldova is one of very few countries where Ukrainian firms are bidding for a stake in privatisation. Ukraine's *Luhanskoblenergo* lost out to a Spanish company at the final stage in the competition for Moldova's regional electricity distribution networks in 1999.

Moldova owes $30 million for Ukrainian electricity supplies. But unlike Russia (to which Moldova owes more than $100 million for gas supplies) or Romania ($22 million for electricity), Ukraine has never used the debt issue to undermine its smaller neighbour. Moscow, on the other hand, has cut off gas supplies on several occasions while Romania has threatened at least once to disconnect Moldova from its electricity grid. Both countries have used the energy issue to put pressure on Chişinău.

But why is Ukraine so 'kind' to Moldova? It is because Kiev also needs Chişinău as a middle-man in relations with Romania. The Ukrainian/ Romanian border treaty took years to reach signature after dozens of rounds of talks. There is a long history of territorial disputes and complaints by ethnic minorities: by Romanians in Ukraine and Ukrainians in Romania. Kiev is also keen to preserve the Moldovan community in Ukraine (up to 300,000 members) and not to bow to Romania's claim that they are ethnic Romanians and *not* Moldovans. Ukraine needs Moldovan support in the Danube Commission, as it has some problems with Romania over shipping in the Danube delta. Ukraine also needs Chişinău as an ally in the CIS, one which shares Kiev's scepticism about re-integration.

Ukraine has also been a guarantor of Moldovan territorial integrity by putting pressure on the Transdniestrian separatists to do a deal with Chişinău. Ukraine, alongside Russia and the OCSE, is an official co-sponsor of the Transdniestria settlement. In early 2003 Kiev backed EU and US travel bans on Transdniestria's top brass imposed in order to speed up a settlement on a federal basis.

But things are not so straightforward. Kiev has been using the Transdniestria issue as a tool for influencing Moldova. Instinctively, as Chişinău moves closer to Moscow, Kiev has started to support Tiraspol. For instance, following Voronin's election victory in 2001 and his initially very pro-Russian policies, Kiev refused Moldovan demands in 2002 for joint Moldovan-Ukrainian customs points on the Transdniestria stretch of the border. 'We will not take part in an economic blockade of Transdniestria', President Leonid Kuchma was quoted as saying. President Voronin retaliated later by accusing Ukraine of 'playing a double game'.

Ukraine also has quite a significant influence in Transdniestria through, for example, its control of the Tiraspol-Odessa highway, a trade lifeline for the self-declared republic. Tens of thousands of ethnic Ukrainians live in the northern part of Transdniestria. Many managers of leading Transdniestrian industrial enterprises are of Ukrainian origin. There are ethnic Ukrainians at the top of the Transdniestrian elite, a tradition which goes back to the days of the Moldovan Autonomous Republic within Soviet Ukraine after World War II, when Leonid Brezhnev was honing his *apparatchik* skills there.

But Ukraine is not playing the 'big Moldovan game', in which certain parties want to divide Moldova or keep the two parts as vassals of Romania and Russia respectively, but rather taking a wait-and-see approach. It all depends on Romania. If things go as the right wing in Bucharest would like and the 'Romanisation' of Moldova deepens, then Ukraine will probably move to develop closer ties with Transdniestria.

'Romanisation' is not dead as an issue. Moldovan ciitizens can now have dual nationality and thousands already have Romanian passports, a tendency likely to grow with Romania's EU membership looming for 2007. Many Moldovans hope they will be able to travel and perhaps work freely in the EU in the future. Romanian President Ion Ionescu told a Russian newspaper during a visit to Moscow in 2003 that with EU membership Romania would become more attractive to Moldova. He even talked about a 'natural union', at Moldova's request rather than Romania's.

Overall, Ukraine has been trying to manoeuvre between Moldova and Transdniestria, trying to preserve its influence in the region and counter that of others, acting as an 'honest broker' in the search for a political settlement of the Transdniestria problem. In the early 1990s some Ukrainian radical paramilitaries volunteered, as they put it, to fight Russian imperialism and Moscow-backed separatists around the former Soviet Union. The exception was in Moldova, where they actually supported the separatists and fought against the Moldovan army, as part of a strategy to keep Moldova from uniting with Romania, as seemed inevitable immediately after the collapse of the Soviet Union. Ethnic Ukrainians in Transdniestria at that time organised rallies calling on 'mother Ukraine' to intervene, but official Kiev declined. When the communist government in Moldova was under threat in 2002 because of pro-Romanian mass protests in Chişinău, the Ukrainian leader sent a special envoy to Chişinău to express support for President Voronin. In all these cases Kiev's strategy was to counter Romanian and Russian influence in Moldova and its separatist region.

Ukraine's main interest in Moldova is to keep Moldovan statehood alive and kicking and to counter overly strong Russian or Romanian influences. If the EU is interested in preserving Moldova's statehood, then Ukraine will be its chief ally.

'Good Brothers', Bad Neighbours: Romanian/Moldovan Relations

Oleg Serebrian

Relations between Romania and the Republic of Moldova are special because of the shared history, language and culture of the people living in these countries. It is noteworthy that Romania was the first country to recognise the Republic of Moldova, only a few hours after its declaration of independence on 27 August 1991. Shortly afterwards, on 29 August 1991, diplomatic relations were established at embassy level. The 'two Romanian states', according to the Romanian President, Ion Iliescu, would build 'privileged' relations of friendship and good-neighbourliness. Subsequently, Moldova was mentioned in all Romania's strategic programmes, alongside NATO and European integration, in projects of regional and sub-regional partnership and collaboration. Romanian diplomacy gave Moldova all the help needed to get her into the Stability Pact for South-Eastern Europe, as recognised by former Prime Minister Cernomaz on one of his visits to Bucharest.

Initially it was thought that the cultural links might serve as a solid basis for deepening bilateral relations and establishing closer collaboration between the two new neighbours, through realistic and coherent policies serving the interests of both nations. Dozens of accords, treaties and conventions in different fields were signed; economic relations were intensified, with more than 1096 joint ventures active by the early 2000s; special Romanian government funds were disbursed for Moldova, thousands of student scholarships allocated etc. However political-diplomatic declarations and actions have not always corresponded to this reality, nor has it prevented tensions arising between the two neighbours. But though relations between Romania and Moldova have known moments of strain and coolness, they never turned completely sour.

Tension between Romania and Moldova began in the early years of Moldovan statehood, under the neo-communist Agrarian government (1994–98), when the concept of 'two Romanian states' (accepted in 1991) was abandoned. From this time on, Moldovan-Romanian relations at the diplomatic level, although in theory 'privileged', and marked by 'friendship and neighbourliness', grew cooler and more distant. This continued during the next two presidencies (Iliescu/Snegur in 1991–97 and Lucinski/Constantinescu in 1997–2001), reaching its most difficult period after the 2001 elections, when the Communist Party regained state power in Chişinău. The return of the Communists to power occurred in the context of a very painful transition, characterised by a sharp deterioration in living standards for the overwhelming majority of the population, by a fragmentation of the so-called democratic political spectrum that eroded people's confidence in the democratic and economic reforms, and last but not least by an electoral system which allowed the Communists to get 71 seats in parliament (out of 101), while only securing the votes of 33 per cent of those participating in the vote.

Even before the creation of independent Moldova, two politico-cultural tendencies were in evidence in Moldova: one pro-Russia (the 'traditional ally'), the other pro-Romania (the emerging 'privileged partner'). The confrontation between these forces increased after the Communist Party came to power and began to implement the measures set down in their electoral programme, ignoring the demands of the parliamentary opposition to refrain from these unpopular reforms and regardless of the possible consequences. Bucharest reacted with some sensitivity to the reform of local government (which involved moving from a Romanian to an old Soviet system), the ban on the use of 'Romanian' as the state language of Moldova, changes in the school history textbook, the suspension of rebroadcasting of Romanian Television in Moldova, etc.) These 'reforms' led to tensions within the country and precipitated one of the coldest and most rigid periods in relations with Romania, as well as raising concern at the international level.

Diplomatic friction between Romania and Moldova came to a head following a speech given by Moldovan Minister of Justice Ion Morei in the context of a hearing at the European Court for Human Rights in October 2001 concerning the Metropolitan Church of Bessarabia. Morei accused Romania of expansionism and undermining Moldova's sovereignty by direct interference in its internal affairs. Morei claimed that legalising the Metropolitan Church of Bessarabia (which comes under the Romanian Patriarchy) would 'make it easier for Romanian expansionism to fish in Moldova's troubled waters'.

The Romanian prime minister responded to this speech by cancelling a visit to Chişinău, stressing that until Chişinău made a clear statement about Morei's speech, bilateral relations at this level were impossible. While Romania was waiting for excuses or explanations, another wave of declarations, tension and even diplomatic conflict started with the demonstrations organised by the Christian Democratic People's Party (CDPP) in January-April 2002 over the new obligation to study Russian in schools, the legal recognition of Russian as the 'second official language' and the replacement of a course on 'The History of the Romanians' by one on 'The History of Moldova'. The Chişinău authorities responded with rhetoric making reference to Romania's 'imperial pretensions' and even more serious accusations. President Voronin accused Romania on transferring funds to the Christian Democratic opposition in Moldova to support the protests in Chişinău.

Official Bucharest said that the actions and attitudes of the Chişinău authorities were intended to serve forces hostile to Romania's integration into Euro-Atlantic structures and to block closer relations between Moldova and European economic and political structures. Some Moldovan analysts and the largest newspapers in Chişinău shared this view.

While the Moldovan authorities were hurling fresh allegations at Romania, the Bucharest parliament, during an extraordinary session chaired by Foreign Minister Geoana, adopted a strategy designed to put an end to the tension between Bucharest and Chişinău. The key word was 'pragmatism' in relations between Romania and Moldova. Romania would focus on economic relations and continue to support Moldova's efforts towards EU integration. This gesture elicited no response from the Moldovan authorities.

At the same time, senior European officials were expressing their concern about the political situation in Moldova and its tense relations with its neighbours. Even Colin Powell, the US Secretary of State, characterised the situation in Moldova as dangerous for democracy and respect for human rights, and in general for internal stability and regional security.

In spring 2002 the Communist leadership in Chişinău, including President Voronin and Prime Minister Tarlev, addressed a series of harsh accusations at Bucharest, accusing it of interference in the internal affairs of Moldova, exercising 'colonial policies' in the land between the Prut and the Dniester, promoting and financing 'creeping unionism' in the Moldovan media, and 'attacking Moldovan statehood'. The tone and frequency of these accusations steadily worsened and reached its nadir when Romania's military attaché in Bucharest was declared *persona non-grata* without explanation. The response from the ministry of foreign affairs in Bucharest was also drastic: it demanded the withdrawal of the minister-counsellor at the Moldovan Embassy in Bucharest.

These tensions were echoed in the field of economic diplomacy. Romania imposed a ban on the import of eggs, meat and tobacco from Moldova on the grounds that these commodities did not meet EU market standards, although neither country was an EU member. The government in Chişinău naturally did not like this measure (exports of animal products account for 15 per cent of all Moldova's exports to Romania, and losses would amount to around $6–10 million annually), and accused Bucharest of imposing the embargo for political reasons. In the first quarter of 2002 alone, Moldova's exports to Romania fell by 29.1 per cent and imports by 37.4 per cent in comparison with the same period the previous year. In an attempt to improve at least economic relations with Bucharest, in June 2002 the Moldovan government dismissed Ion Godonoaga, president of the cooperation committee with Romania, and Mihai Moraru, the economic counsellor at the Moldovan embassy in Bucharest, claiming that they had not made sufficient effort to solve the problem of meat and dairy exports. The situation provoked a further row between Romania and Moldova; eventually the WTO got involved, with the result that Romania was required to pay compensation to Moldova.

Conclusions

Relations between the two neighbouring countries started off with strains and stresses. At a time when the government in Chişinău is exhibiting pro-CIS and anti-European behaviour (the EU being proclaimed as one but not the main priority, the political aim of the Communists being Moldova's integration into the Russia-Belarus Union), it is hard to envisage goodneighbourly relations between Moldova and either of its neighbours: Romania, with its exclusive pro-Western orientation, and Ukraine, whose European message is becoming more and more consistent. In speaking of their Euro-Asian orientation the Moldovan authorities continue to think in terms of bipolar geopolitical rivalry. For the Communist authorities in Chişinău, as for Gennady Zhuganov, Vladimir Zhirinovsky and Alexander Lukashenko, Euro-Asian integration means the creation of an opposition to 'Western imperialism'.

Many people say that Moldova is suffering from an 'identity crisis'. The current administration's main preoccupation has been strengthening its own hold on power rather that solving its external problems. At the domestic level the Communist administration is conducting a crusade against the country's

'Romanian roots', its history and language, in particular by promoting the idea of a 'Moldovan language', a concept foreign to linguists and most others, including the other ethnic groups living in Moldova. This reached ridiculour proportions when the Moldovan authorities recently attempted to publish a Moldovan-Romanian dictionary in order to prove the existence of two distinct languages. This action precipitated a revolt by the Moldovan and Romanian academic community in summer 2003. Eventually President Voronin was forced to deny publicly the need for such a dictionary, but he did not renounce the idea of a 'Moldovan language'.

'Goodneighbourliness' is indispensable, especially for Moldova. In this context the declaration made by Bodo Hombach, former special coordinator of the Stability Pact for South-Eastern Europe, in Chişinău in 2001, is very significant. Hombach stressed that relations with Romania were of vital interest to Moldova, and that the Romanian government was insisting on Moldova joining the Pact and working intensively in that framework. For Romania, a NATO member and candidate for EU membership, stable relations with its neighbour are also important, quite apart from the emotional historical and cultural ties.

As a future EU member, and with its responsibilities as a country on the EU's eastern border, Romania has a direct interest in encouraging democratic development in Moldova. Romania has acquired a certain amount of experience of the road to European integration, and it is ready to share this experience with its neighbour. But Moldova does not seem eager to accept this offer, and is not yet very clear about its future orientation. Furthermore, Chişinău has not yet abandoned its accusatory rhetoric against its Romanian neighbour, which gives rise to a certain amount of scepticism that any solution will be found in the near future.

Baltic States and Moldova: Lessons of Success and Failure

Liliana Vițu

When communism collapsed and the Soviet Union imploded in 1991, many leaders in Chișinău considered that Moldova and the Baltic states were starting out on a similar footing as independent states and members of the European family. This was because of their common post-war history, reinforced by the close contacts between the Moldovan and Baltic Popular Fronts and their mutual support in fighting for independence. As the Lithuanian academic Tomas Venclova put it, 'Moldovans were regarded as allies in the common cause of liberation from the Russian yoke.' However, it has not worked out like that. While the EU summit in Copenhagen in late 2002 confirmed that the Baltic states would be part of the first wave of EU enlargement in 2004, Moldova lagged far behind. The reasons for this can be found in modern politics and diplomacy, as well as in the clash of history and culture on the territories of these countries.

The only non-Slav nations in the western part of the former USSR, Estonia, Latvia, Lithuania and Moldova differed from the rest of the Soviet Union in having had a separate national existence in the inter-war period. The Baltic countries gained their independence from Soviet Russia in 1920, and Moldova returned in 1918 to its mother country, Greater Romania, after being annexed in 1812 by the Russian Empire. The signing of the Molotov-Ribbentrop Pact on 23 August 1939 signalled the end of Baltic independence and Moldova's existence as part of Romania; all were absorbed into the Soviet Union the following year.

Strong Baltic resistance

By the time of their forcible annexation in 1940, the Baltic states had built up substantial experience as independent nation-states, with a strong national identity and attachment to their territory. This made their cultural absorption into the Soviet Union almost impossible. These Baltic societies were highly literate: the first Estonian school was opened in 1631 in Tallinn and the first printing press and university were established in Tartu in 1632, while the creation of Vilnius University in 1579 animated the cultural evolution of both Lithuania and its neighbouring counties. The inter-war period gave birth to a wide-ranging culture with flourishing literature, music, press, arts and theatre. The Baltic languages resisted the introduction of Russian words largely thanks to their use of the Latin alphabet, a permanent mark of difference. Also, the reestablishment in Estonia in the late 1950s of private contacts with foreign countries opened a 'window on the West' which had long-term effects and eventually prepared the Baltic peoples for their vanguard role in extending Gorbachev's perestroika. The Nordic connection was important mainly in ensuring the survival of Western links and attitudes throughout the Soviet period, a fact that did not admit the full absorption into the USSR of the Baltic countries. Despite their decades of isolation from the West, the Baltic peoples remembered the Europe of the 1920s-1930s, when they were independent. This is why, when Soviet communism started to collapse, the sense of national identity brushed aside all social divisions and led to the national unity that ultimately played a major role in achieving Baltic independence.

More importantly, the Baltic peoples preserved their identity thanks to the strong religious influence of centuries of Germanic and Scandinavian settlement. The Lutheran Church remained mainly under German administration until the late 19th century in Estonia. In Latvia most people belonged to the Evangelical Lutheran Church; eastern Latvia was predominantly Roman Catholic and only a small minority were Russian Orthodox. Most Lithuanians and ethnic Poles belonged to the Roman Catholic Church, while Russian Orthodoxy was the largest non-Catholic denomination. Thus, religion was a crucial factor in forming identities in the Baltic states and determining the attitudes of the EU countries towards them once independence was gained.

Confused identity in Moldova

After the eastern part of the Principality of Moldova, later known as Bessarabia, was annexed to the Russian Empire in 1812, ethnic Romanians underwent a period of russification. Restrictions were placed on the use of their mother tongue, and a policy of resettlement brought in Bulgarian and Găgăuz refugees from the Balkans and Russians and Ukrainians from further east. A century later, when Bessarabia's National Assembly proclaimed union with Romania and its own dissolution (27 November 1918), most of the ethnic Romanians felt more comfortable with their newly-acquired Moldovan identity within the Russian Empire.

After 1940, when Bessarabia was annexed by the Soviet Union, national identity became even more confused. The Soviet authorities immediately took steps to create a separate and distinct Moldovan nation, lest a new Romanian government should claim the annexed territory back on ethnic and historical grounds. Stalin proceeded with a policy of elimination of the Romanian identity through mass deportations to Siberia and the promotion of a 'Moldovan' language based on archaic Romanian and imported Russian/Slavonic vocabulary and written in the Cyrillic script. The Metropolitan Church of Bessarabia, canonically dependent on the Romanian Orthodox Church, was abolished and the new church of Moldova was subordinated to the Russian Patriarchy, which has historically been closely linked to, and a tool in the service of, Greater-Russian expansionism. Having destroyed the Romanian intellectual elites in Bessarabia, the Soviet leadership replaced them with Russian-speakers brought in from the centre. So it is not surprising that by 1991, when Moldova became independent, it could not count on a clear national identity, given its multi-ethnic population and after 50 years of suppression and denigration of all aspects of the Romanian identity.

Thus, while inter-war independence strengthened the national identity of the Baltic peoples, Moldova's period of independence as part of its mother country gave rise to even more confusion among the population in terms of history, language and homeland. This explains the diverging paths taken by Moldova and the Baltic states after the fall of the Soviet Union in 1991, when it looked, superficially, as though they all started on the same footing.

Diverging paths

Various internal and external factors influenced developments in Moldova and the Baltic states after independence, but a few were crucial in determining their treatment by the EU and their future after the collapse of the USSR.

First, the forcible incorporation of the Baltic states into the Soviet Union was never recognised by three major Western powers, Britain, France and the United States, which viewed the post-1991 states as legal successors to the interwar republics. This was not true for Moldova, whose union with Romania in 1918 was not accepted internationally. This was because the Americans were unhappy with the lack of a referendum in Bessarabia, while Britain and France were loath to threaten the Tsar's interests while he was still fighting the Bolsheviks.

Historical and cultural proximity played an important role in the European integration efforts of the Baltic states. The Nordic countries and Germany made sure they were included in the association process as soon and as deeply as possible, becoming a model for economic and political reform for other newcomers. As a result, the three Baltic states became less dependent on the Russian market, developing more important links with the Nordic economies.

Second, Moldova's involvement with Europe was considerably weakened by its lack of the credibility needed for any prospect of EU membership. At the domestic level, the first thing that strikes an observer about Moldova is the incompetence of its obsolete political class; few have a proper education and up-to-date knowledge and experience, compared with the Baltic politicians who enjoyed the assistance of a strong and well-qualified diaspora and had trained as specialists outside their own countries. Also, a lack of political will with regard to reform and European integration has led to sluggish and incoherent economic progress, whereas laying the foundations for a competitive market economy is a key factor in the association process.

In addition to its lack of credibility, Moldova experienced a lack of effective advocacy in contrast to the Baltic states, whose case was powerfully supported by Germany and the Nordic countries. Romania was no longer seen as an advocate for Moldova once the pro-independence current in Moldova emerged as opposed to unification with Romania, whose patrons – France, and to a lesser extent Italy – opposed more generous concessions to the East European applicants because of domestic constraints and scepticism. Moldova's appeal to the most ardent supporters of the East-Central European countries, such as Germany and Britain, remained weak, and it proved rather unpopular with Western investors and exporters.

Moreover, the political leaders who came to power in Moldova were and still are closely linked to Russia due to their past as Soviet bureaucrats. Unlike the Baltic states, Moldova was unable to withstand the sort of Russian-inspired secessionist movements seen in the region after the collapse of the Soviet Union. The presence of Russia's 14th Army on Moldova's territory since 1992 has severely undermined its independence, serving as a tool for direct Russian political pressure on the Moldovan leadership. More importantly, Moldova has hesitated to make a clear choice in favour of a European orientation and has signed up to various CIS programmes. In this it differs again from the Baltic states, which did not wish to be part of a Russia-led post-Soviet community that might constrain their freedom to set their own foreign policy.

Since independence, Moldova's leadership, as well as its population, has been divided between those dedicated to withdrawal from the CIS as a precondition for European integration, and those favouring closer links with Russia. Although Russian influence has hampered Moldova's efforts to integrate with the EU, the confusion that has dominated the domestic political scene, together with the lack of a clear national identity or national consensus in favour of the European vector in Moldova's foreign policy, were the most important factors behind Moldova's failure on its road 'back to Europe'. The EU in consequence placed Moldova in the same basket as Ukraine and Belarus, rather than with the Baltic states, to which so many Moldovans felt akin when they gained their independence.

Moldova and the OSCE: a History of Failed Initiatives

Adrian Severin

The history of Moldova's relations with the Organisation for Cooperation and Security in Europe (OSCE) is a history of failed initiatives. Originally looked upon with hope, the OSCE has come to be regarded as incapable of meeting the expectations placed upon it.

Moldova became a member of the OSCE as a successor state to the USSR. Relations between the two have been focussed on Moldova's problems over its inheritance, which are also international questions relating to the management of the legacy of the Soviet empire.

The OSCE has been called upon to find a way of ensuring the security of Moldova and the region, both endangered by the 'Transdniestria crisis'. This crisis has two intertwining components. First and foremost, it is about the presence in Transdniestria of troops, arms and ammunition belonging to the former 14th Army of the USSR. The withdrawal of these to Russia after Moldovan independence was 'postponed'. This has been justified over time by: a) Russian security needs in its 'near abroad', then b) the need to keep under control the Romanian-speaking and Russian-speaking communities, which were in violent confrontation over the secessionist policy of the Russian-speaking leaders in Tiraspol, then c) the desire that troop withdrawals should coincide with a political solution to Transdniestrian separatism and, finally, d) technical difficulties caused by opposition from the Transdniestrian secessionist authorities to the withdrawal of troops, which they claimed guaranteed stability in the area; and of arms, which they claimed belonged to them as heirs to the USSR. Secondly, there was an attempt to find a solution to Transdniestrian separatism itself, a solution which would both maintain the territorial integrity of Moldova and allow it to exercise sovereignty over its whole territory in peace.

From the very beginning, the international community has argued that the presence of Russian troops in Transdniestria is a source of insecurity. In their turn, the Moldovan authorities have unwaveringly claimed that they can ensure stability in their entire territory and asked that the foreign troops be withdrawn. Sometimes the Moldovan authorities have stressed that, far from calming Transdniestrian secessionism and controlling the excesses of the warring parties, the presence of foreign troops has bolstered the activities of the illegitimate authorities in Tiraspol. Russia has stood out against such a view. The ensuing disputes have been, over the years, the subject of numerous discussions in the OSCE Permanent Council and at ministerial conferences.

The OSCE Summit in Istanbul (1999) finally agreed that Russian troops, arms and ammunition should be withdrawn from Transdniestria by the end of 2002. A year later, the Austrian chair of the OSCE drew attention to the fact that Russia was not taking action to fulfil the obligations it had assumed in Istanbul. On the other hand, in 2001 the Romanian chair claimed that Russia had fulfilled its obligations, arguing that most of the heavy weaponry had been repatriated and that the Russian government and the OSCE had agreed that the ammunition and certain weapons should be destroyed *in situ*. The next chair, Portugal, saw things differently. Nevertheless, the ministerial conference in Porto in December 2002 failed even to adopt a decision firmly calling on Moscow to observe the Istanbul provisions and setting a new deadline. The conference only acknowledged the Russian position, i.e. reconfirming its wish to withdraw but without giving a particular date and suggesting that the timing should take into account progress in solving the political crisis relating to Transdniestrian secession. Thus, it can be said that the OSCE's involvement in safeguarding Moldova's sovereignty by eliminating the remains of Soviet military power in Moldova had, thus far, been a failure.

The OSCE Permanent Mission to Chişinău, set up by the OSCE Permanent Council on 4 February 1993, was originally mandated to facilitate a long-term political solution to the Transdniestria conflict; to assist the parties in strengthening Moldova's independence and sovereignty by concluding an agreement on a special status for Transdniestria; to gather information on conflicts in the area; to support measures related to the withdrawal of foreign troops from Moldova; to assist in defining Transdniestria's special status, to include observance of human rights, the rights of minorities and the principles of democracy; and to provide support for the repatriation of refugees. It should be noted that this mandate focused on safeguarding the territorial integrity of Moldova as a unitary state with a special status for Transdniestria. It could be inferred that this status was intended to be similar to the autonomy already granted to Găgăuzia. However the leaders of Transdniestria, under the protection of Russian troops (which would have prevented the authorities in Chişinău returning to Transdniestria in force to exert their sovereign powers there), have insisted on either independence or a confederal system. That is why the withdrawal of foreign troops was a priority for the OSCE.

On 9 December 1999, in pursuit of the decisions adopted by the Istanbul Summit, the OSCE Permanent Council decided to extend the mandate of the OSCE Mission to Moldova by including the task of providing transparency to the withdrawal and destruction of the Russian ammunition and weaponry in Transdniestria, as well as coordinating technical and financial assistance to facilitate these movements. Over time, as the Russian troops have declined in number, the retention of the weaponry and ammunition in Moldova has posed a threefold threat, geopolitical, criminal and environmental, namely: a) the rapid re-commissioning of a Russian army capable of operating in foreign territory and modifying the ratio of forces in Central Europe; b) the illegal transfer of arms and ammunition to the paramilitary forces of the Tiraspol secessionist regime; and c) an ecological disaster caused by deterioration of the ammunition.

The mandate of the OSCE Mission was exercised under an agreed system involving three brokers and guarantors of the negotiations between the Moldovan authorities and the Transdniestrian separatists: Russia, Ukraine and the OSCE. Under this mediation system several compromise formulae have gradually been mapped out. These have been enshrined in the Memorandum on the Basics for Normalising Relations between the Republic of Moldova and Transdniestria (Moscow, 8 May 1997); the Agreement on Confidence-building Measures and the Development of Contacts between the Republic of Moldova and Transdniestria (Odessa, 20 March 1998), followed by a Joint Statement by the Mediators (21 November 1998); and the Joint Statement of the Participants in the Kiev Reunion regarding the Normalisation of Relations between the Republic of Moldova and Transdniestria (Kiev, 16 July 1999). These documents allow, in principle, for the maintenance of common borders and the joint management of the economic, juridical, social and defence spheres. Unfortunately, these agreements, even where partially observed, have failed either to facilitate dialogue by increasing trust between the parties or to find a basis for compromise which would permit a political solution to the crisis. In fact, the direct negotiations have always come to a standstill, sometimes even being formally broken off.

In order to facilitate dialogue and build confidence, particularly when demarches at governmental level were blocked or dramatically hampered, the OSCE Parliamentary Assemby (OSCE-PA) decided, in January 1999, to set up an ad hoc Committee for Moldova. The mandate of this Committee was to promote peace, stability and the rule of law, while insisting on the unity of the Moldovan state. This formulation underlines the initial preference of the OSCE-PA for the idea of a unitary state. However, this approach has not been pursued in practice.

The three general principles underlying the work of the Committee for Moldova were: respect for Moldova's territorial integrity; observance of relevant previous agreements; and solving the conflict exclusively by political means. In order to permit consideration of solutions that the parties were not willing to discuss during the official negotiations, the OSCE-PA, together with the Finnish Parliament, organised a seminar in Finland in May 2001 on issues related to self-government. Two other seminars were held in Chişinău and Tiraspol in April and September 2003, this time to analyse the formula for federation. The OSCE-PA adopted more resolutions on Transdniestria during its annual sessions in Bucharest (July 2000), Paris (July 2001), Berlin (July 2002) and Rotterdam (July 2003).

The Paris Resolution is particularly interesting because it draws attention to certain aspects of the problem that have been less discussed. Thus, the OSCE-PA talked about the need for a balanced pursuit of investment and infrastructure development on both banks of the Dniester, suggesting that unequal economic evolution could make the reintegration of all the Moldovan territories under a single sovereignty more difficult. At the same time, the OSCE-PA called on OSCE member-states to act so that trade with economic agents on either side of the Dniester should not facilitate the development of organised crime or the strengthening of illegal entities that might undermine Moldova's territorial integrity. In this context, it was suggested that some international trade with Moldova had merely served to fund the separatists. Finally, the OSCE-PA suggested that economic solutions should also be analysed with a view to overcoming the crisis.

The Berlin Resolution particularly focused on the need to fight organised crime, thus connecting the political and criminal aspects of the crisis.

The OSCE's involvement in the Transdniestria crisis is an acknowledgement that the crisis has regional and global relevance. Unfortunately, the OSCE has not recognised another aspect of the crisis: the criminal dimension. With the passage of time, the presence in Transdniestria of illegitimate authorities, behaving and often being treated as representatives of a genuine state but (since the state is not a subject of international law) not integrated into the international order and accepting no responsibility before the international community, has resulted in the development of a safe haven for organised crime. Criminal groups operating under the protection of this pseudo-state have penetrated the European, Euro-Atlantic, and Euro-Asian markets, doing lucrative business. Significant funds have stemmed from this business, thus consolidating the power of the Transdniestrian authorities and allowing them to escape being entirely subject to Moscow's policies. Thus, a point was reached when Tiraspol was able to impose its views even against Russia, thwarting the enforcement of the latter's understandings with the OSCE.

In order to be able to negotiate a political solution which would also be enforced by the Transdniestrian leadership, the OSCE has chosen not to tackle the ever more relevant criminal aspects of the crisis. This has done nothing but aggravate the problem. Only in 2003 did the EU finally understand the (criminal) nature of the situation and decide to ban admission of the illegitimate leaders in Tiraspol to EU member-states. Even this did not result in an embargo on economic relations between firms in the democracies and the Transdniestrian regime. An OSCE-PA resolution in July 2001 implicitly recommending such an embargo had no effect. It was not supported even by the governmental structures of the OSCE.

However, the OSCE was more effective when, in 2000, it rejected the 'common state' project, which equated Moldova, a sovereign state and subject of international law, with Transdniestria, a secessionist region of Moldova. This project had been submitted by Evgeny Primakov, former Russian Foreign Minister, who was appointed by President Yeltsin to head a working group charged with enforcing the decisions of the Istanbul Summit. The OSCE did not accept the idea of a confederation which would maintain only formally the territorial integrity of Moldova.

At a meeting of the parties concerned, held in Kiev in July 2002 at OSCE initiative, the mediators in the Transdniestria conflict tabled a draft agreement aimed at ensuring the territorial integrity of Moldova while accommodating the Transdniestrians' demands for independence. This 'Kiev document' defined the Republic of Moldova as a 'federal state'. Implementation of the agreement was to be subject to monitoring and guaranteed by Russia, Ukraine and the OSCE.

This step displayed both the virtues and weaknesses of the OSCE in trying to resolve the crisis. What is important and positive is that the OSCE succeeded, to a great extent, in bringing the two parties involved to the point of accepting, in principle, a federal-type solution, and negotiating a coherent and comprehensive text aimed at solving the problem within a new constitutional framework. It is also healthy that, thanks to the OSCE, the process is now unfolding in a transparent manner. This enhances the chances of the results of the negotiations being accepted by the population and thus being legitimised. If the OSCE solution proves viable, it could also be applied to other areas of conflict such as the Caucasus.

The OSCE's weak points result from its dependence on those member-countries which have a direct interest and which control the Organisation's decisions through their virtual right of veto. As a consequence of this, the OSCE has formulated a draft that does not guarantee the stability of the proposed federation. Under pressure, the OSCE started from the false premise that Moldova is a multi-national state, while in fact it is only multi-ethnic; and that the tensions in Transdniestria are of ethnic origin, when they are in fact geo-political. Hence the temptation to create an ethnically-based federation within which Transdniestria would be a Russian area, whereas it is Ukrainians who are actually in the majority there. It is the same false premise that has given rise to the idea of including Ukraine and Russia among the guarantors, while those countries have direct and often conflicting interests in the region. This would be to make those countries both players and referees. From both the European and global perspective, the OSCE position is also open to criticism because it gives a false impression of internationally balanced involvement, while the OSCE is actually a mere interface that lends respectability to the direct involvement of the 'brokers' in the conflict. This is to say that, in this case, the OSCE, as a multilateral organisation specialised in collective and cooperative security, can work effectively only if Russia and Ukraine – the other mediators and future guarantors – allow it to do so. Since the pertinent decisions should be taken by consensus, Russia and Ukraine are always able to block the adoption of a decision by their opposition, while, in return, the OSCE cannot stop them acting according to their wishes. Whenever these countries block a consensus, they are the only parties (since a mediator with a vested interest in the business is, in fact, a party) able to act freely. Thus, the only genuine players are those having a direct vested interest in the dispute, while the Euro-Atlantic West is kept to the fringes of the playground. That explains why the obligations assumed by Russia at the Istanbul OSCE Summit remain unfulfilled: because the OSCE has not been able to take any measures to press Russia to improve the situation.

Besides this criticism of principle, an objective evaluation of the federalisation draft proposed by the OSCE suggests the following aspects that need to be clarified as soon as possible:

a) The draft does not state precisely how many subjects the federation is to include: two (including Transdniestria), three (including Găgăuzia) or four (including Taraclia). The answer to this question is essential to defining what kind of federation Moldova is to become: symmetrical or asymmetrical.

b) The list of powers shared between the federation and its subjects is very long, which increases the risk of future power struggles. Establishing some exclusive powers would be a better solution, but this will be difficult as long as there is no political will to keep Moldova a united (even if federal) state.

c) According to the draft Constitution, all conflicts should be solved by the federal authority. Such a hierarchical principle has been proved to be quite inefficient in the case of conflicts between government entities representing different cultural communities.

d) The presidency of the future federation is to have both executive and arbitration powers, which may involve the presidency in a clash of interests leading to conflict between the subjects of the federation.

e) The draft does not stipulate the political and judicial mechanisms to be used for solving any domestic disputes. Given the absence of such provisions, and especially if the federation is an ethnically-grounded one, federal stability will be at stake.

f) The list of guarantees is long and often unrealistic.

g) The working mechanism for the three guarantors and the nature of their powers are not set out. OSCE and CoE experience of other cases could offer some interesting examples (eg the appointment by the European Court of Human Rights of national members to conciliation and arbitration courts set up to solve domestic disputes). In the absence of such provisions, abuses could occur like those behind the long and still-unresolved Cypriot crisis.

h) There is no mechanism for revising the Constitution.

i) There is no reference to electoral mechanisms intended to promote moderate candidates capable of securing cross-ethnic legitimacy.

Efforts to find a political solution to the Transdniestria crisis have always cut across two theses mainly supported by Russia. One is that stability should be secured in Moldova by military means until a political solution is found. The other is that the chosen political solution should be enforced by military means as well. Thus it was argued that the presence of Russian troops was a stabilising factor which prevented further outbreaks of social unrest. In addition, it was said that such a presence should continue after a solution was found in order to make it effective. If the international community had refused to agree to the presence of Russian troops (as the Istanbul Summit required), then the

Russian troops could have been replaced by others flying the OSCE 'flag'. This now seems to be impossible, not only because the OSCE's structure does not allow it to carry out military tasks, but also because the replacement would have been merely formal, given that the OSCE military mission was to be created on the basis of the Russian army. Otherwise Russia would have blocked the consensus, rejecting the entry of other military troops in an area considered to be her own security zone. With no consensus, the Russian army would have remained there under the pretext that her presence was a transitional solution intended to avoid a vacuum in international authority.

In an attempt to get out of this vicious circle, in April 2003 the OSCE Dutch Presidency moved that the constitutional agreement promoted by the OSCE should be guaranteed through the deployment of military units formed through cooperation among OSCE members to replace the Russian troops leaving Transdniestria. This operation should include military contribution not only from the neighbouring states (Russia's 'near abroad' concept), but also from other states (a so-called 'multi-ethnic military unit' yet undefined). It is clear that this proposal was intended, on the one hand, to find a way round Russia's insistence on the need to keep foreign troops in the area and, on the other, to ensure the practical involvement of the Western democracies in solving the crisis.

It is uncertain how far this initiative will succeed, so other ways are being explored of ensuring the participation in the process of powers with no direct interest in the dispute. The OSCE seems likely to have to either give up its role gradually or share it with the EU, which has declared its readiness to act to solve the Transdniestria issue. So far it is not clear how the EU will approach the question, or whether it has any chance of succeeding, but the intention is welcome, given that the OSCE seems to have reached deadlock and the crisis cannot be overcome without genuine international participation.

Part 4
Moldova and the EU

The EU and Moldova: a Neglected Relationship

Marius Vahl

Introduction

EU-Moldovan relations have been largely neglected since the disintegration of the Soviet Union, both among policy-makers and by academics. In contrast to the considerable EU efforts in Central and Eastern Europe[1] and the Balkans, Moldova has received limited attention in the EU. Moldova's policy vis-à-vis the EU has been hesitant and contradictory, as it struggles to find its place in post-Cold War Europe. Largely as a result of the unresolved Transdniestrian conflict, Moldova has the dubious honour of having become the poorest country in Europe. This, combined with the enhanced powers of the Union and the relative progress in EU policy towards its other neighbours, raises the prospects of a stronger EU engagement with Moldova. This may indeed be required if a settlement of the Transdniestrian conflict is to be achieved, itself a precondition for the completion of Moldova's transition to a stable and prosperous European democracy, the long-term aim of both Moldova and the EU.

Establishing EU-Moldova relations after the collapse of the Soviet Union

The European Community (EC) was arguably even less prepared than other Western actors for the dissolution of the Soviet Union and the emergence of 15 new independent states. Formal diplomatic relations with the Soviet Union were only established in June 1988 with the Luxembourg Joint Declaration on mutual diplomatic recognition. A trade and co-operation agreement between the EC and the Soviet Union was signed in December 1989, providing for most-favoured nation treatment (MFN) on tariffs and duties and political dialogue through a Joint Committee.[2]

The EC began to provide economic assistance to the Soviet Union in 1990, initially in the form of emergency assistance. Subsequent aid was provided through the much broader Tacis programme established in 1991. The creation of a special programme for the former Soviet republics, rather than including them in the Phare programme for Central and Eastern Europe, was an early indication that the EU would follow a different policy towards the former Soviet bloc than towards the region on which it was increasingly focused, Central and Eastern Europe.

In spite of intensified fighting and armed clashes in Transdniestria in Spring 1992, the Transdniestrian conflict remained far down the list of concerns of the EC and its member states, and direct EC involvement was never seriously considered. To the extent that West European states were to get involved in the conflict, it was through other international institutions, primarily the OSCE and its Mission, established in 1993, the World Bank and the IMF. Indeed, the limited violence relative to other concurrent conflicts and the early ceasefire led the EC to regard the Transdniestrian conflict as a good example of conflict management for other post-Soviet crises.[3]

The differentiated EU approach towards Eastern Europe and the limited attention it paid to Moldova were evident also in the first Stability Pact proposed by French Prime Minister Balladur in April 1993. Through a series of EU-sponsored conferences and round tables in 1994–95, the Stability Pact promoted over 100 bilateral agreements between the countries of Central and Eastern Europe. Although Moldova participated in the Pact, the focus was elsewhere and no significant agreements between Moldova and its neighbours were concluded. Relations between Moldova and its two neighbours, Romania and Ukraine, have been more conflictual than between other Central and Eastern European countries. Many of the difficult issues which gave rise to these periodic tensions in Moldova's relations with Romania and Ukraine were resolved by the kind of bilateral agreements concluded elsewhere in the region as a result of the Stability Pact.

The EC-Soviet agreement became obsolete with the collapse of the Soviet Union in late December 1991. In October 1992, the EC agreed that Partnership and Co-operation Agreements should be concluded bilaterally with the former Soviet republics. Following two rounds of negotiations in Spring 1994, the Partnership and Co-operation Agreement between Moldova and the

EU was signed on 28 November 1994.[4] The PCA focuses mainly on trade and economic co-operation, and represents only a modest extension of the 1989 EC-USSR agreement, in particular if compared with the Europe Agreements between the EU and the countries of Central and Eastern Europe. As in the EC-USSR agreement, the EU and Moldova grant each other MFN status for trade in goods, but with exceptions in important sectors such as textiles. In contrast to the earlier agreement, the PCA envisages the approximation of Moldova's legislation to that of the Community, as well as the prospect of an eventual free trade area. Co-operation is envisaged in a large number of areas, but with very limited legal commitments to push this co-operation forward. The PCA establishes the usual set of institutions, with a ministerial-level Co-operation Council assisted by a Co-operation Committee of senior officials and a number of expert working groups, as well as a consultative Parliamentary Co-operation Committee.

Moldova's 'European Choice'

Moldova became increasingly involved in European and international organisations in the mid-1990s. It joined Partnership for Peace in March 1994, and parliament ratified CIS membership one month later. In July 1995, Moldova became the first member of the CIS to join the Council of Europe. But while Moldova began to participate in these institutions immediately, partnership with the EU was not activated until the entry into force of the PCA in July 1998. And although EU economic assistance to Moldova through Tacis and macro-financial assistance was gradually increased, the amounts were small relative to the assistance provided by other international organisations.[5]

The EU as such thus played a limited role in West European policy towards Moldova. The EU's agenda was dominated by EMU and institutional reform, and when external relations did make it to the top of the agenda, attention was focused on other issues such as the Balkans and enlargement. As far as the Transdniestrian conflict was concerned, the EU was only indirectly represented through the OSCE and its (American) ambassador in Chişinău.

From the middle of the 1990s, however, Moldova paid increasing attention to the EU. The idea of eventual accession was first raised officially in December 1996 by the then recently-elected President, Petru Luschinschi. EU membership was adopted as a strategic objective for Moldova in the Foreign Policy Guidelines for 1998–2002 adopted by the new government formed after parliamentary elections in March 1998. These Guidelines called for the creation of institutional structures to administer a more pro-active policy geared towards eventual EU accession, with upgraded contractual relations through an Association Agreement as a priority in the medium-term.

The marginalisation of Moldova in the EU's proximity policy

The PCA between the EU and Moldova entered into force on 1 July 1998, more than three and a half years after it was signed. This was the third PCA between the EU and a CIS country to become operational, following those with Russia in December 1997 and Ukraine in March 1998. The first meeting of the ministerial Co-operation Council took place on 14 July 1998.

The following month saw the start of the Russian financial crisis, which was to have a devastating effect on Moldova. After its first year of economic growth in 1997, the Moldovan economy contracted by more than 10 per cent in the following two years. Although a study on an eventual free trade area was commissioned, it was clear that there was no credible alternative to what the studies concluded: that the Moldovan economy was not structurally ready for free trade, and priority should be accorded to accession to the WTO.

Furthermore, the rhetoric of European integration was not followed up in practice by successive Moldovan governments in the late 1990s. The institutional structures called for by the Foreign Policy Guidelines were not established, and many of the reforms required, including Moldova's PCA commitments, were either not introduced or remained unimplemented.

By mid-2003, the Co-operation Council had convened five times, and four meetings of the Parliamentary Co-operation Committee had taken place. Sub-committees were established to assist the Co-operation Committee, reflecting the emphasis on economic issues in the PCA. A regular and institutionalised multi-level dialogue between the EU and Moldova was thus established, accompanied by increasing amounts of economic assistance. The commitments made under the Tacis programme were tripled during the 1990s, from 10.1 million ecu in 1991–1993, to 32.7 million euros in 1997–1999.

Although the PCA focuses mainly on economic relations between Moldova and the EU, non-economic issues have become gradually more prominent in the overall relationship. This is particularly true of justice and home affairs (JHA), which have received growing attention, as seen for instance in the joint statements issued after the Co-operation Councils. In addition to the JHA issues covered in the PCA (mainly money laundering, illegal migration and customs co-operation against drugs and arms trafficking), the list of issues has been extended and made more specific to include enhanced co-operation against trafficking in human beings, smuggling of goods such as cigarettes and alcohol, and the fight against terrorism.

The late 1990s were thus a period of enhanced co-operation and strengthened political dialogue between the EU and Moldova, even if the EU was unwilling to acknowledge Moldova as a potential member and reluctant to enter into discussions on an eventual Association Agreement. The increased activity and the gradual broadening of the scope of co-operation could be interpreted as reflecting a readiness for deeper engagement on the part of the EU, and as a response to the 'European choice' made by the Moldovan government.

However, the increased contacts at political and expert level were the direct result of the entry into force of the PCA, which, it can be argued, represents merely a resumption of 'normal' relations, partially suspended since the dissolution of the Soviet Union. A perhaps more plausible explanation for the broadening of the EU-Moldova agenda is the growing competences on non-economic issues accorded to the EU by the Amsterdam and Nice Treaties, rather than an increased focus on Moldova in the EU. Indeed, in spite of the deepening and widening of EU-Moldova relations from the end of the 1990s, this period witnessed a relative marginalisation of Moldova in EU policy towards non-EU Europe. This was due to the EU's more substantial co-operation and integration with almost all of its other neighbours from the second half of the 1990s.

The principal development was the initiation of accession negotiations between the EU and five accession candidates in 1998, a process widened two years later to include an additional seven countries, among them Moldova's neighbour Romania. In addition to drawing attention and resources away from Moldova (and other European countries not considered candidates for EU membership), the EU enlargement process, while probably positive for Moldova overall and in the long run, has had unfortunate consequences in the short term. In December 2000, the EU Council decided to take Romania off its list of countries whose citizens require visas to enter the Schengen area, a decision implemented from early 2002. This has induced hundreds of thousands of Moldovans to acquire Romanian citizenship, adding to the demographic drain on a country where as many as a fifth of the total population are thought to live and work abroad, many of them illegally.

Secondly, the EU's role in the Balkans was significantly enhanced following the Kosovo conflict in spring 1999, mainly through its Stability and

Association Process, under which the prospect of eventual EU membership was offered in May 1999. Substantially increased assistance was allocated to the Balkans in the 2000–2006 EU budget, whereas the relative share of the CIS was slightly reduced. The EU is also a key actor in the multilateral Stability Pact for South-Eastern Europe created in July 1999.

Thirdly, the EU set out an increasingly detailed strategy for its relations with those of its neighbours not then considered candidates for EU membership, culminating in the 'Common Strategies'. These were one of the principal innovations of the EU's Common Foreign and Security Policy introduced by the 1997 Treaty of Amsterdam. The decisions at the December 1998 Vienna European Council concerning the Common Strategies to be developed following the entry into force of the Amsterdam Treaty in May 1999 provided yet another indication of the relative marginalisation of Moldova. Four such documents were envisaged, on Russia, Ukraine, the Mediterranean region and the Western Balkans, leaving Moldova as one of the few neighbours of an enlarged EU not covered by a Common Strategy. In the end, however, only the first three strategies were adopted, and the instrument as such has come in for considerable criticism, from both outside and inside the Union.

The EU pursued an essentially undifferentiated policy towards the countries of the former Soviet Union in the early 1990s. One economic assistance programme, Tacis, was established covering all the CIS countries, and a new type of bilateral agreement, the Partnership and Co-operation Agreement, was envisaged for all CIS countries. But as the EU has strengthened its relations with its non-CIS neighbours, there has been a gradual divergence in level of co-operation between the EU and the various CIS countries, mainly because of a strengthening of relations with Russia, and to a lesser extent Ukraine. The sequencing of the process of negotiating and ratifying the PCAs provided an indication of the EU's priorities as far as the CIS was concerned: Russia, then Ukraine, then Moldova. And although the PCA with Moldova is to a large extent a copy of the previous PCAs with Russia and Ukraine, the absence of regular summits results in a more limited political dialogue between the EU and Moldova. Finally, there have been numerous bilateral EU-Russia initiatives in recent years, starting in 2000 with the creation of an energy dialogue and enhanced co-operation under the Common Foreign and Security Policy. In 2001, there were initiatives to create a common European economic space, and on bilateral EU-Russia co-operation on European Security and Defence Policy, and discussions on a visa-free regime from Autumn 2002. Although it is understandable and indeed perhaps inevitable that the EU focuses more on relations with its biggest and most powerful neighbour, this has further fuelled perceptions of exclusion in Moldova.

In short, EU policy towards its neighbours overall has been considerably strengthened since the second half of the 1990s. Paradoxically, in the light of the closer relations between the EU and Moldova in the same period, this process of differentiated EU engagement with its 'near abroad' has entailed a relative marginalisation of Moldova in EU proximity policy.

Beyond EU Enlargement: Moldova and the 'Wider Europe' Initiative

Since 1998, the implementation of the PCA has been the EU's main priority in its relations with Moldova. The principal aims of Moldova's policy towards the EU, on the other hand, have been to be acknowledged as a candidate for membership in the long term, and to upgrade the relationship in the medium term through negotiation of an Association Agreement along the lines of the Stability and Association Agreements (SAAs) concluded with the countries of the Western Balkans.

The EU has so far been unwilling to acknowledge Moldova as a potential candidate for EU membership. This is in part because of a general preoccupation in the EU with internal issues and with the fifth (eastward) enlargement, the biggest and most challenging enlargement in its history. On the Moldovan side, the continuation of the Transdniestrian conflict and in particular the lack of reform in Moldova reduced the credibility of its aspirations for EU membership. However, a greater willingness in the EU for a stronger engagement with Moldova has emerged in recent years. The first signs of a change in EU policy came with the endorsement by the EU Council in December 2000 of elements of a common EU approach towards Moldova. Moldova was invited (together with Ukraine, and then Russia) to join the European Conference in 2001. This forum was set up by the EU in late 1997, initially as a forum for political dialogue between the EU and all candidate states (i.e. also those such as Turkey which had not been invited to initiate accession negotiations). The Conference was later expanded to include the EFTA members and the countries of the Western Balkans, and with the inclusion of Moldova, Russia and Ukraine, the European Conference now has 40 participating states.

Moldova was also admitted to the Stability Pact for South-Eastern Europe in 2001, as it had been requesting since 1999. This was part of a new Moldovan strategy of gaining participation in South-East European structures and processes, including requests for an SAA, as a route to being considered as a potential candidate for EU accession. However, EU acknowledgement of

Moldova's EU aspirations is unlikely to be forthcoming as a result of geographic labels, but rather as the result of a sustained commitment to domestic reform and implementation of European rules and values.

In early 2002, the Swedish and British governments proposed an EU initiative on strengthening relations with the 'new neighbours' of the EU after enlargement, identified initially as Belarus, Moldova and Ukraine. The EU decided in November 2002 to launch a New Neighbours Initiative, tasking the EU institutions to come up with proposals on how to strengthen relations between the EU and Ukraine, Belarus and Moldova. By then the EU had cooled somewhat to the idea of entering into new comprehensive commitments with the three countries, as suggested by some EU member states in early 2002 and proposed by the Polish government. This reduced enthusiasm was mainly due to developments in Ukraine, in particular the scandal over Ukraine's possible sale of military equipment to Iraq and the massive demonstrations against the president in autumn 2002. There were also concerns that the initiative might be interpreted as an implicit promise of eventual EU membership.

However, political developments in Moldova also played a role. The electoral victory of the Communist Party in Moldova in 2001 was a source of mild concern in Western Europe. Relations with the EU had hardly figured in the Communists' electoral campaign, though at the fourth Co-operation Council in May 2002 the EU extracted from the Moldovan government assurances of their pro-European orientation. The Moldovan government's handling of numerous controversial issues relating to fundamental questions such as the freedom of the media and of religion has been criticised by the European Parliament and the Council of Europe. Furthermore, certain elements of the 'Slavic choice' of the new government, such as the goal of full membership of the Eurasian Economic Community (EURASEC), are in the long run incompatible with Moldova's 'European choice' and undermine the credibility of its pursuit of integration into the EU.

On the other hand, the reorientation of Moldova's foreign policy has improved relations with Moscow, as seen with the conclusion of a Friendship Treaty in 2002. It may also have contributed to the accelerated withdrawal of Russian military forces and equipment from Transdniestria from early 2003. In practice, however, the 'Slavic choice' appears to have become as diluted as the 'European choice' of previous governments, and the Communist government is increasingly emphasising its support for European integration and the objective of full membership of the EU. In September 2002, President Voronin launched the process of establishing political and administrative structures along the lines of those called for in the Foreign Policy Guidelines of 1998 to co-ordinate efforts towards integration with the EU.

By the time the European Commission unveiled its proposals for 'wider Europe' in March 2003,[6] the initiative had been expanded to include Russia and the Mediterranean partners, none of which aspire to EU membership. The new EU Neighbourhood Policy proposed by the Commission aims for considerable integration and co-operation across all policy areas between the EU and its neighbours, falling short, however, of the prospect of EU membership.

The substance of this policy is to be developed through bilateral *Action Plans* setting out common objectives and a time-table for their achievement, to be completed in 2004. These are to be agreed with the partner countries, given political endorsement by the EU and the partners, and reviewed annually within existing arrangements. It is suggested that the Action Plans should 'supersede Common Strategies to become the Union's main policy document for relations with these countries over the medium term.' From the EU perspective, this replacement of one of the main CFSP instruments, the Common Strategy, is the most significant proposal in the Communication. This would reverse one element in the relative marginalisation of Moldova, one of the few non-EU, non-candidate states in Europe not covered by a Common Strategy.

The possibility of concluding new *Neighbourhood Agreements* is one of the key elements of the 'wider Europe' initiative. The scope of these is to be examined once existing agreements – the PCA in the case of Moldova – are implemented. It is stressed that these should not override current agreements, and would supplement existing contractual relations. A new *Neighbourhood Instrument* for economic assistance is also being developed which is likely to have an increased focus on assistance for the approximation of legislation. Furthermore, the communication also suggests extending EIB lending, so far limited to Russia, to the CIS countries.

On the economic side, the 'wider Europe' initiative is in the short to medium term unlikely to lead to important changes in EU-Moldova relations. Indeed, Moldova is singled out as a country with which the establishment of a free trade area, a key short- to medium-term goal of the new Neighbourhood Policy, is not an immediate option. Although the proposals in the field of justice and home affairs are limited, a gradual liberalisation of the regime for the movement of persons is envisaged, a key issue for Moldova considering the hundreds of thousands of Moldovans with Romanian citizenship.

The long-term aim of the new Neighbourhood Policy is to establish close relations similar to those enjoyed by the EFTA states in the European Economic Area (EEA). However, the latter enjoy considerable participation in EU institutions in various ways, while no role in EU institutions is envisaged for the countries covered by the new neighbourhood policy. On the key issue of prospective membership, the communication states that this would not be given in the medium term. On the other hand, it does not exclude this for Moldova in the long run, a position reiterated in spring 2003 by Enlargement Commissioner Verheugen, who is in charge of developing the new policy.

Transdniestria (Re-)Visited? Moldova and the ESDP

Another sign of change in EU policy towards Moldova is a willingness to consider greater involvement in the Transdniestrian conflict. A number of proposals for an EU role in peacekeeping in Moldova emerged in 2003, from the Dutch OSCE chair and from think-tanks, and has been discussed internally by the EU. In September, President Voronin invited the EU to get more involved in finding a solution to the Transdniestrian conflict. The increased EU focus on Transdniestria has been accompanied, and indeed caused, by a growing awareness of the linkages between the unresolved conflict and Moldova's difficult economic and political situation. Concerns about the impact of the Transdnistrian 'black hole' of smuggling and transnational crime on the EU itself are rising as enlargement brings the EU closer to Moldova. Such fears have intensified since the terrorist attacks in the US, and provide the context for the apparent growing willingness of the US government to engage with Russia over the Transdniestrian conflict, as seen during the Bush-Putin summit in the summer of 2002.

The more pro-Western and pro-EU foreign policy of Russia under President Putin could further facilitate a settlement of the Transdniestrian conflict. The development of the EU-Russian 'strategic partnership' has also put Moldova and Transdniestria on the agenda. Although no common position has been reached as of autumn 2003, the conflict has regularly been discussed at the biannual EU-Russia summits. And even if the 'wider Europe' proposals on any possible EU involvement in the Transdniestrian conflict are modest, envisaging at most post-settlement support in civil security with a vague promise of enhanced economic assistance for reconstruction, the EU Council of Ministers also appeared more willing, at its meeting in April 2003, to consider a more active role for the EU in finding a settlement to the conflict. The suggestion from the Greek Presidency that the EU should focus its efforts in the 'wider Europe' on one issue, and that that one issue could be the

Transdniestrian conflict, received considerable support. The EU's opportunities for playing a more prominent and effective role in Moldova is enhanced by the widening of EU competences, particularly in the field of justice and home affairs (for instance on visas and asylum) and foreign, security and defence policy (most notably the establishment of an EU peacekeeping force). The increasingly comprehensive set of policy instruments available to the EU makes it better equipped – perhaps better than any of the other international organisations and actors present in Moldova today – to play a leading role in finding a settlement to the Transdniestrian conflict.

More tangible evidence of a greater EU role started to emerge in 2003. Following an EU initiative and trilateral meetings hosted by the EU, Ukraine and Moldova reached an agreement in May 2003 on joint border control at the Ukrainian-Transdniestrian border, for years one of the most difficult issues in Moldovan-Ukrainian relations. The EU participates as an observer and adviser to the Joint Commission on a constitutional settlement established in mid-2003 following a proposal by President Voronin at the beginning of that year.

Conclusions

The EU played a very limited role in Moldova throughout the 1990s and Moldova was far down the list of priorities for the EU. The EU-Moldova relationship in the 1990s focused on establishing bilateral relations, mainly through the negotiation and signing of a Partnership and Co-operation Agreement in 1994 similar to those with other former Soviet republics. Increasing economic assistance was provided, primarily through the Tacis programme, although EU assistance was much more limited than that provided by the World Bank and IMF.

The end of the 1990s was a period of enhanced co-operation between the EU and Moldova, following the entry into force of the PCA in July 1998. But paradoxically, Moldova inadvertently became marginalised in EU proximity policy in the same period, as the Union focused on other issues and other areas, such as the enlargement process, the Western Balkans and relations with Russia. Moldova had by then made its 'European choice.' The EU, however, was unwilling to acknowledge its aspirations for eventual EU membership, and has focused on Moldova's implementation of the mainly economic provisions of the PCA. Moldova repeatedly solicited EU support for an Association Agreement in the medium term and acknowledgement of the possibility of full EU membership in the long term. These divergent objectives dominated the relationship from the end of the 1990s.

Moldova is unequivocally European, and as long as EU membership is open to all European countries, cannot in principle be denied such prospects indefinitely. Moldova is unlikely to be acknowledged as a potential EU member as a result of its efforts to be considered part of South-Eastern Europe. A key lesson of current and previous EU enlargements is that candidate status is achieved as a result of internal reforms and a commitment in practice to European rules and norms, and not geography.

But with the introduction of the euro, the accession of ten new members in 2004, and relative stability in the former Yugoslavia, the EU is increasingly focusing its attention on its eastern neighbours. In the light of Moldova's economic and social plight and the still unresolved Transdniestria conflict, and as Romania's accession to the EU, possibly in 2007, approaches, Moldova is likely to rise up the EU's policy agenda in the next few years. The complex and comprehensive nature of the Transdniestrian conflict and its effect on Moldova's political, economic and societal development requires a comprehensive response. With the growing competences of the EU in non-economic areas, it is now better equipped to play a more active role in Moldova and Transdniestria.

Greater EU involvement could be facilitated by recent geopolitical developments. The terrorist attacks on New York and Washington have increased concern about the dangers posed by 'weak' and 'failed' states, leading to enhanced co-operation among major actors such as the US, Russia and the EU. After the intra-European divisions over the war on Iraq, settling the Transdniestrian conflict may provide a common cause for such co-operation.

The author gratefully acknowledges the support of the Belgian Federal Office for Scientific, Technical and Cultural Affairs for his research on Europeanisation and conflict resolution in the wider Europe.

Notes

[1] Central and Eastern Europe includes here 10 countries, the eight new EU members in the region, Romania and Bulgaria.
[2] *Agreement between the EEC and Euratom and the USSR on Trade and Commercial and Economic Co-operation*, Official Journal L 68/1, 15 March 1990.
[3] See for instance the *EC statement to the UN General Assembly* in October 1992.
[4] *Partnership and Co-operation Agreement between the European Communities and their Member States and the Republic of Moldova*, Official Journal L 181, 24/06/1998 p. 0003 – 0048.

[5] Approximately 52 million euros of assistance to Moldova was committed through Tacis from 1996 to 2001. The World Bank's contribution of $252 million was almost five times as large in the same period, and the $310 million provided by the IMF was ten times the 30 million euros of macro-economic assistance committed by the EU.

[6] European Commission, *Wider Europe – Neighbourhood: A New Framework for Relations with our Eastern and Southern neighbours*, COM (2003) 104 final, 11 March 2003.

Moldova and the EU: a View from Chişinău

Andrei Neguţa and Alexandru Simionov

Since independence, the situation in the Republic of Moldova and its neighbouring region has changed considerably. Europe is no longer divided into spheres of influence. East-West confrontation is giving way to cooperation and partnership. The European Union has transformed the Old Continent from the scene of centuries of bloody carnage into a peaceful and prosperous space united around democratic values.

The evolving EU is becoming a world power thanks to its economic weight and human potential. Its Common Foreign and Security Policy is gradually transforming the process of European integration and giving the EU greater influence on policy at both the European and global level. Its institutions are already seeking efficient mechanisms in the field of security and defence. The EU has the capacity to affect the future of other European states. The stability, security and prosperity it affords its members make it the most important pole of attraction for these states.

The EU is attractive to all European countries. However, it is most attractive to those that need to affirm their statehood, strengthen their security and become more stable. Moldova's desire to adhere to the EU is explicable and natural given its culture and customs, which make it part of European civilisation. Although Moldova is the poorest country in Europe by some measures, its reason for acceding to the EU is similar to that of other Central and East European countries: to become, as quickly and profoundly as possible, a secure and stable state. A peaceful and prosperous Moldova would be a source of stability and security in the region and a reliable partner for its friends in both East and West. Moldova's integration into the EU with the support of other European countries would be the shortest and the most reliable way of achieving security and establishing a friendly and prosperous climate at the domestic level, in accordance with the wishes of its population. The common values and objectives shared by Moldova and the EU provide the basis for a strategic partnership. The journey travelled by the Central and East European countries over the last decade shows that European integration should not be a priority in Moldova's foreign policy alone, as conceived up to now by its government, but a priority at the state level, implemented consistently in both domestic and foreign affairs.

The adoption of such an approach is even more important now that the EU is undergoing an unprecedented enlargement to the east, and the accession of new members is impinging for the first time on Moldova's interests.

On 12 December 2002, the European Council in Copenhagen decided to admit in May 2004 ten new member states, eight of them former socialist countries in Central and Eastern Europe, and three former Soviet republics, Estonia, Latvia and Lithuania. This leaves Moldova as the only South-East European state to which the EU has not, at least for the moment, offered the prospect of accession. In the face of this discrimination, Moldova cannot seize the opportunities and advantages enjoyed by the other member states of the Stability Pact for South-Eastern Europe. A favourable attitude from the EU would persuade the countries in the region to accept Moldova as a fully-fledged member of all the regional cooperation and integration processes, and primarily the Stabilisation and Association process.

Despite all the difficulties that Moldova is confronting, its political leadership has acknowledged the importance of the South-East European route as the shortest and most natural path to achieving its strategic goal of admission to the EU.

Although the EU is undergoing reforms to retain its viability after the accession of the new member states, the Union does not intend to curtail its enlargement but on the contrary is deepening its relations with its new neighbours. Its neighbourhood policy does not exclude the long-term prospect of EU membership for them. The EC Communiqué of 11 March 2003 on 'Wider Europe' proposes a framework for the development of the EU's relations with its new neighbours, including Moldova. However, the EU cannot, for the time being, set definite deadlines for the next wave of accession or estimate Moldova's chances of joining the Union. Still, the consequences of the coming waves of eastward enlargement depend not only on the EU's policies but also on Moldova's foreign and domestic affairs and how far the political leadership in Chişinău can attract EU support.

Moldova will only be able to take up a definitive position on European integration if the East moves closer to the West, ie if Russia moves closer to the EU. Moldova favours a process which would increase the compatibility and complementarity of the structures of cooperation and integration over the whole continent, as well as between the former Soviet republics and the EU. Moldova was the first CIS country to launch the idea of harmonisation of CIS legislation and standards to those of the EU. Moldova is convinced of the need to create a common European democratic, economic and security space, based on common values and objectives, which would facilitate and accelerate the solution of the manifold political and socio-economic problems of Moldova and the region. Only then would it be possible to unify and mobilise Moldovan society around its European future. The external factor is very important to Moldova. Moldova's geo-political situation, economic characteristics and ethnic composition require the development of a harmonious relationship with both East and West. Moldova wants to be in a position to choose freely, without external pressure, the regional structures with which it wishes to cooperate and integrate.

This is the main political reason why Moldova welcomes the EC Communiqué on 'Wider Europe'. This strategic document will define the future course of the EU's relations with those European states which are not included in the current eastward enlargement but with which the Union wants to extend and deepen its relations. The document establishes a new differentiated approach towards each of the new neighbours of the enlarged EU, including the four western countries of the CIS, Moldova, Ukraine, Belarus and Russia. The extent of EU assistance to its neighbours in the east will depend above all on the progress of political and economic reform at the domestic level. This will be set out in an individual Action Plan for each of the four countries, followed by a Neighbourhood Agreement, which will not however be an Association Agreement as Moldova would wish.

The new political-juridical framework will offer the prospect of only partial integration into the EU. The programmes and agreements will create favourable conditions for integration into the EU's internal market, the European energy, transport and telecommunication links, the common environment and scientific space, etc; and for the free movement of goods, capital, labour and services. The document does not exclude, in the long run, the full integration of any of the four states into the EU, so institutional and political integration is also possible. Eventually, everything will depend on the EU's readiness to accept new members and the degree to which the new neighbours fulfil the membership criteria. Although at present the EU puts Moldova in the category of states without a clear prospect of accession, the close neighbourhood links will improve Moldova's chances of enjoying a differentiated strategic approach. Moldova needs to be able to integrate with the Union at its own pace, maintaining its relations with both East and West. Such a policy will not damage Moldova's links with its Eastern partners. On the contrary, it will bring more clarity, pragmatism and predictability to the relationship.

Moldova's political self-identification as a South-East European state was not first adopted by its leadership in response to the EC Communiqué. By late 1998 – early 1999, Moldova had already formally expressed its wish to participate in the first EU initiative towards South-Eastern Europe, the Royaumont process. Afterwards, by acceding to the Stability Pact and other regional initiatives, Moldova established its own way of getting closer to the EU. The Moldovan authorities thought, and still think, that this option will allow for its natural and progressive integration into the South-East European area which will in the future become part of the EU. Currently, Moldova needs to be treated by the EU in the same way as other members of the Stability Pact, through its inclusion in the Stabilisation and Association programme. This would offer the country a clear European perspective and benefit not only Moldova but also the EU.

Moldova's obvious European vocation and the foreign and domestic policies adopted by its present leaders point to the need for a more flexible attitude from the EU. Moldova's well-motivated and consistent requirements are backed by its increasing participation in various regional initiatives and projects. Moldova's process of European integration is deepening even as it becomes more complex. In addition to the 1993 Copenhagen (membership) criteria, the EU has also underlined the need for structural reforms in the candidate countries. Despite the existence of these criteria, the EU has the ultimate say on when a new member can be accepted.

Even if it is not part of the EU's current eastward enlargement, Moldova has already achieved some results as regards the Copenhagen criteria. As the first CIS member of the Council of Europe, Moldova has made considerable progress in creating democratic institutions and the rule of law, and enforcing respect for fundamental human rights and freedoms including the rights of national minorities. In the economy, structural reforms have been undertaken and a programme of privatisation implemented with the support of the international financial institutions. However, the Moldovan authorities will not rest on the results already achieved but continue to work to fulfil the membership criteria. Given the experience of the Central and East European countries, Moldova's leadership believes that the EU should establish a list of minimum further requirements for the launch of accession negotiations.

Such an approach would speed up political, economic and institutional reform in Moldova and its ability to meet European standards and the Copenhagen criteria. The Moldovan authorities need to prepare the country for accession to the EU and take action to eliminate the remaining obstacles.

Although the candidate countries started their European integration on a different footing, their inclusion in the current round of enlargement has brought them considerable advantages. Since Moldova is not considered by the EU a potential candidate for accession, it would be premature to weigh up the advantages and disadvantages of its eventual adherence to the EU.

Settlement of the Transdniestrian conflict has become a priority not only for Moldova but also for the region and the whole of Europe. This problem is the major obstacle to Moldova's modernisation and to the enforcement of security and stability on the forthcoming eastern border of the EU. Thus, the EU and Moldova have a common interest in seeing this issue solved as soon as possible.

As for economic reform, the prospect of EU membership would map out a clearer and more coherent path. Economic transformation would be accelerated if it had the political support and assistance of the Union's member states.

Moldova's inclusion in the EU accession process would create the most favourable conditions for the free movement of Moldovan citizens into the European space and vice versa, which would in turn stimulate economic and trade links as well as foreign investment. Moldovan citizens would have access to high-quality goods and services, while their rights and interests would be respected and defended in accordance with the highest European standards.

Current state of affairs between Moldova and the EU

Moldova's collaboration with the EU can be considered to have begun when Moldova became (as a successor state) a contracting party to the Agreement on Trade and Economic-Commercial Cooperation signed between the USSR and the EU on 18 December 1989. This agreement formed the juridical basis for Moldova-EU relations up to the conclusion of the Partnership and Cooperation Agreement (PCA). This established a new institutional and legal framework. The PCA was signed on 3 October 1995, but entered into force only on 1 July 1998, after a long process of ratification by the national parliaments of the EU member states.

The agreement is valid for ten years and sets out the general framework for EU-Moldova cooperation, covering the development of political dialogue; the promotion of long-term investment and economic links; economic, commercial, social, cultural and scientific cooperation; and support for Moldova's efforts to strengthen democracy and complete the transition to a market economy. Both sides undertook to respect the principles of democracy and the market economy, as well as international law and human rights as defined in the Helsinki Final Act and the Paris Charter.

Moldova was the third CIS state to sign a PCA with the EU, after Russia and Ukraine. This can be considered a mark of recognition of Moldova's importance to the EU.

Although the EU leadership did not comment directly on the possibility of Moldova's acceptance as an associate member in the foreseeable future, by signing the agreement and making provision for its implementation as soon as possible it gave a positive indirect political signal. In this respect, Moldova is better placed than other countries with a PCA.

It is clear that rapid and rigorous implementation of the agreement will amount to a practical rapprochement with the EU and a first step towards an accession process leading to full membership. However, it is rather difficult for Moldova to put the provisions of the PCA into practice because it is an unbalanced agreement, in that 80 per cent of the action and effort is required from Moldova's side and only 20 per cent from the EU. It does not, for example, allow for the kind of programmes the Central and East European countries benefited from under Phare.

Implementation of the PCA takes place on two levels: execution of those articles which are clearly and precisely formulated with fixed terms, and which are the routine subjects for bilateral meetings; and measures relating to general provisions such as feasibility studies for an eventual Free Trade Zone or EU credits for Moldova.

All the instruments used by the EU towards Moldova contribute to the country's political and economic reform and socio-economic development, and to steady rapprochement between the two parties. In this way, Moldova is gradually becoming a trustworthy partner in the promotion of general European values and the strengthening of peace and stability in Europe and in the region. In the five years since the agreement came into force, Moldova has achieved considerable results in all fields of cooperation with EU member states, in harmonising its legislation with that of the Community, promoting reforms and overcoming the inherent difficulties of transition, thanks to political and financial assistance from the EU. The two sides are doing their best to make maximum use of the PCA, in accordance with common priorities. One proof of this is the growing trade links, Moldovan exports being the most dynamic on the Community's market, registering a 20 per cent rise in 2002 and over 40 per cent in the first quarter of 2003.

The present political and legal framework does not however allow for a shift from cooperation and partnership to European integration. Moldova has repeatedly asked the EU to examine the possibility of offering the country the prospect of accession, though without asking for a definite date for membership. The conclusion of a Stabilisation and Association Agreement would establish a historic perspective for the country, would help to reintegrate and unite society behind the idea of EU integration, and would accelerate transition and the fulfilment of the Copenhagen criteria. The present leadership is convinced that progress on its way to Europe would strengthen Moldova as a state and increase its ability to contribute to a more peaceful, united and prosperous Europe.

Officially, the EU has not categorically refused Moldova's request for accession to the EU, but nor did the country receive any clear signals in this respect. Although the Commission insists on the need for further reform and implementation of the PCA provisions, it has avoided setting preliminary conditions for Moldova to meet in order to become an associated member of the EU.

Association: the first stage in Moldova's admission to the EU

The EU is constantly demonstrating how important it is for Moldova's future. Its commercial, technical, financial and humanitarian assistance are playing an increasing role in political, economic and social reform, and in Moldova's harmonious development. The EU has become more receptive to Moldova's wish to be included in its South-East European initiatives. The EU's active political support is contributing to the consolidation of this young state. Lately, Moldova's relations with the Union have turned into a strategic partnership. It is extremely significant that, with Moldova moving closer to the EU, the leadership in Chişinău is more aware of the need to eliminate the obstacles on Moldova's path to European integration. The political will is greater, real measures are being taken, and positive trends can be observed.

In order to join the EU, Moldova would have to pass through the association process, even if it were treated by the EU as a neighbour for a time. Before launching negotiations for an Association and Stabilisation Agreement, the EU will examine how far Moldova meets the EU's requirements. Since the country does not meet certain criteria, with foreign troops on its territory and a lack of control over the eastern part of the country, it would be premature to submit an application at the moment. Unlike other Central and South-East European countries, Moldova is moving towards European integration without having addressed any formal request to the EU, aware that the country could not possibly be given the status of associated member until it eliminates the current obstacles on its road to European integration. To achieve this, a more intensive and structured political dialogue is needed, with a higher degree of flexibility and mutual engagement.

As mentioned above, the Transdniestrian problem is a major obstacle on Moldova's road to Europe, as well as a serious threat to national and regional security. This unresolved conflict is hindering economic reform, preventing a unified customs system, and encouraging the black economy and a proliferation of trans-frontier problems (organised crime, corruption, contraband, money laundering, illegal trafficking, including human trafficking, etc.) The conflict is thwarting Moldova's socio-economic development and its fulfilment of the EU's accession criteria.

The shortest route to EU integration for Moldova is via South-Eastern Europe. Moldova is the only post-Soviet country in this region, and is profoundly attached to it. The country is facing a number of problems common to other South-East European states, and shares the same interests and objectives. Participation in the Stability Pact and other regional initiatives allows Moldova to join the other countries in the region in seeking to solve existing problems and transform this part of the continent into a zone of goodneighbourliness, peace and stability.

Since the EU has not for the time being included Moldova among the future accession states under the Stabilisation and Accession process in South-Eastern Europe, the Moldovan authorities are facing concurrently various tasks: to seek a political settlement to the Transdniestrian conflict, to be admitted as a South-East European state in all fields of activity, and to come nearer to fulfilling the Copenhagen criteria. These tasks are determined by Moldova's internal characteristics and its status as at once a former Soviet republic and a South-East European state. The fulfilment of these goals must be coordinated and synchronised with measures under the Action Plan for Moldova provided for in the EC Communiqués of 11 March 2003. The first stage might cover

EU involvement in the political settlement of the Transdniestrian conflict, to encourage the negotiating parties to reach a speedy and lasting solution in order to secure Moldova's eastern frontier (through joint measures to eliminate illegal traffic on the Transdniestrian segment of the Moldovan-Ukrainian border); linking Moldova to the Stabilisation and Association Process for South-Eastern Europe; the establishment of an asymmetric free trade regime; and EU financial assistance.

Moldova should also be included in the CARDS programme for South-Eastern Europe. Simultaneously, Moldova will do its best to conclude a Stabilisation and Association Agreement and define its strategy for accession to the EU. The transition period could end with the enactment of this Agreement and strategy.

Moldova will submit its request to become an associate member with the prior agreement of the Union, the date for this to be decided by the two parties. Unlike some South-East European countries, Moldova's particular situation makes it impossible to predict the actual terms and date for Moldova's inclusion in the stabilisation process. But the move would be important since it would spell out the tasks and obligations Moldova has to meet in order to become an associate member.

In short, in the short to medium term Moldova will act to achieve the following goals: further political, economic and institutional reform aimed at better fulfilment of the accession criteria; implementation of the PCA and Moldova-EU Action Plan; inclusion in the CARDS programme and all the Community's initiatives in South-Eastern Europe; a durable settlement to the Transdniestrian conflict with EU involvement and participation; implementation of the National Economic Growth and Poverty Reduction Strategy with regular financial assistance from the EU and other international donors and financial organisations; study of the European integration experiences of Central and South-East European countries; a major increase in commercial links between the EU and Moldova, through an asymmetric free trade zone in the region; an increase in European investment in Moldova; and full integration into South-Eastern Europe through links with all the EU's programmes and initiatives in the region.

Special attention will be paid to regional projects, which will be adjusted to fit in with European projects such as the integrated electricity market or the European Charter on Small Enterprises. Also, Moldova will do all it can to encourage tourism and cultural-humanitarian cooperation in the region; to train specialists in European integration for every ministry and department; and to maintain close and cooperative relations with the CIS on the basis of mutual interest and its adjustment to EU standards. Moldova will take part, with EU agreement, in a CIS free trade area if this is based on WTO norms. Moldova will not take part in integrationist or other activities that would damage the country's European aspirations, or adopt a foreign policy that would go against the EU's Common Foreign and Security Policy.

In order to achieve all these tasks, the following institutions have been established: a National Commission for European Integration, which elaborated the Concept and Strategy for Moldova's Association with the EU and coordinates integration and cooperation activities (with inter-ministerial groups responsible for each of the 31 chapters in accession negotiations); and a Department for European Integration in the Ministry for Foreign Affairs, which will consolidate national institutional capacity to promote the strategic priorities for Moldova's European integration and make Moldova's participation in the Stability Pact more effective. The Parliamentary Commission for European Integration is responsible for the harmonisation of national legislation with the basic law of the Union.

Conclusions

All this represent a strategic approach to furthering Moldova's European integration as well as improving the country's external image. European intergration is a historic opportunity for Moldovan society, and especially for the younger generation. The advantages of getting closer to the EU will be seen in the political, economic and welfare fields. Politically, it will mean a continuation of democratic development, and greater security both internal and external. Economically, the 'peripheral economy' syndrome will be overcome, with an increase in access to European markets, common development funds, investment and technology. Socially, we will approach European standards in health, education, social protection, the environment and IT. In order to achieve all this we shall have to strive for legal harmonisation, economic restructuring, training for a new work-force, modernisation of infrastructure, etc. But we will also increase Moldova's competitiveness and set her on an easier and faster path to the EU.

Moldova and the European Union: a Missed Opportunity?

Jan Marinus Wiersma

I have to tell even educated people in Brussels the name of the capital of the Republic of Moldova. This is an indication of the lack of knowledge about or interest in this country. Moldova is small and seems far away, and has no direct strategic value. It is seen as a backwater that was once an unimportant part of the USSR. This explains the EU's low level of engagement in Moldovan affairs. Even the fact that Moldova is the poorest country in Europe makes no difference. When people do show concern, it is about the trade in women. Checking the list of statements made by the EU over the last few years, one will find only a few relating to Moldova.

At the official level, this will of course be denied. The EU has offered Moldova a Partnership and Cooperation Agreement (PCA), effective since 1998, and other (mainly macro-financial) assistance. But while this kind of support has had very positive effects in countries which are candidates to join the EU, Moldova has not benefited. Some say the Moldovans themselves have failed to use the opportunity. There is truth in this, but there has also been a lack of will on the part of the EU to tailor its assistance to Moldova's circumstances.

Moldova is not just any post-Soviet state. It is unique in its difficulties. Its backwardness stems from its centuries-old history. When reacting to Moldova's economic and financial problems, the EU usually hides behind the IMF and the World Bank, which treat it on the basis of the famous Washington consensus. And the IMF can be very strict! But should we simply follow macro-economic indicators? Moldova was part of the USSR and before that part of the Tsarist empire, and did not distance itself very rapidly from that past after the collapse of communism. That might explain the EU's reticence. Meanwhile the Baltic states are soon to join the EU. This contrast is explained by the different transition processes. While the Baltics went for a complete rupture with the past, the Moldovans joined the CIS, remaining within Moscow's orbit. The question remains whether they did this because there was no alternative, or because they really wanted to.

The PCA provides for the establishment of a political dialogue and has provisions in a number of areas ranging from trade to the rule of law. It has a suspension clause which can be invoked in the event of human rights violations. It also provides for a structure for consultation at different levels. In general one could say that the PCAs aim to bring partners closer to the EU on the basis of shared principles such as the market economy and liberal democracy. Financial support is available for implementation of PCAs through the Tacis programme. In the case of Moldova, substantial funds have been made available, though overall the NIS have received far less than the countries participating in the corresponding CARDS programme for South-Eastern Europe: CARDS has double the funding for only a tenth of the population of the NIS states. Looking at the statistics, one could argue that in the case of Moldova the PCA and Tacis have failed completely. Though the country receives trade preferences, the balance remains in favour of the EU at a very low level. This is due to the lack of free trade arrangements, which already exist for a number of Mediterranean countries. The EU has been especially slow in opening up the agricultural market. The EU is still not satisfied with Moldova's regulatory environment. It is no coincidence that this is also the main issue in the complicated relations between Moldova and the IMF in dealing with the country's debt.

Moldova scores very low on the UN human development index: its per capita GDP is 1.8 per cent of the EU average and roughly one third of its 1989 level. Looking at these figures it is obvious that nothing has been done to alleviate the poverty of the average Moldovan. On the contrary. Many Moldovans have been forced to leave their country to find jobs elsewhere. They actually keep the country afloat by sending money back from abroad.

The EU wants to create a 'ring of friends' on its new borders. This concept is in line with the new CFSP emphasis on conflict prevention. But it takes a lot of mental creativity to see the western NIS countries as stable partners. They show the symptoms of failed states and as such could still become a security risk. Not in the traditional sense – they do not pose any military threat – but as safe havens for all kinds of illegal activities that would endanger the EU. Already there are many examples. It is no surprise that countries like Poland demand a much more forthcoming approach by the EU because they are afraid of becoming frontier states bordering an insecure zone.

One cannot accuse the European Parliament (EP) of not being active on Moldova's behalf. It has taken seriously its PCA obligation to develop intensive (parliamentary) relations with Moldova. The Joint Parliamentary Cooperation Committee (JPCC) has given the EP the opportunity both to monitor developments in the country and to discuss in depth where it is going. Moldovans often express their frustration at neglect of their problems, especially by the EU. The overriding problem is that of the country's territorial integrity. Moldovans are convinced that their state cannot develop fully without a solution to the conflict with the breakaway statelet of Transdniestria, which endangers Moldova as a whole. But there are also complaints about the lack of knowledge of the country's special economic problems. Moldova has lost part of its agricultural market in the former Soviet Union, but the EU has not offered a real alternative that would allow the country to reorient its trade to the west. So it remains dependent on old relationships to the east in this and other areas like energy.

Moldovans do not want their country to become a nowhere land. There have been many debates in the last ten years about where they should be 'embedded', to use a modern concept. The fighting that led to the establishment of the separatist regime in Transdniestria was partly motivated by the fears of Russians and Ukrainians living there that Moldova would become part of Romania, as advocated by some politicians. That never materialised. Whatever doubts one may have about Moldova, it has become an independent state and will stay that way. No-one is any longer propagating the idea of unification with Romania. Bucharest has been wise enough not to play on these feelings.

Lately there has been speculation about a reorientation towards Russia. When they won the last election, the Communists were discussing the possibility of joining the Russia-Belarus Union. Once in government they came to the conclusion that this would be an empty gesture. The main political forces in Moldova still distrust one another on the issue of political orientation, but at the same time they have found some common ground in concluding that their country's destiny lies in Europe, and more specifically in the EU. The government has set up a number of institutions to deal with the EU and intends to bring all its laws into line with EU legislation. In July 2003 the communist President Voronin stated that his country could become an associate member of the EU in 2007, when Romania hopes to join. How serious Moldova's EU ambitions are, only time will show. But the EU must respond. It remains to be seen how Moldovans would really react should EU membership become a real option. Many would welcome it because of Moldova's old links with Romania, but it would make others nervous. Some would argue that by voting communist the majority of Moldovan voters had shown they were against reform. And being against reform would destroy any EU aspirations, given the need to implement the Copenhagen criteria (democracy, market economy, implementation of EU rules). This argument has some validity. But the outcome of the last election was also a vote against an inefficient and corrupt government.

One step towards 'embedding' was the inclusion of Moldova in the Stability Pact for South-East Europe set up after the recent violent conflicts in the Balkans. This gives the country a regional anchor. It offers a chance to learn and take part in activities in wide-ranging areas such as regional trade, security, and justice and home affairs. It was a priority for the JPCC to make this possible. At a time when the President of the Commission, Romano Prodi, was offering something to everyone in a speech about EU enlargement just before the Helsinki Summit, he forgot to mention Moldova. The JPCC protested immediately, claiming a place for Moldova in EU-supported European structures. Though it took some time to convince the member states, this ambition was fulfilled. Of course the Moldovans hope that active participation in regional cooperation will lead to the opening of negotiations for a Stabilisation and Association Agreement with the EU along the lines of those designed to bring the countries of former Yugoslavia into the European integration process.

In 2003 Moldova held the chairmanship of the Council of Europe. In Chişinău this was seen as an opportunity to show Moldova's democratic credentials. It did a decent job given its limits as a small and poor country. Wanting the job also meant accepting the interference of the European community in national affairs. It was the Council of Europe that had to act when, after the last election, government and opposition became engaged in a too-fierce battle including big demonstrations. The mediation effort supported by the EU was successful, but pressure is still needed to persuade the opposition to accept a legally-elected government and the government not to abuse its position. Politicians must be able to do their work without being harassed, while the media must be an expression of pluralism. The few resolutions on Moldova adopted recently by the EP have dealt with these issues, and they were also the spur for a special mission to the country in 2002. The JPCC is often the place where both opposition and government parties can discuss their differences without the usual verbal violence. This is a useful adjunct to the Council of Europe's mediation efforts.

The Transdniestria issue is not the direct responsibility of the EU but of the troika: the OSCE, Russia and Ukraine. But since it also affects relations between the EU and Moldova, it cannot be ignored. Though the case of Cyprus shows otherwise, most Moldovans believe that EU membership will remain a dream unless a permanent solution is found to this conflict. Furthermore, the existence of a semi-criminal, uncontrolled mini-state in the midst of Europe threatens the interests of the EU in a number of areas like illegal immigration. It is hard to explain why the EU can be so active in the former Yugoslavia while at the same time neglecting a security problem a little further to the south-east. Only slowly is the EU showing signs of accepting any responsibility. The attempt to put pressure on the Tiraspol regime to cooperate in finding a compromise that respects the territorial integrity of Moldova by installing a limited visa ban was an important first step. One nervous reaction from the authorities in June 2003 was to ban an EP delegation from entering Transdniestria. There is no place in Europe for Smirnov, the leader of Transdniestria, and his like. But he has survived so far because two of the responsible troika members have not been prepared to put sufficient pressure on him. Not until 2003 did the Russians start withdrawing their troops and munitions from the area in line with earlier OSCE decisions. And only after many international demands did Ukraine agree to strengthen the customs regime along the Transdniestrian border. But the measures seem to be having an effect. Both sides have now agreed to negotiate a new constitution for a Moldova that will include Tiraspol.

However, a huge gap has to be bridged on this issue. Chişinău only wants to discuss a kind of political autonomy for Transdniestria, while Smirnov wants to follow the Serbia-Montenegro model. The EU has agreed to be an observer at the constitutional talks. It has also indicated a willingess to play an active part in the peace process by taking over peace-keeping activities from Russia. The EP has welcomed this initiativce, which could be exercised under the auspices of the European Security and Defence Policy. But working out a formula for an EU military presence will not be easy. The Russians might not be keen to leave this role entirely to the EU, while the Americans seem to favour a stronger role for NATO.

The EU should put its weight behind the OSCE proposals for the federalisation of Moldova. I do not agree with those who consider it is possible for Moldova to move forward without Transdniestria. We need to get a grip on that part of Europe, and cutting it loose from Moldova would create a lasting sore. But I would be against a federalisation which united two systems in one state, one democratic and transparent and the other autocratic and corrupt. The best way to avoid this would be to put the federalisation process in the context of a strengthening of democracy all over the country, including Tiraspol.

In March 2003 the European Commission published a communication entitled 'Wider Europe', which deals with relations with the new neighbours of the enlarged EU. Though the element of differentiation is underlined, the same document deals with both the southern and eastern border regions. This creates the impression that, say, Moldova and Morocco are in the same basket. The Commission refuses to address the question of whether any of the countries can become member of the EU, though it does quote Article 49 of the EU Treaty, which says that any European country can apply for membership. 'Wider Europe' offers the new neighbours participation in all EU policies but not in its institutions. A 'proximity instrument' will be developed covering the actual policies to be implemented and the financial envelope attached. The Commission promises to consider the establishment of Neighbourhood Agreements to replace the PCAs after their full implementation. The reaction to all this in Moldova has been one of disappointment. In recent years Moldova has said explicitly that it wants to become a member of the EU, while recognising that this will not be an easy goal to reach. I have the impression that Moldova would prefer a more individual approach based on an Action Plan leading to a Stabilisation and Association Agreement. The EP has not yet responded in detail to the Communication but its earlier statements were more positive about the ambitions of countries like Moldova. The EP recognises Moldova's right to become member of the EU. It has also acknowledged that, in the case of Moldova and Ukraine, some form of association should not be excluded. This would mean that these states could move from partnership to association, leaving the door open for the final option of EU membership. Basically, the EP does not exclude the further enlargement of the EU to include Moldova.

The Commission is confident that what it is offering will have the same beneficial effects as the prospect of EU membership. I am less optimistic. Given the need for drastic reform and the need to push local elites forward, more leverage is necessary. Asking countries to implement the Copenhagen criteria without being clear about the reward will not work.

Nevertheless, the new policies proposed by the Commission and likely to be supported by the Council would not block future alternatives. On the contrary, they could enable Moldova to prove that it can participate fully in all EU policies, especially in the area of the four freedoms (persons, goods, services, capital). Theoretically Moldova could reach the same position as countries like Norway. That would require a good deal of reform, but that would be a good thing in itself. But it would also need a lot of rethinking on the EU side. The European Conference is not a good political platform. A different and more effective forum is needed to enable Moldova to really align itself with the EU's Common Foreign and Security Policy. A free trade area should be part of the deal, but also a concrete action plan in the field of justice and home affairs. The financial instrument should be different from Tacis and look more like Phare, with more opportunities for investment and a strategy for poverty reduction. In the past the EU has used the ECHO programme for much-needed support in the area of health. ECHO's goals changed, so Moldova was phased out. But the situation in Moldova is still so bad that the EU might consider developing a post-emergency instrument for European countries with specific poverty problems.

Moldova should demand a much clearer road-map with benchmarks and deadlines. The Commission has also promised to create a new Neighbour Instrument intended to promote cross-border and regional cooperation. Maybe that could be used also to support an 'Eastern Dimension' based on the model of the Northern Dimension, involving a comprehensive approach to regional cooperation.

Let me end with a plea that has been part of almost every JPCC statement: that the EU finally open its own embassy in Chişinău. Not having official representation in a neighbouring country would be considered offensive in diplomatic circles. The EU should show more respect for the people of Moldova.

River Prut: a Softer Iron Curtain?

Oxana Guţu and Valeriu Gheorghiu

Once EU enlargement to include Romania is declared irreversible, Moldova will become a prospective neighbour of the EU: hopefully, in 2007.

Luckily, Moldova has a number of years to show its new neighbour that stability and security are not alien concepts. The political rationale for the current enlargement can be summarised as follows: 'Enlargement will create stability, prosperity and security over the entire European Continent.' But Moldovans fear that enlargement will at the same time lead to the creation of a new (Schengen) Iron Curtain. Moldova felt the first breath of EU enlargement in 2001, when Romania introduced a passport regime for Moldovan citizens crossing the Romanian border. All the Central and East European countries which are to join the EU in 2004 introduced visas for Moldovan citizens in the period 2000–2002. The passport regime imposed by Romania and the visa regimes imposed by Central European countries have dramatically curtailed the cross-border trade which was previously an important source of income for many Moldovans.

Relations between Moldova and the external world have been and are determined by the history of the region and, particularly, by the country's geographical position and the borders of the state. Moldova's borders with its two neighbours, Romania and Ukraine, run for 1905 kilometres. That with Romania (683 km) was part of the former USSR-Romania frontier. That with Ukraine coincides with the former administrative border between two Soviet republics, the Moldavian and Ukrainian Soviet Socialist Republics. It runs for 1,222 km, but 443 km of this is under the control of the local separatist authorities in Transdniestria.'[1]

Borders

The border with Ukraine is in practice transparent and porous. Since Ukraine's borders with Russia and Belarus are also transparent, this means that people and goods from the CIS can cross Moldova's eastern border virtually unchecked. This permits widespread smuggling and the illegal traffic of arms, drugs and people. In the territory controlled by the separatists, smuggling of cigarettes, alcoholic beverages and oil products takes place on a vast scale. Arms trafficking is not uncommon, and increases every time a conflict emerges within the CIS or elsewhere in Europe. This encompasses both minor light arms and complete rocket-launching installations. There is also significant trafficking of women from Russia, Belarus and Ukraine via Moldova, Romania and Cyprus to Western Europe through this part of the border.

The western border with Romania along the River Prut has a special significance for the Moldovan people: the first customs post was at Ungheni, created immediately after the annexation of Bessarabia by Tsarist Russia in 1812. The Ungheni customs post was the crossing-point between Romania and Moldova after the Second World War. The Moldovan-Romanian border is better organised and controlled than the Moldovan-Ukrainian border. In fact, the Moldovan-Romanian border (like that between Ukraine and Poland) is the first CIS barrier to illegal migrants from the Asia-Pacific region into Europe. Nevertheless, there are still frequent cases of smuggling and illegal border-crossing.

The borders of Moldova can be crossed in both eastern and western directions by train and by car. There are three international airports, but transit through them is much less important.

Migration

This relative freedom of movement is particularly significant at a time of great change. Whereas in the early nineties Western Europe was unknown to most Moldovans, nowadays there is no family in Moldova which does not have relatives, friends or acquaintances who have travelled abroad. Migration has taken place in three main stages: 1990–1993, 1994–1998 and 1998 onwards.

The first wave of travellers abroad were determined emigrants. Most of them knew where they wanted to go and were determined never to come back. They emigrated (for permanent residence, repatriation, to join their families, etc) to Israel, West Germany, the USA and Canada. Only a few Moldovans, the curious ones, travelled as tourists or to visit friends and relatives.

The second wave of migration involved adventure-seekers and businessmen. People started leaving for other countries to seek jobs. Although at first most Moldovans focused on Russia, more and more people turned to the West.

The third wave, that of the desperate and disillusioned, mostly resulted from the critical condition of the national economy, in part due to the economic crisis of August 1998 in Russia. During this period, people working in Russia started returning to Moldova, where information about job opportunities in the West became widely spread.

It is not possible to determine the exact number of those staying abroad illegally. Official statistics, published for the first time by the Department of Statistics and Sociology at the beginning of 2003, indicated that no more than 234,000 Moldovans were working abroad both legally and illegally. According to State Migration Service data, however, about 500,000 citizens of Moldova were permanently resident abroad (ie were working there). Remittances from abroad are huge. Official statistics covering money transferred through banks or money transfer systems indicate that the figure rose from $88.3 million in 1999 to $275 million in 2002. The illegal cash flow is difficult to estimate; cash is simply hidden and not declared at customs by bus drivers operating shuttle services between Moldova and Italy/Greece/Spain. The National Bank has estimated that the illegal cash flow in 2002 was at least $150 million, giving a total cash flow of $425 million in 2002. By way of comparison, state budget revenue for 2003 is put at $288 million.

Because of its geographical location and current economic situation, Moldova has emerged as a major country of origin for trafficking in women and children. However, there are no official figures to assess the dimensions of the problem. A rough picture can be gained from the efforts of the International Organisation for Migration, which in 2002 assisted almost 1000 Moldovan women victims of trafficking.

Despite the extremely tight visa regimes imposed by European countries, hundreds of ways of reaching the EU have been devised, including participation in international seminars, sports competitions, studying abroad, invitations from relatives, colleagues, etc. The resourcefulness of those wanting to go abroad is unlimited, and it will probably remain so until the economic situation in Moldova becomes at least tolerable.

Another 'escape strategy' leads thousands of Moldovan citizens to apply for Romanian citizenship. Under Romanian law, anyone with a parent or grandparent who lived in what was then Romanian territory in 1918–41 is entitled to (re-)apply for Romanian citizenship. (In an attempt to avoid fraud, applicants have been required since summer 2003 to apply in Romanian and in person.) A Romanian passport has become even more attractive since Romanian citizens have enjoyed visa-free entry to the Schengen area. The Romanian government's EU negotiating position is that Moldovan citizens wishing to travel to Romania will need a visa to cross the border from the date of Romania's accession to the EU. Hence the rush to apply for passports and the queues outside the Romanian Embassy in Chişinău. The Moldovan authorities have no data on the number of citizens who hold passports from other states, whether Romanian, Russian or Israeli. Romania and Russia have refused to supply such information. Media estimates range from thousands to several hundred thousand holders of other countries' passports.

Visas

In this situation Europe has become more and more concerned about the flood of cheap labour, which has brought with it numerous problems, often of a criminal nature. Since 1999, West European embassies have reviewed their visa regimes and introduced certain restrictions which have led to the disappearance of many travel agencies, while Central and East European countries have also introduced visa regimes. However, the number of Moldovans eager to work abroad has continued to rise, and phantom (unlicensed) companies have sprung up which focus on sending Moldovan citizens abroad. Visa costs have increased tremendously, reaching $1500–3000, although the official price for a three-month Schengen visa is 25 euros.

To understand how this has happened, it is necessary to bear in mind that of the 76 embassies accredited to Moldova, only 11 are located in Chişinău, the others being in Moscow, Kiev, Bucharest, Budapest, Sofia, Athens, Ankara and Prague. Three EU member states have embassies in Chişinău – Germany, France and Britain – but only the German embassy issues Schengen visas. Of the other nine embassies only three (Bulgaria, Poland and Hungary) issue national visas.

This means that Moldovans often have to go through a tortuous process to obtain a visa. For instance, to get a visa for Slovenia they must first queue at the Hungarian Embassy (a transit country with a significant flow of travellers) and pay about $60, and then, having obtained a Hungarian visa, travel to Budapest to request a visa for Slovenia. Thus, for a visa that costs $40, they will have to pay travel expenses amounting to about $550, or almost 14 times the cost of the actual visa. If Moldovan citizens want to obtain a visa for

Canada, they have to go to the nearest Canadian diplomatic post, which is in Bucharest. For Albania, they have to travel to Moscow. For Mexico, to the Greek consulate in Odessa (Ukraine) to get a visa for Greece, and then to Athens to apply for a Mexican visa. In these circumstances it is no wonder that Moldovans do not want to do all the travelling themselves and are ready to pay to avoid the hassle.

In some cases visa procedures are not only expensive but offensive. For example, Moldovan citizens applying for a tourist visa, a business visa or a visa based on an invitation from the Czech Republic must pay a $400 deposit, in cash, when they get their visa, as well as submitting a return travel ticket or green card for the car. The Italian Embassy in Bucharest requires Moldovans (male or female) to submit a special certificate confirming that the applicant has not changed his/her name in the past, which certificate must be translated into Italian and witnessed by a notary, by the Ministry of Justice, and by the Ministry of Foreign Affairs of Moldova. This is stressful, costly, and offensive.

In this way a visa, which should be available to ordinary people, becomes a privilege for the rich, who can bribe consular officers.

Experience so far does not suggest that visas are a very effective instrument for curbing either criminal activity or illegal immigration. People who have to pay $2000 to go to Europe will do everything they can to remain abroad and earn some money. Visa restrictions will not stop the penetration of organised crime, but may prove an insurmountable obstacle for thousands of ordinary citizens. The policy of zero migration, tight borders and a vast array of enforcement methods cannot eliminate the immigration push towards the wealthy parts of Europe. The growing migration pressure from the east has multiple and complex causes, the most significant being the massive unemployment and poverty in Eastern Europe.

What is to be done?

The EU seems to regard visa requirements for citizens of non-member countries and rigorous control of migration as an adequate response to these fears and risks. The negative consequences of restricting travel across the borders of the wider Europe are obvious. New EU members are compelled to make their borders impenetrable, which will inevitably have a negative effect on relations with their neighbours to the east; the liberalisation of movement of people and goods will be suspended for several years. At the same time, the benefits expected from lifting border controls between old and new members, and the freedom to take up employment, will be delayed for several years after accession.

Taken together, these requirements will not only have a negative impact on future EU neighbouring countries, but also make new members feel like second-class citizens.

The establishment of new EU borders in the east of the continent and a new dividing line in Europe will generate frustration among the non-candidate states. The peoples left out of the EU will feel isolated from the rest of the continent, and in the case of Moldova also suffer a new separation from their natural Latin and European cultural space.

The question is: how can this situation be avoided? What should be done with countries not involved in enlargement? Or maybe another question: what should the countries not involved in enlargement do in order to benefit from the EU's stability, prosperity and security while at the same time ensuring the security of the EU's border?

It seems that a solution for Moldova is on the way to being found. In 2002 Moldova was included in the British Initiative to grant 'New Neighbour' status to Ukraine, Moldova and Belarus, and in the Polish Initiative known as the 'Eastern Dimension',[3] which also covers the other two countries plus Russia. Alongside a regional approach these documents reflect an initial attempt to treat each country individually, including Moldova. However, the European Commission's 2003 Communication 'Wider Europe – Neighbourhood: a New Framework for Relations with our Eastern and Southern Neighbours', which sets down EU policy for the next decade, seems to take EU external policy back ten years, putting an end both to debate in the EU and to Moldova's hopes of joining the EU in the foreseeable future.[4]

At first glance, Moldova's relations with the EU should make marked progress in the 'Wider Europe' context, since the Communication offers the possibility of collaboration with the EU in areas ranging from market regulation and liberalisation to legal migration and transit of persons; from security to conflict management; from the promotion of human rights to the integration of transport, energy and telecommunications networks; and much more. The problem is that these possibilities are offered not only to Moldova but also to Russia, Ukraine and Belarus, adopting a 'one size fits all' approach. Without being opposed to this, we have to note that it is hard to believe that, for example, free movement will be permitted in the near future to over 210 million people from the western CIS, even if not all of them want to travel concurrently.

Moreover, the Commission's Communication does not take into consideration, nor does it even mention, the fact that Moldova is a member of the Stability Pact for South-Eastern Europe. Thus, the EU has in practice ignored all the efforts made by Moldovan diplomats since 1999, again placing Moldova only in the CIS context. This could be viewed by Moldovans as exclusion from the new Europe, which could have a profound effect on the country's political identity, foreign and security policies, and progress in democratic and economic reform.

Viewed from the other side, the demographic situation (a dramatically ageing society and birth-rate below replacement level) in the countries of both Western and Central Europe, and its implications for employment, pensions and health care, demonstrate clearly that Europe needs immigrants.

For this reason, entry to the EU for hundreds of seasonal workers should be legalised. The existing policy involves immense hypocrisy. Member states pretend to abide by stringent and restrictive laws, while tolerating the existence of extensive areas of the shadow economy based on immigrant labour, from which they undoubtedly benefit. Immigration, insurance and tax regulations need to be reconsidered, as they provide the soil in which pathologies grow. At the same time, the EU is moving towards a common internal immigration policy. This is a thorny issue, as immigration touches some of voters' most sensitive nerves. However, bearing in mind the ultimate goal, 'a secure and prosperous Europe', and the demographic problems faced by the EU, it is time to press ahead with long-planned measures such as removal of the veto on migration issues, which makes progress agonisingly slow; improved statistics on migration at the country and Community level; incorporation of more and more immigration issues in relations with countries of origin, to promote 'burden-sharing'; exploration of all options while drafting and debating the future Action Plans with New Neighbours in order to ensure full and reliable cooperation in the field of justice and home affairs; extension of EU programmes in the field of research, education and culture to New Neighbours, including visits programmes; granting resident permits to victims of trafficking, which would help in the uncovering, investigation and punishment of smuggling schemes and criminal groups; establishment of readmission mechanisms, in line with the Commission's Green Paper; and approval of the 'family reunification' directive in order to make the EU more attractive for the specialists needed in EU member states.

For its part, the Moldovan government, confronted by huge external debts and significant budgetary shortages but aware of what is to come, is attempting to solve some problems and avoid new ones by, among other things, planning to introduce an automated control and verification system for people crossing frontiers. Readmission agreements are already in force with Poland, Hungary and Romania, have been signed with Ukraine, Lithuania and Italy, and are envisaged with the Czech Republic, Belgium, Netherlands, Luxembourg, Switzerland, Albania, Croatia, Slovakia, Portugal, Germany, France, Latvia, Spain and Austria. As a beneficiary of the Stability Pact for South-Eastern Europe, Moldova signed the Palermo Declaration on Trafficking in South-Eastern Europe; a national action plan to deal with human trafficking is being implemented as funding allows. Moldova needs to exploit further Stability Pact initiatives.

Conclusions

Moldovans, like other Europeans, perceive the EU as a beacon of stability, prosperity and security in Europe. However these benefits can be obtained only through a joint effort by the EU and non-member countries, so that geographical borders reunite rather than separate people, and new relationships can be built on the European continent as outlined in the 'New Neighbourhood' Communication. Success will depend very much on the perspective offered to Moldova and other non-candidate countries: to be neighbour-outsiders, or, albeit in the far distant future, members of the EU.

Notes

[1] O. Graur. The Border Guard Troops' role in controlling and ensuring the functioning of the State Border. '*New Borders in South Eastern Europe. The Republic of Moldova, Ukraine, Romania*', Chişinău, 'Stiinta', 2002, pp.121–140.

[2] V. Gheorghiu. New Schengen Borders and their impact on the Relationships of the Republic of Moldova and Romania. '*New Borders in South Eastern Europe. The Republic of Moldova, Ukraine, Romania*', Chişinău, 'Stiinta', 2002, pp.88–100.

[3] Wlodzimierz Cimoszewicz. The Eastern Dimension of the European Union. The Polish View. *Speech at the Conference 'The EU Enlargement and Neighbourhood Policy'*, Warsaw, February 20, 2003.

[4] 'Wider Europe – Neighbourhood: A New Framework for Relations with our Eastern and Southern Neighbours'. *Communication from the Commission to the Council and the European Parliament*, Brussels, 11.03.2003, COM (2003) 104 final.

Has EU Development Assistance Helped?

Vic Heard

Moldova has received more aid in proportion to its population than almost any other country of the former Soviet Union, and the EU through the European Commission (EC) has provided its share. After an initial 1 million euros in 1991 the EC's Tacis programme has provided some 10–12 million euros annually in technical assistance. Over the same period, the EC gave 87 million euros in balance of payments support, 16 million from the Food Security Programme plus humanitarian relief and some small, specialised EC programmes. The World Bank, IMF and EBRD have of course provided more, but the EC is the second largest technical assistance donor after the USA. Germany, the UK and Sweden have significant programmes, and other EU member states, Canada, Japan, Turkey and the UN also provide assistance. Nevertheless, more than 10 years after independence, Moldova, once one of the richer parts of the USSR, is now the poorest country in Europe.

The Moldovan government's openness to change and reform attracted donors from the first days of independence. As the Economist commented in 1994, it was 'a country of sound reforms and a suitable laboratory for experiment'. Not all experiments worked. Tacis, perhaps, experimented less than some, focussing mainly on three areas: agriculture, private sector development, and administrative and social reform.

Agriculture

Moldova is primarily an agricultural country, and reforming agriculture was a sound choice. Some Tacis projects were designed to improve the quality of farm produce or agricultural information, but the flagship programme was land reform. When, uniquely among ex-Soviet countries, the Moldovan government embraced land reform, Tacis responded in 1994 with a pilot project to design property survey programmes and plan collective farm privatisation while preserving irrigation systems, veterinary and other services, milk collection systems and the rest of the rural economy. The 1996 Programme was to implement privatisation, provide agricultural advice, and strengthen the Agricultural Restructuring Agency (ARA) to take privatisation forward. (The ministry of agriculture, the obvious partner, was unenthusiastic). However, the 1994 project duplicated the work of USAID and, to some extent, the World Bank. USAID had produced a privatisation plan which divided state farms among farm workers, and the World Bank had a loan ready to support it. There were no implementation funds ready for the Tacis plan, so the Moldovan government chose the US version.

In 2000, an evaluation found that the Tacis land-reform work had had no impact and that ARA was ineffective. Ten years on, it is hard to see how communications between donors could have been so bad. It is also possible to wonder whether rural poverty would be so deep had the Tacis plan been adopted. Instead of privatising the farms, the USAID plan gave farm workers 1.6 hectares each consisting of separate pieces of arable land, vineyard, pasture, etc. Some workable co-operatives were formed with 50 or more landlords. However, when 50 people shared a tractor or an irrigation ditch these mainly fell into disrepair. Reportedly, the way farm animals were shared was by eating them. In 2003, most Moldovans, who once helped feed the USSR, got less than the required daily calorie intake. The Russian financial crisis was partly to blame, but much must be put down to land reform and poor donor co-ordination.

Private sector development

Many donors expected to reap political and commercial rewards from aid to the former Soviet Union. The first private sector projects in Moldova under Tacis were, therefore, in defence conversion, privatisation and banking, paving the way for EU investors. Apart from Agroindbank, banking was soon left to USAID. Priority went to defence conversion as, with the loss of defence markets, high-tech Moldovan enterprises would soon lose their cutting edge. An early project converted six enterprises to civil production, with limited success. A real success story came later with a company which previously designed missile control systems. This now has joint venture agreements with two major Western partners and expanding exports. Its engine-tester can diagnose faults in virtually any car, rivalling Western designs, and sensors previously used for monitoring rocket exhausts now control high-temperature ovens. No one could have predicted this success at the outset. Tacis should take credit but, unfortunately, the conjunction of marketable technology, a dynamic executive and an intact work-force was pure luck.

This company had previously been restructured by ARIA, the Association for the Restructuring of Enterprises set up by the World Bank with Tacis and other donors. ARIA is probably one of the most successful enterprise projects in the whole former Soviet Union. It brings substantial numbers of Moldovan enterprises into profit, boosts exports, and wins restructuring contracts abroad against international competition. ARIA piloted innovative techniques in restructuring by transforming the huge Alpha factory on the outskirts of Chişinău, bankrupt since switching from defence production to televisions, into a profitable combination of business park and incubator – a model now being replicated in Bălţi. However, ARIA was *not* an experiment. The Bank followed the original Marshall Plan model, which set up the enormously successful German equivalent to ARIA, GTZ.

In small and medium enterprise (SME) development, the Tacis Business Communication Centre continues to help small businesses. However, the far greater effort on privatisation has had virtually no impact. Policy advice given to the privatisation department was sound, but the department was ineffective and government commitment unpredictable. The main problems arose over preparing companies for privatisation. Privatisation contractors are paid by donors, but take their profits from success fees negotiated independently with governments. This can produce a conflict between donor demands for large numbers of privatisations and the contractor's interests being best served by privatising only a few major enterprises. Tacis contractors in Moldova handled this by privatising a few enterprises themselves and a larger number of small ones through local sub-contracts. However, by 2000, opinion in Brussels was that Moldova would be better off using market forces to privatise through success fees alone. It was noted that the contractor stayed on after the project and privatised more in the subsequent months than in the years before. With hindsight it can be seen that initial ambitions to privatise state wineries and tobacco companies were unrealistic. Few were capable of attracting investors. Most were Soviet monsters like *Moldcarton*, the Moldovan manufacturer that once supplied cardboard cartons from the Caucasus to the Arctic. The costs of transporting waste paper to make the boxes from an even larger area put paid to any prospect of profit or chance of investment.

MEPO, the Moldova Export Promotion Organisation, which was supported by Tacis from 2000, made a promising start and after only a year reported substantial export contracts following outward trade missions. The project-trained Moldovan trade advisers now have a constant stream of visitors. MEPO provides advice on both Western and traditional Eastern markets. It achieves some cost recovery and may have a bright future if the government underwrites its shortfall, as is done in the West.

Administrative and social reform

A Partnership and Cooperation Agreement (PCA) underpins EU relations with Moldova and there is a long-running, successful PCA support project, which includes bringing Moldovan legislation and standards into line with EU norms. Tacis has also focused on three other issues: higher education in economics and business, social security, and public administration. However, work in higher education appears to have had little impact, and two other donors launched MBAs at about the same time as Tacis – again, once more reflecting poor co-ordination. Work on social security also suffered because of differences of approach among donors. Sadly, work consolidating local government into 7 counties (*judets*) had barely started when the new communist government decided to reinstate the earlier system of over 40 *oblasts*.

Other initiatives

Tacis includes small projects called 'facilities', which may have had as much impact as the main projects. This is especially true of policy advice programmes, which have allowed Tacis to help the government explore issues and have generated some of the best Tacis projects, including MEPO. For several years Tacis provided an adviser to the president, prime minister and foreign minister. It can also take credit for advice leading to WTO membership. Here also, though, coordination failed when Tacis and another donor produced rival draft civil codes. Other 'facilities' helped with customs, statistics, border management, university links (Tempus) and management training. The Food Security Programme's 15 million euros in foreign exchange released the equivalent amount in leu (national currency) from the national budget to support vulnerable groups (pensioners and children), and the associated system of financial control helped the government improve its financial management.

Some major projects fell outside the main policy areas. One, a confidence-building gesture, involved repairing a shell-damaged bridge leading to Transdniestria. Others were linked with railway privatisation, the Giurgeleşti oil terminal, statistics, border crossings, environmental studies on the River Prut, and securing the eastern borders.

Current programmes

For the 2001–2004 Programme, the Moldovan government selected three focus areas from a list of six in the new Tacis instrument. They chose Private Sector and Economic Development, Administrative and Legal Reform, and the Social Consequences of Transition. These maintained the earlier focus, but an attempt was made to use them as cross-cutting themes to produce an integrated programme rather than unconnected projects. For the first time the programme had poverty-reduction goals. It broke new ground in other ways: other donors were allowed to contribute to project design, and local expertise was used to a greater extent in implementation.

Social Consequences of Transition. A child poverty committee including the Moldovan government and all donors (except USAID) was allowed a major role in designing the Tacis social development project. The project helps the most vulnerable children while being so well integrated with other donors' programmes that it cements together much of their work. An additional project on disease prevention and health improvement deals with food hygiene and sanitary standards in schools and public institutions.

Private Sector and Economic Development. This large project combined SME and restructuring work using the substantial numbers of Moldovan business management consultants trained on other projects. Tacis had earlier piloted the use of minimal EU contractor inputs and reliance on local consultants in Armenia, but in Moldova this was done on a larger scale. The project was linked with another, financed by the cross-border programme, promoting trade across the Prut. It also had a pilot component in Găgăuzia, which is avoided by other donors except for Turkey despite being the poorest region. There was also to have been an SME poverty-reduction project for Găgăuzia, but Brussels switched the resources to border management with a view to strengthening the enlarged EU frontier.

Institutional, Legal and Administrative Reform. These projects trained the civil and commercial judiciary and strengthened the Standards Institute. Both supported private sector as well as legal reform objectives. However, the border management project referred to above has stalled as it envisaged Moldovan customs units operating in Ukraine to police the Transdniestrian frontier. The reluctance of the Ukrainian government to permit this might have been foreseen.

Table 1: EC Assistance to Moldova 1991 – 2002 (Commitments in million euros)

Programme	1991	1992	1993	1994	1995	1996	1997	1998	1999	2000	2001	2002	2003	Totals
Tacis Action Programme	1.0	9.0		10.0	9.0	13.0		14.7		15.3	14.8		30.0	116.8
Small Projects Programme						4.9		4.8		5.7	5.2			20.6
Cross border Cooperation Programme						2.0	2.7	1.3	0.7	4.0	3.0	3.7		17.4
Tacis total	1.0	9.0	0.0	10.0	9.0	19.9	2.7	20.8	0.7	25.0	23.0	3.7	30.0	154.8
Macro-Financial Assistance (Grants)		27.0		25.0	20.0	15.0							10.0	97.0
Food Security Programme										5.5		10.5	10.0	26.0
ECHO (Humanitarian Assistance)								4.0		0.81		0.8		5.61
Total	1.0	36.0	0.0	35.0	29.0	34.9	2.7	24.8	0.7	31.31	23.0	15.0	50.0	283.41

For comparison, over the period 1993 to 2001 USAID provided US$267 million to Moldova

Transdniestria has been an awkward issue for Tacis in other ways too. The EU member states all regard it as an illegal, breakaway part of Moldova, and neither they nor Tacis give it any assistance. The Moldovan authorities take the same line, doggedly insisting that it is an integral part of their country. However, while the member states might agree a 'nothing for Transdniestria' clause, the Moldovans would not accept the implication that it was not part of their country. Tacis instruments are, therefore, silent on the issue, and the programmes theoretically cover Transdniestria as part of Moldova. In practice, no assistance provided to the Moldovan government could reach Transdniestria. The exceptions have been MEPO, which has handled export enquiries from Transdniestria, and the Gula Bîcului bridge across the Dniester itself, which Tacis repaired as a confidence-building measure in the peace process. Both Chişinău and Tiraspol allowed their officials to accompany an EC mission to the middle of the bridge, then ornamented with a Russian tank, to examine two large shell-holes, and later collaborated over the repair and the eventual re-opening ceremony. Neither side would say who had done the damage.

The Tacis programme approved in July 2003 retained the same three priority areas as the 2001 programme. It has continued some of the earlier initiatives including assistance to MEPO and work on SMEs, the PCA and the child poverty projects. It will also assist Moldova's WTO membership. The total package will be 50 million euros: half from the Tacis National Programme, 10 million euros each from the Food Security and Macroeconomic Programmes and 5 million from the Regional Programme.

Conclusions

An EC evaluation in 2000 concluded that Tacis in Moldova had been generally positive, timely and appropriate. But what was the impact? Privatisation programmes achieved little, the land reform project was ignored, and much work in education and agriculture has had little result. The border management project in the 2001 programme shows that Tacis can still back the wrong horse if the aim is Moldova's development. In the past Tacis ignored Moldovan expertise and used exclusively EU consultants. Recent work with the private sector may signal a change. Some of the best projects, including ARIA, MEPO and the recent Social Development Project, have resulted from collaboration with other donors. This is no problem with the Food Security Programme, but Tacis procedures are so long-winded that partners are unwilling to wait. The pressure for projects 'with an EC flag' is unhelpful, and the US and the World

Bank are still sometimes seen as competitors, echoing Tacis's original commercial and political overtones.

By 2003 Moldova was the poorest country in Europe, a time bomb ticking on the enlarged EU frontier. The country did not spend 10 years becoming poorer because donors got it right, and there are lessons to be learned all round. For Tacis, the lesson may be that the EU and Moldova could both benefit greatly if the EU abandoned political and commercial aims, worked as closely as possible with other donors, used local expertise, and focused only on Moldova's development. There is now a Poverty Reduction Strategy in Moldova to which all donors have signed up as a common task for the future. Above all, Tacis should recognise that the days of stand-alone projects and ring-fenced programmes with national flags on them are past. Moldova's development is too important for the EC to go it alone. It is time to go with the rest of the international community.

Moldova: Where Next?

Ann Lewis

It would be a rash observer who, in late 2003, would predict Moldova's course over the next few years with any confidence. The economy, the social structure, the body politic and the very future of the state seem to hang in the balance. Will it become another failed state, endangering not only its region but the wider community? Or can it, with international help, find a way out of its difficulties?

This short tail-piece will not attempt to summarise the various contributions to this book, but rather draw out a few threads and indulge in a little speculation.

But first, why should we bother with Moldova? It is small, far away, quiescent if not peaceful. It barely impinges on the consciousness of the outside world. If it is a mess, what does it matter? If it fractures, or parts are absorbed by its neighbours, some might argue that that would be a perfectly satisfactory solution for the world at large. The search for a united, stable and prosperous Moldova might well be long and painful: is it worth the effort?

Moldova is undeniably part of Europe, and the EU must as a matter of principle wish to see the country embrace the best European values and standards. As the EU enlarges, it has an increasing interest in promoting regional stability and resolving any potential conflicts near its borders. In more practical terms, Transdniestria provides a dangerous haven for illegal traffic in arms, drugs and people. Given the international threat from terrorism, this is a hole that needs to be plugged.

Many authors have drawn attention to Moldova's weak sense of national identity as underlying many of its problems. It has been described as a state that has not yet become a nation. The country has indeed never before existed as an independent entity within its current borders, which simply perpetuate the arbitrary borders imposed in Soviet times. Polls suggest that the majority of people (where opinion can be tested) do feel 'Moldovan', but this finds little expression in the political process. Attempts on the one hand to redress the inequities inflicted on the Romanian-speaking population through 50 years of russification, and on the other, to combat perceived discrimination and total 'romanisation', have created a dangerous polarisation of attitudes and an unwillingness to seek consensus on the highly symbolic cultural and language issues. Cutting across the ethnic divide, the political parties have been fractious and fragmented, some looking eastwards, some westwards, some leaning towards democratisation, others tending to the authoritarian, many highly personalised. The radical wings are outspokenly hostile to and deeply suspicious of each other.

All this has made it hard for Moldova, even excluding Transdniestria, to maintain any kind of coherent and consistent policy line round which the people can rally and which can get the country out of its difficulties. To the outsider it seems clear that the only identity open to Moldova is that of a multi-ethnic and multi-cultural society with good relations with both East and West. As it is, many Moldovans are already hedging their bets. Many Russian-speakers hold Russian passports, while increasing numbers of Romanian-speakers are acquiring Romanian citizenship. Huge numbers already live and work abroad. Hardly a sign of commitment to Moldova.

Moldova's most urgent need is to stem its long-term economic decline. The economists writing in this book, whether from Chişinău, London or Washington, are agreed on what is wrong: excessive dependence on the agricultural sector (subject to the vagaries of the weather); excessive dependence on the CIS for markets (subject to economic swings) and imports especially of energy (subject to political pressures and leading to massive indebtedness); institutional weakness leading inter alia to increasing corruption (Moldova sank to no 100 on Transparency International's 2003 corruption index, down from 93 in 2002 and 64 in 2001); a stop-go process of reform; and a poor climate for investment both foreign and domestic, without which Moldova will never achieve real growth and development. The separation of Transdniestria has deprived Moldova of a potentially substantial industrial base.

All of this is greatly aggravated by the very high level of emigration, which has deprived the country of much of its educated and energetic young workforce removed a natural constituency in favour of change and reform, and propped up the budget through remittances, thereby obscuring the urgent need for action. It has also led to acute social problems and the danger of a downward spiral of deprivation and breakdown in the social fabric, fuelling yet more emigration.

The advent of the Voronin administration with a large majority in parliament offered the chance of greater stability in policy-making. But in the event the leading party is itself divided and not much progress has been made. Economic gains stem largely from short-term factors rather than reflecting any fundamental improvement in the economic base. Prospects for the future look unclear. If the communists lose votes in the next round of elections, this could lead to the adoption of more coherent and centrist policies; but equally it could result in further fragmentation. The situation presents a challenge to the centre-right parties.

To be or not to be?

Given the current rifts and contradictions, it is worth asking the question: can and should Moldova survive as a single state? It is already run de facto as two separate states. Why not regularise this? Some in Moldova already believe that the country's path to European integration would be easier without the burden of undemocratic Transdniestria. In the case of Transdniestria, formal recognition by the international community would bring it back under international law and undermine its position as a safe haven for crime. Against this, it is by no means clear that Tiraspol wants to be burdened by the trappings of full statehood. Both new countries would need substantial external support. And for the West simply to recognise the current Transdniestrian leadership would go against all its commitments to state sovereignty, democracy and human rights. Furthermore, the international community, through the OSCE, has generally taken a negative view of border changes other than in exceptional circumstances.

This last objection would also apply to a further option: for one or both parts of Moldova to be absorbed into larger states. In the case of Transdniestria this could scarcely be Russia, to which many already owe allegiance, since there is no common border – unless Russia were prepared to contemplate another exclave like Kaliningrad, which seems unlikely. But Transdniestria could join neighbouring Ukraine, given its 30 per cent of ethnic Ukrainians, which would solve the problem of the regime's illegality. As for the majority Romanian-speaking area, some Romanian nationalists have long hankered after union with Romania – essentially a return to the pre-war situation. This might begin to look appealing to many more with the approach of Romanian accession to the

EU. The idea of absorbing a part of Moldova has at various times been raised as a possible eventuality in both Ukraine and Romania, though neither seems keen at present on such a solution, and Ukraine has enough internal divisions already without taking on another major liability. Certainly, neither country would advocate it publicly, and both would be wary of any possible damage to their budding relationships with the EU. The idea might begin to look quite tempting to the wider community however (if not to one or both of the potential partners) if there were a general breakdown in Moldova.

All options for splits or dismemberment come up against one major objection: while Moldova may be on a fault-line, the fault does not run neatly down the Dniester. Both parts are ethnically mixed, and there are no doubt divergent political attitudes throughout the country. This, together with the complementarity of the economies, suggests that it is worth a major effort to reunite the state on a viable long-term basis. Hence the efforts of the OSCE and others over a decade to find a settlement.

What kind of Moldova?

The Transdniestria issue is immensely complex. Readers interested in gaining a full understanding of its ramifications and the history of the negotiations are advised to look at the full text of the ICG report 'Moldova: No Quick Fix'. The Executive Summary is printed as an appendix to this volume, but this does not do justice to the main report.

There are some fundamental contradictions involved in any attempt to solve the Transdniestrian problem by reintegrating the statelet. While a settlement may be in the long-term interest of Moldova's people and regional stability, many in the current political elites involved, whether in Chişinău or Tiraspol, Moscow or Kiev, have a vested interest, often economic as well as political, in the status quo. And if there is to be a settlement, there are fundamentally opposing ideas about the basis for any new state. Tiraspol is seeking the greatest possible degree of independence for Transdniestria, perhaps in a weak confederation, while Chişinău wants a strong central government with some autonomy for Transdniestria.

Against this background it is not surprising that, while all parties paid lip-service to the need for agreement, the mediation process involving Russia, Ukraine and the OSCE staggered on for nearly a decade with almost no progress towards a settlement. In the circumstances it is something of an achievement that the mediators managed to produce the outline for a possible settlement known as the 'federalisation plan' or 'Kiev Document'. While many in the international community hailed this as a helpful step forward, the text met with a barrage of criticism from some political analysts and NGOs from the Romanian-speaking community.

Critics of the federalisation plan complain that it would legitimise the undemocratic, illegitimate and corrupt regime in Tiraspol, give Transdniestria undue influence over the central government and enable Russia to exercise influence or control over Moldova via Transdniestria; that the putative guarantors of the settlement (Russia, Ukraine and the OSCE – in which Russia has veto powers) are too heavily weighted to one side; that the people of authoritarian Transdniestria could not express their opinion freely in a referendum; and that, in sum, it would deliver Moldova back into the Russian orbit and get in the way of any moves towards the EU.

Some of these objections have substance and others show the deep well of mistrust for the other side. From the outsider's point of view, it is hard to see how a viable federation can be established unless all parts have a broadly similar political structure, or how international organisations dedicated to democracy, such as the EU and OSCE, could endorse a structure that is not based on democratic principles.

These issues need to be addressed if a settlement is to be achieved. The OSCE undoubtedly made tactical errors in drawing up the Kiev Document, especially in starting from a Russian model, which was bound to evoke suspicion that it was all a Russian fix. The document itself also failed to address some crucial questions, including the number of units in the federation and the distribution of competencies.

Those so vociferously opposing federalisation have not so far come up with a viable alternative way of securing an independent and united Moldova. They agree that, given the historical background, Transdniestria will have to have a good deal of autonomy, but see this as being exercised within a strong unitary state. How this is to be brought about is far from clear. One idea seems to be that the West should use its leverage to persuade Russia to secure the removal of the current Tiraspol regime, the establishment of democracy in Transdniestria and its subordination to a unitary Moldovan state. This is a tall order. If the opposition are serious about an alternative approach they need to produce a comprehensive strategy for the parties to consider. At present the federalisation plan is, to quote Western diplomats, 'the only show in town'.

President Voronin's proposal in February 2003 that the two sides draw up a new constitution and a draft agreement kick-started another round of negotiations, bolstered by the EU visa ban on Transdniestrian officials and the withdrawal of a large number of Russian troops. The negotiations, to take place on a broader base than the Kiev Document, offered a new opportunity to the parties and the wider community. But progress in the first few months was slow.

As of late 2003, a number of alternative approaches have been aired. One is that set out in the ICG report, which charts a possible path to the creation, on a longer time-scale, of a federal state acceptable to all sides and the wider community. This would involve the development of a new power-sharing model (perhaps an asymmetric federation with several constituent units, of which Transdniestria would be one); a campaign to improve public understanding of the issues; steps by the international community to reduce the benefits of the status quo to those involved through a variety of sticks and carrots; and the strengthening of democratic processes in both Transdniestria and the rest of the country. The proposals deal in great detail with the complex economic, political and military issues involved. To this observer, the most difficult part of the process seems to be to find ways of inducing the Transdniestrian leadership to accept any process of democratisation which would weaken their own position. In the end a generous exit strategy might be the price of their cooperation – perhaps a price worth paying to end the conflict and reunite the country.

This plan, like any other for the future of Transdniestria, depends crucially on Russian willingness to cooperate, especially by putting pressure on the Transdniestrian leadership. This raises the question of what Russia actually wants for Moldova. There are clearly some in Russia who profit from illegal activities in Transdniestria. It is less clear how far the interests of the political leadership are involved in this. Looked at more widely, does Russia want to see Moldova a stable and prosperous democracy with good links with the West? Or would it prefer to retain Transdniestria as a dependency, albeit a not always malleable one, with the scope that offers for political, economic and military influence in the region? Russia's direct military interest would seem limited, given that Ukraine serves as a substantial barrier between the two countries, and East-West tensions in the region are largely a thing of the past. But Romania's membership of NATO from 2004 will no doubt induce caution. What may be decisive is how far Russia is interested in making common cause with the West in general, and the EU in particular, in resolving this issue.

It may well be that views are divided in Moscow. Some probably see Transdniestria as a niggling issue which is capable of settlement and could be used as a 'quick win' in relations with the EU, possibly in return for some concession from the EU in other fields. Others will regard any diminution in Moscow's influence and position in the region as a blow to national prestige.

Some will undoubtedly hope that a settlement can be reached which will gain Moscow international credit while entrenching its indirect influence over the whole of Moldova: the very scenario most feared by opponents of federalisation. The EU will have to be wary of being lured into unwise concessions through the desire to reach a settlement.

If the parties involved, with help from the wider community, cannot find a settlement acceptable to all, Moldova seems stuck with an indefinite continuation of the status quo, and a steady economic decline possibly leading eventually to economic and social collapse and open conflict.

What relationship with the EU?

Moldova's attitude to the EU has always been ambiguous. It feels, rightly, part of the European mainstream by virtue of its history and culture. In the nineties the EU was seen by many as a beacon of hope offering promise of a more stable and prosperous future. Central and South-East European countries, even the Baltic states, were gradually being accepted as potential EU members and receiving substantial help in reforming their economies and societies.

Moldova has had a problem positioning itself in relation to the EU. Some Moldovans felt the country should be treated like the Baltic states, given their similar history of pre-war independence. But Moldova's 'independence' was as part of Romania, and it never had the powerful sense of national identity which made the Baltic states such distinctive entities even in Soviet times, and enabled them to grab at and adjust rapidly to independence and democracy.

More recently Moldova has aligned itself with 'South-Eastern Europe', the somewhat amorphous entity extending from Romania and Bulgaria to the Western Balkans covered by the Stability Pact. Moldovan politicians have viewed their acceptance as part of this grouping as a way of jumping the EU queue through the Stabilisation and Association process, which offers its members the long-term prospect of EU accession.

For the EU, however, Moldova has always been placed firmly in a box for the westernmost FSU states: Ukraine, Belarus, Moldova and, depending on context, Russia. It is not surprising that Moldova is unhappy at always being grouped with its Slav neighbours, when it feels so different. But the EU is unlikely to want to change this (for it) convenient arrangement, and for the moment Moldova would do well to make the most of what is currently on offer if it wishes to make progress in relations with the EU.

These countries are now covered by the EU's latest 'Wider Europe' initiative. This notably does not offer the prospect of EU membership even in the long term, though this cannot explicitly be excluded under current EU law. But the Moldovan government is in any case ambiguous in its attitude to the EU. It would like the benefits of membership, and claims that the prospect of membership would enable it to secure domestic acceptance of radical reforms – a familiar theme, used by other countries in the region. But this betrays a misunderstanding about EU membership. Membership is not something the EU offers as a carrot to bring in new members, but as recognition that a country is committed to and actively pursuing the highest European standards. The best way to secure membership is to become fully qualified. So far Moldova's commitment seems to be restricted to declarations and organisational changes. There is little sign of movement towards more democratic structures, and there has even been some movement backwards, for instance in the area of press freedom, under the Voronin administration. The EU will be looking for more tangible signs of commitment.

If Moldova is serious in its intentions towards the EU, it will at some point have to consider how far EU accession and its WTO membership are compatible with membership of the CIS and, if this becomes an option, participation in the Common Economic Area (or Single Economic Space). The EU for its part has no interest in damaging Modova's links with Russia, which will remain the country's key trading partner for the foreseeable future.

Moldova's aspirations to get closer to the EU, reaffirmed by President Voronin after an early tilt to the East at the beginning of his term of office, give the EU the opportunity to play a more influential role in developments in Moldova in general, and the settlement of the Transdniestria crisis in particular. Greater EU involvement in the settlement process would help reassure those in Moldova who deeply mistrust the current arrangements and the current mediators, or simply want to see a more balanced process.

Among the steps the EU could take in Moldova, depending on how events develop, these are the following:

- Play a more active role in encouraging and assisting institutional change. The EU's new Action Plan under the 'Wider Europe' initiative provides a good framework. This should if possible cover Transdniestria as well. Any EU technical assistance should be carefully coordinated with that of multilateral and bilateral donors to prevent wasteful overlap.

- Provide expertise to those trying to devise a new legal and constitutional framework for a unified Moldova, encouraging best international practice in areas such as minority rights.

- Promote more informed public debate about the political, constitutional and other issues involved in any settlement.

- Provide more help in strengthening controls on all Moldova's borders, to help reduce illegal traffic and stem the drain on the economy.

- Be ready to increase pressure on Transdniestria's leadership eg through targeted sanctions, to reduce the benefits of separation and encourage a sensible settlement.

- Consider how best to take part in any joint peacekeeping effort, operating under an EU, NATO or OSCE umbrella.

- Be ready to offer substantial support for a newly united Moldova, in such areas as military observers, arbitration mechanisms, and aid for reconstruction.

The EU could also consider, as the ultimate carrot, offering Moldova the prospect of long-term association and then membership of the EU once it is united, peaceful, democratic, and committed to operating to the highest European standards.

Abbreviations

ADR	Alliance for Democracy and Reform
ARA	Agricultural Restructuring Agency
ARIA	Association for the Restructuring of Enterprises
BBC	British Broadcasting Corporation
CARDS	Community Assistance for Reconstruction, Development and Stabilisation
CIS	Commonwealth of Independent States
CCA	Audiovisual Council
CDM	Democratic Convention of Moldova
CEA	Common Economic Area
CEPS	Centre for European Policy Studies
CFSP	Common Foreign and Security Policy
CPRM	Communist Party of the Republic of Moldova
CPSU	Communist Party of the Soviet Union
CSCE	Conference on Security and Cooperation in Europe
DFID	Department for International Development (UK)
DMR	Dniester Moldovan Republic
EBRD	European Bank for Reconstruction and Development
EC	European Community
EEA	European Economic Area
EFTA	European Free Trade Area
EIB	European Investment Bank
EMU	Economic and Monetary Union
EP	European Parliament
ESDP	European Security and Defence Policy
EU	European Union
EURASEC	Eurasian Economic Community
FDI	Foreign Direct Investment
FSU	Former Soviet Union
GDP	Gross Domestic Product
GNI	Gross National Income
GTZ	Gesellschaft für Technische Zusammenarbeit GmbH
GUAM	Georgia, Ukraine, Azerbaijan, Moldova
GUUAM	Georgia, Ukraine, Uzbekistan, Azerbaijan, Moldova
ICG	International Crisis Group
IFI	International Financial Institution
IMF	International Monetary Fund

JHA	Justice and Home Affairs
JPCC	Joint Parliamentary Cooperation Committee
LC	Letter of Credit
MASSR	Moldavian Autonomous Soviet Socialist Republic
MBA	Master of Business Administration
MDPM	Movement for a Democratic and Prosperous Moldova
MEPO	Moldovan Export Promotion Organisation
MFA	Ministry of Foreign Affairs
MSSR	Moldavian Soviet Socialist Republic
NATO	North Atlantic Treaty Organisation
NGO	Non-governmental Organisation
NIS	Newly-independent States (of the former Soviet Union)
ODIHR	Office for Democratic Institutions and Human Rights
OSCE	Organisation for Security and Cooperation in Europe
OSCE-PA	Parliamentary Assembly of the OSCE
PACE	Parliamentary Assembly of the Council of Europe
PCA	Partnership and Cooperation Agreement
PDF/PFD	Party of Democratic Forces
Phare	Technical assistance for Central and Eastern Europe (originally PHARE: Poland and Hungary: Action for Restructuring the Economy)
PPCD	Christian Democratic People's Party
PRCM	Party for Revival and Conciliation in Moldova
RBU	Russia-Belarus Union
SAA	Stability and Association Agreement
SME	Small and Medium-sized enterprise
SSR	Soviet Socialist Republic
TA	Technical assistance
Tacis	Technical assistance to the NIS and Mongolia (originally Technical Assistance to the CIS)
Tempus	Trans-European Mobility Scheme for University Students
WTO	World Trade Organisation
UNHCR	United Nations High Commissioner for Refugees
UNDP	United Nations Development Programme
USAID	US Aid Program
USSR	Union of Soviet Socialist Republics

Notes on Contributors

Petru Clej

Editor since 2000, broadcast journalist since 1991, Romanian Service, BBC World Service. Organised BBC office in Chisinau, 1998. Former journalist on *Romania Libera,* Bucharest. Has covered elections in Moldova since 1994.

Alexandru Canţîr

Head of Chisinau Bureau, Romanian Section, BBC World Service, since 1993. Chairman, NGO Committee for Press Freedom since 1994. Editor in social–political department at the independent news agency BASA–press since 1993. Previously worked on various newspapers and journals.

Prof William Crowther

Professor of Political Science, University of North Carolina at Greensboro, USA, and Director of the Parliamentary Documents Center for Central Europe. Author of a number of works on politics in Moldova and Romania.

Dr Valeriu Gheorghiu

Programme Director for projects on European integration, Institute for Public Policy, Chisinau. Member of Moldova's National Commission for European Integration.Head of political analysis and regional cooperation departments, MFA, Moldova,1993–2000. Author of articles and co–editor of three books on European integration and border issues.

Anatol Gudîm

Executive Director, Centre for Strategic Studies and Reforms (a Moldovan NGO). Areas of research: macroeconomics, transitional processes, regional development. Formerly at Institute of Economics, Academy of Sciences, Moldova (researcher 1965–1985), State Institute of Planning (director 1986–1990), World Bank and UNDP Project 'Strategy for Development' (national coordinator 1997–1999). Vice–Minister of Economy 1994–1997.

Oxana Guţu

Legal consultant within a European Commission Tacis project for the implementation of the Partnership and Cooperation Agreement between the EC and Moldova. Master of Arts from the College of Europe. Lecturer at the State University of Moldova. Special interest in justice and home affairs and EU enlargement.

Gottfried Hanne

Political scientist specialising in conflict and ethnic studies and comparative politics (Doctoral thesis on Transdniestrian conflict due for completion early 2004), Institute for International Politics and Regional Studies (Berlin). Member of OSCE Mission to Moldova 1999–2002, covering human and minority rights, democratisation and (internal) political affairs in Moldova.

Vic Heard

Has worked in international development since the 1960s, for the EC, for the UK's Department for International Development (DFID) and Foreign and Commonwealth Office, at headquarters and in the field, and in the Boards of UN agencies. EuropeAid Programme Coordinator for Moldova and Central Asia, 2001–2002. Currently DFID representative in Honduras.

Stuart Hensel

Senior Analyst, Central and Eastern Europe, Economist Intelligence Unit, London, since 1998. Worked on democratisation projects in the Balkans at the National Democratic Institute in Washington, 1996–98. Canadian.

Rostyslav Khotin

Editor, Ukrainian Section, BBC World Service since 1998. For most of the 1990s, reported for Reuters news agency from Kiev, covering Ukraine, Belarus and Moldova. Graduate of the Journalism Department, Kiev State Shevchenko University.

Ann Lewis

Free–lance consultant. Former member of British Diplomatic Service. Spent most of her career dealing with Central and Eastern Europe, including postings in Moscow and East Berlin. Editor of 'The EU and Ukraine: Neighbours, Friends, Partners?' and 'The EU and Belarus: between Moscow and Brussels'.

Prof Peter Maggs

Professor of Law, Clifford M. and Bette A. Carney Chair in Law, University of Illinois at Urbana–Champaign. Specialises in the law of Eastern Europe, Russia and Central Eurasia. Played an active role in preparation of a draft Civil Code for Moldova.

Dr Ala Mîndîcanu

Editor-in-chief, weekly newspaper *Democratia,* since 2001. Involved in politics since 1988. Member of Parliament 1994–2001, President of the Subcommittee on Equal Opportunities since 2001. Vice–President, Social–Liberal Party since 2001.

Veaceslav Negruţa

Senior economist, Policy Analysis Centre, Chisinau, focussing on economic and monetary policy, banking sector development and country debt management. Expert, Centre for Strategic Studies and Reforms, 1997–99. Senior economic adviser to the Moldovan Prime Minister, 1999. Director, Monetary Policy and Research Department, National Bank of Moldova, 2000–01.

Andrei Neguţa

Chairman of the Foreign Affairs Committee of the Moldovan Parliament. Communist Party (PCRM) MP since 1998. Head of Moldova's delegation to the Parliamentary Assembly of the Council of Europe 2001. Secretary of PCRM 1997–1998.

Dr Claus Neukirch

Press and Public Affairs Officer at the OSCE Mission to Moldova since 1 September 2003. Also served at this Mission in 1996 and 1997. Former Researcher at the Centre for OSCE Research in Hamburg. Consultant for the International Crisis Group, summer 2003. Has served on several OSCE Election Observation Missions.

Dr Oleg Serebrian

Vice–Rector, Free University of Moldova since 1995, President of Social–Liberal Party and President of European Movement of Moldova since 2001. Moldovan Ministry of Foreign Affairs 1993–1999, Programme Director, Soros Foundation, Chisinau, 1996–97. Visiting Professor at Cluj University, Romania, since 1998.

Dr Adrian Severin

Member of the Romanian Parliament. Member of the Parliamentary Assembly of the Council of Europe. Former President of the Parliamentary Assembly of the OSCE 2000–2002. Deputy Prime Minister of Romania and Minister for Foreign Affairs 1996–1997, Minister for Privatisation 1991–1992, Deputy Prime Minister for Reform and Relations with Parliament 1990–1991.

Alexandru Simionov

Senior Adviser, Foreign Affairs Committee, Moldovan Parliament, responsible for regional cooperation in South–East Europe and European integration since February 2003. Project Assistant, UNHCR office, Chisinau, 2001–2002. Lecturer on international relations, Moldova State University, since 2001. MFA department for international relations, 2002–2003.

Vlad Spanu

Senior Fellow and Member of the Advisory Board of the Institute for Development and Social Initiatives in Chisinau. Senior Moldovan diplomat 1992–2001, latterly as Minister–Counsellor in Washington and Head of International Organisations Division, MFA. In 2003 gained Masters in public administration from a mid–career programmme at Kennedy School of Government, Havard.

Ion Stăvilă

Deputy Minister of Foreign Affairs of the Republic of Moldova. Former Director of the Department of European Security and Political and Military Issues, and Director of the Department of General International Security at the MFA.

Dr Ion Sturza

General Manager of *Rompetrol Moldova*. Engaged in various business activities up to 1998. Became Minister of Finance and First Deputy Prime Minister of Moldova 1998, and Prime Minister 1999. Expert with various IFIs. Member of Balkan Political Club and collaborator with Bertelsmann Foundation.

Dr Elizabeth Teague

Research analyst, Ministry of Defence, London. Previously research analyst at the Foreign and Commonwealth Office and analyst of Soviet politics for Radio Free Europe/Radio Liberty.

Liliana Viţu

MA in Modern European Studies, London Metropolitan University, 2003. BBC World Service (Romanian section) correspondent in Moldova, 1998–2002. Analyst of Moldovan domestic politics in the Transition Department, Economist Intelligence Unit, 2001–2002.

Marius Vahl

Research Fellow, Centre for European Policy Studies (CEPS), Brussels, working on the Wider Europe programme. Recent publications include 'Just Good Friends? The EU–Russian 'Strategic Partnership' and the Northern Dimension' (March 2001),'Navigating by the Stars: Norway, the EEA and the EU' (February 2002), and 'Europe's Black Sea Dimension' (June 2002). Norwegian.

Jan Marinus Wiersma

Member of the Foreign Affairs Committee of the European Parliament and chair of its delegation for relations with Ukraine, Belarus and Moldova. Former international secretary of the Dutch Labour Party. Currently Vice–President of the Party of European Socialists.

Angelina Zaporojan-Pirgari

Lawyer. Masters degree in Human Rights and Democratisation, Venice. Worked at OSCE Mission in Moldova 2001–2002 as Human Rights Assistant handling individual complaints, many about violations of minority rights. Previously involved in UNDP project on judicial reform in Moldova, and OSCE/ODIHR Election Observation Missions in Moldova and Bulgaria.

Appendix
MOLDOVA: NO QUICK FIX[1]

Executive Summary

The conflict in the Transdniestrian region of the Republic of Moldova is not as charged with ethnic hatred and ancient grievances as others in the area of the Organisation for Security and Cooperation in Europe (OSCE), and it is more conducive to a sustainable settlement. However, a "quick fix" in 2003, as envisaged by the Dutch Chairmanship of the OSCE, is also unlikely. To reach the sustainable agreement that is required if the forthcoming European Union (EU) enlargement is not to be compromised by a nearly open border with international crime and serious poverty, a comprehensive approach is needed that takes into account the root causes of the original conflict and the factors that have blocked the settlement process since 1992.

The Transdniestrian authorities are not recognised by any state and have been subjected to targeted sanctions such as travel bans by the EU and the U.S. but they have acquired for their small territory on the left bank of the Dniester River with barely one-sixth as many people as Moldova some of the attributes of a state. They have gained control over local enterprises and the customs service covering their section of the Ukraine-Moldova border and their side of the internal Moldovan boundary. This enables them to profit not only from legal trade but in all likelihood also from the trafficking of other goods in transit to Moldova and beyond. Such illicit activities pose a threat to the security of the wider region. The EU, which will share a common border with Moldova after the accession of Romania in 2007, has a particular interest in settlement of the conflict and regularisation of Transdniestria's status.

[1] Report of the International Crisis Group, ICG Europe Report No 147, Chişinău/Brussels, 12 August 2003. The full text of the report is available on the ICG website, www.crisisweb.org

The Transdniestrian elite (and others) prefer the status quo to any negotiated agreement. An important part of a settlement process, therefore, must be to design steps that would reduce and even abolish the benefits that flow from that tainted status quo – for example, the imposition of sanctions on Transdniestrian leaders and enterprises and help for the Moldova government to establish a unified customs system along its entire border.

The vested interests of elites on either side of the river do not necessarily correspond to the interests of the broader population. Although the majority on both sides would certainly profit from increased investments and trade after settlement of the conflict, there is no general awareness of the real costs of separation and the political stalemate. Moreover, the authorities in Transdniestria hinder the development of civil society, free media and party pluralism. As a result, there is no opportunity to express views freely on the future of the region. Another important pillar of the process, accordingly, must be the fostering of an open society in Transdniestria. A settlement that merely cemented the Smirnov regime in place would be unacceptable.

At the same time, economic transformation, democratisation, rule of law, freedom of the media and human rights are also deficient on the other side of the river. The third pillar of a comprehensive approach to a final settlement, therefore, should be to make Moldova more attractive for the Transdniestrians in order to provide incentives for them to support an agreement. Joint benchmarks for legislation and its implementation in Moldova and Transdniestria should be worked out and reviewed regularly, with clear rewards for compliance and targeted punitive measures for non-compliance. For Moldova, this initially could mean not getting loans or access to aspects of the European market. For Transdniestria, it would include further visa restrictions, the freezing of individual and enterprise assets and perhaps a ban on trade with Transdniestrian companies not registered with the Moldovan authorities. Additional aims of this process would be to harmonise the legislation of Moldova and Transdniestria and reintegrate state structures that have developed in parallel for more than a decade, in order to prepare the way for reintegration.

The fourth pillar would have to be a fair proposal for a final settlement tabled by the Moldovan side. A federation – preferably asymmetric and multimember – would be the best political system for a unified Moldova; it would not only give Transdniestria broad autonomy but also keep it in constant interaction with the central authorities. It should include a framework for a functioning dispute settlement mechanism to cope with new disputes.

Finally, any agreement would need political and military guarantees. The former should include a functioning dispute settlement mechanism. The latter are important to prevent spoilers from provoking violence, including military people on both sides until they are decommissioned, and should come in the form of an international security presence mandated by the OSCE.

RECOMMENDATIONS
To the OSCE, the EU and the U.S.:

1. Plan a comprehensive settlement process involving simultaneous democratisation on both sides of the Dniester River, with a special emphasis on the left bank (Transdniestria).

2. Establish an international security presence under an OSCE mandate, led by the EU and including troops from Russia and other interested OSCE participating states, to take over from the current trilateral peacekeeping forces in Moldova by 1 January 2004.

3. Urge Ukraine and Moldova to come to an agreement on joint customs posts and on the presence of independent observers, both to be located on Ukrainian territory if Transdniestria continues to refuse to allow Moldovan customs to operate on its territory.

4. Establish a trust fund under international supervision into which all revenues collected by Moldovan authorities from Transdniestrian enterprises would be deposited and which pending a final agreement between the two sides would be used exclusively for financing economic development, infrastructure, education, public health and social welfare.

5. Draw up a reconstruction program for a unified Moldova based on a co-ordinated approach by international donors.

6. Increase aid for language education and social integration programs in both Moldova and Transdniestria.

To the EU:

7. Open a full European Commission delegation office in Moldova.

8. Draw up and assign priority to an Action Plan for Moldova that sets clear benchmarks – worked out in close cooperation with the OSCE and the Council of Europe – for development of democracy,

rule of law and human rights, including specific benchmarks to be met in Transdniestria.

9. Target the Transdniestrian leadership with further sanctions if it continues to block the negotiation process and removal of Russian ammunition or fails to meet the benchmarks in the EU Action Plan for Moldova described above, and urge Russia to join such measures and refrain from helping the Transdniestrian regime consolidate its power.

To the OSCE:

10. Increase the OSCE Mission to Moldova by at least three international staff members responsible for promoting reunification, including democracy and rule of law, especially in Transdniestria.

11. Include economic experts, inter alia from the International Monetary Fund, among the international experts working with the Joint Constitutional Commission.

12. Conduct an awareness-raising campaign in Moldova on the nature of power-sharing, especially through various federal models, as a conflict resolution tool.

13. Strengthen co-operation between Transdniestria and Moldova at non-official levels (for example, economic agents, NGOs, and the media) by organising and/or supporting such measures as round-tables, workshops, and summer schools.

14. Have the donor states agree that the OSCE voluntary fund for destruction or withdrawal of ammunition can be used to finance destruction of the ammunition also in Russia after it has been withdrawn or establish a new voluntary fund for that purpose.

15. Task the Strategic Police Matters Unit of the OSCE Secretariat to conduct a full scale needs assessment in Moldova and to prepare a program for police training with a special view to the need for increased policing in a security zone after final settlement of the conflict.